Urban Pollution

Environmental Anthropology and Ethnobiology

General Editor: **Roy Ellen**, FBA
Professor of Anthropology and Human Ecology, University of Kent at Canterbury

Interest in environmental anthropology and ethnobiological knowledge has grown steadily in recent years, reflecting national and international concern about the environment and developing research priorities. `Studies in Environmental Anthropology and Ethnobiology' is an international series based at the University of Kent at Canterbury. It is a vehicle for publishing up-to-date monographs and edited works on particular issues, themes, places or peoples which focus on the interrelationship between society, culture and the environment.

Urban Pollution

Cultural Meanings, Social Practices

Edited by
Eveline Dürr and Rivke Jaffe

berghahn
NEW YORK · OXFORD
www.berghahnbooks.com

First published in 2010 by
Berghahn Books
www.berghahnbooks.com

Library of Congress Cataloging-in-Publication Data

Urban pollution : cultural meanings, social practices / edited by Eveline Dürr
and Rivke Jaffe.
    p. cm. -- (Studies in environmental anthropology and ethnobiology ; vol. 15)
Includes bibliographical references and index.
 ISBN 978-1-84545-692-4 (hardback) -- ISBN 978-1-84545-848-5 (institutional
ebook) -- ISBN 978-1-84545-848-5 (paperback) -- ISBN 978-1-78238-509-7 (retail
ebook)
 1. Urban anthropology. 2. Urban pollution. 3. Human ecology. 4.
Environmental degradation. 5. Taboo. 6. Purity, Ritual. 7. Primitive societies. I.
Dürr, Eveline. II. Jaffe, Rivke.
 GN395.U74 2010
 363.7309173'2--dc22

           2010018552

British Library Cataloguing in Publication Data

A catalogue record for this book is available from the British Library

Printed on acid-free paper

ISBN: 978-1-84545-848-5 paperback
ISBN: 978-1-78238-509-7 retail ebook

Contents

List of Figures

Acknowledgements

The editors would like to thank a number of individuals and organisations for their help in realising this volume. The first versions of a number of chapters were first presented at three conference panels. The first conference panel, 'Differential Explanation of Space in Urban Environment', convened by Eveline Dürr and Soheila Shahshahani (Shahid Beshti University, Iran), was held at the Inter-Congress of the International Union of Anthropological and Ethnological Sciences (IUAES) in Göttingen, Germany, 17–21 July 2001. Generous European funding facilitated organisation of and participation in the second panel, 'Environmental and Ecological Issues in Cities: An Anthropological Approach', European Association of Social Anthropologists (EASA), Biennial Conference, Vienna, 8–14 September 2004. The third conference panel, titled 'Neue Perspektiven in der Stadtethnologie', convened by Christoph Brumann (University of Cologne, Germany) and Eveline Dürr, was held at the Conference of the German Anthropological Association (GAA), Halle, 4–7 October 2005. We would like to express our thanks to three anonymous reviewers for their insightful comments which have helped to focus our analysis of urban pollution and have led to a much improved final version. We are also grateful to the Director of the French Institute of Pondicherry for granting permission to reproduce three of the figures from the Mayamata (edited and translated by Bruno Dagens) in Chapter 3.

CHAPTER 1

Introduction: Cultural and Material Forms of Urban Pollution

RIVKE JAFFE AND EVELINE DÜRR

In an increasingly urbanised world, environmental degradation is a crucial factor in the development and liveability of cities. Air quality, garbage, noise, stench and other forms of pollution both reflect and influence human habits and social behaviour. Urban environmental and public health policies are products of political ideologies, dominating important aspects of city life and the physical environment. Simultaneously, vernacular understandings of the city can influence or undermine environmental and social policy. While urban environmental management has received increasing attention in recent years, technological and economic approaches are generally privileged over attention to social and cultural perspectives on pollution. Surprisingly little is known about perceptions of pollution and environmental degradation in cities, how such perceptions are embedded in the everyday lives of city dwellers, or how they interact with urban space, power and identity.

Social and cultural aspects of the urban environment are important to urban and environmental scholars alike. However, environmental anthropology and sociology have often neglected the urban, tending to focus on natural resource management and conservation, and on issues of depletion rather than pollution. With a few notable exceptions (Aoyagi et al. 1998; Checker 2001, 2005), urban sociology and anthropology have rarely focused on the environment,[1] retaining a stronger emphasis on more traditional topics such as urban poverty and informal sector activities;

---

1. Urban historians have displayed a stronger, though also relatively recent, interest in environmental issues and specifically pollution (see Melosi 2000; George 2001; Gandy 2002; Pellow 2002).

ethnicity and cultural pluralism; rural-urban migration and consequent adaptations; and crime and violence. Recognizing the socio-cultural significance of pollution and environmental degradation, references to environmental and ecological perceptions have been increasing in urban studies, with a particular focus on social movements such as the environmental justice movement (e.g. McKean 1981; Bullard 2000; Checker 2005). These studies of urban environmental movements have largely been based in industrialised countries such as Japan or the United States. Urban planners and policy makers have also tended to neglect the important cultural and social aspects of urban environmental management. Despite growing attention to the local dimensions of rural environmental problems and the possibilities as well as the complications of participatory management, the consequences of this discourse for the urban have not been fully incorporated. In addition, sustainable development experts have a propensity for macro-level analyses, neglecting more ethnographic accounts.

An anthropological approach to urban pollution provides insights overlooked in more technocratic models of pollution. An emphasis on the emic perspective allows a critique of such standard, often developmentalist, environmental knowledge and enables a more intimate and nuanced comprehension of the social production of pollution. Anthropology contributes to urban environmental studies extensive ethnographic research and a contextual framework for understanding the seemingly universal processes of garbage removal, sewage systems and so on. As Hajer (1995: 18) notes, 'to analyse discourses on pollution as quasi-technical decision-making on well-defined physical issues … misses the essentially social questions that are implicated in these debates'. The work of, for instance, urban planners, policymakers or sustainable development experts is complicated by such emic constructions and perceptions of environmental issues, and the cultural context, including interpretations of the urban environment and nature, that shapes them. An anthropological approach to urban pollution focuses on cultural meanings and values attached to conceptions of 'clean' and 'dirty', purity and impurity, healthy and unhealthy environments. It addresses the implications of pollution as it is related to discrimination, class, urban poverty, social hierarchies and ethnic segregation in cities. Pollution is used as a lens through which to dissect the social and cultural intricacies of the urban environment, space, power and capital.

In this edited volume, pollution is conceptualised broadly as having both imagined and material aspects. Many studies of pollution, including much of the work in this volume, analyse local understandings and articulations of urban pollution. Within these studies, there are distinct analytical categories, that do tend to overlap to a certain extent. A first concern is with symbolic forms and cultural perceptions of pollution and how these are manifested and expressed in urban space. Its parallel focus is on concrete, physically measurable forms of urban pollution – garbage, sewage, air pollution – and anthropological methods are used to understand more clearly the issues of power, class and ethnicity surrounding the production and removal of such wastes. Such a symbolic-material dualism only holds true up to a point, as these categories are, of course, overlapping and interrelated. The materiality and sociality of urban pollution are relational entities that produce each other – this relational materiality itself, as well as the hybridity of pollution, can be the focus of study. The social life of garbage – material waste – can be explored just as the materiality of symbolic pollution needs to be understood more precisely; an analysis of the continued significance of 'modern' distinctions between the natural and the symbolic (cf. Latour 1993; Law 1999) within pollution is also a promising avenue for future research. The 'pure' distinction between material and symbolic pollution reflects the performed distance between 'technical' environmental engineers and urban planners dealing with 'material' garbage, on the one hand, and 'cultural' anthropologists studying 'symbolic' social pollution on the other. While this volume, containing mostly anthropological contributions, has an inbuilt bias towards the latter position, ultimately, an interdisciplinary study of urban pollution needs to take account of such hybridity, for instance by acknowledging and analysing the agency or effectivity of garbage, water and so on (e.g. Swyngedouw 2004; Hawkins 2005; Kaika 2005; Heynen et al. 2006; Gille 2007). Medical anthropology and biosocial studies of human bodies 'polluted' or afflicted by non-human elements provide another, though not always explicitly urban, field of exploration (see Schell and Denham 2003; Nguyen and Peschard 2003; Obrist et al. 2003).

While acknowledging the constructed nature of this broad material-symbolic dualism, the rest of this introduction remains organised within it, while attempting, as many of the following chapters do, to complicate the 'purity' of such distinctions. Re-examining classical work on pollution and concepts of purity and order, this volume engages with modern expressions of these themes in urban areas, which are particularly affected by processes of globalisation, including increasingly neoliberal urban policy, privatisation of urban space, continued migration and spatialised ethnic tension within cities.

Cultural pollution

Cultural constructions of pollution: meaning and identity

The seminal work in terms of cultural pollution is Mary Douglas' *Purity and Danger* (2002), first published in 1966. Her structuralist approach and the definition of dirt – the unclean – as 'matter out of place' (Douglas 2002: 44) inextricably link pollution to the cultural specifics of a social order.

Defining dirt involves classifying and sorting, the drawing of boundaries and margins. Pollution results from boundary transgression and, in being defined as pollution, contributes to the marking and safeguarding of the same boundaries. What is out of place depends on the nature of the social order as inscribed in the scheme of cultural categories and reflected in the way meaning is created. Dirt is a cultural construct, existing in the eye of the beholder (2002: 2), rather than a universal category. Given the centrality of the social order in definitions of dirt, pollution, according to Douglas, is essentially disorder. It is that which transgresses the social order, disturbing rules and classifications set by religion, science or ideology. Dirt disrupts and disturbs this order – which is perceived as a naturally given order – as boundaries are crossed. Dirt threatens the balance and stability provided by the social order; the ensuing imbalance is a danger and is regarded as wrong and immoral. Pollution, therefore, is not so much a matter of hygiene as it is a framing of moral symbols. Consequently, transgressions must be resolved through punishment or ritual purification. Many religions, for instance, include concepts of pollution, often accompanied by guilt, and associated with specific rites of purification. Ascribing phenomena with the status of dirt, and so classifying them as potential dangers, amounts to the symbolic maintenance of boundaries and contributes to the stability and safeguarding of a specific social structure. Boundaries may be conceptualised in corporal, social, spatial and geographical terms and consist of for instance the skin of the human body, walls, crossroads or national borders. Particularly likely to be classified as pollutants are the anomalous, the ambiguous, the liminal and the transitional; dealing with them reduces uncertainty and increases the logic of a social order and the unity of a society. Concepts of symbolic or ritual pollution serve to create and maintain social categories, to establish inside and outside worlds, to mark and protect the difference between what is safe and what is dangerous, what is acceptable and what is unacceptable.

Critique of Douglas' theory focused on the deterministic relationship between cosmology and social environment, in particular her understanding of culture as existentially determined by social organisation. Her work – popular in part because of its wide applicability – has been classified as overly universalistic, to the extent of ignoring social and historical contexts. In arguing that establishing order through concepts of purity is universal, Douglas' theory posits a unidirectional movement from chaos to order, discounting social forces that might seek to transform order into ambiguity, disorder or hybridity. This neglect of the hybrid led to criticism of her excessive dependence on a Levi-Strauss-inspired dualist paradigm, as her theory of purity and pollution relies heavily on the concept of binary oppositions. This is also in conflict with postcolonial approaches in cultural theory which reject dichotomies but emphasise the dynamic nature of culture as a constantly changing process. They posit that culture is negotiated and framed by both local and global conditions (Hall 1997; Inda and Rosaldo 2008). Mary Douglas' own tendencies towards unmitigated dualism or structuralism, however, are sometimes reproduced by scholars in ways that disregard the social and technical complexities underlying social and cultural realities. Notwithstanding these points of criticism, Douglas' work is still fundamental to research on pollution and purity.

In addition to such conceptual critiques, the constructivism typifying Douglas' approach to dirt can lead to a disproportionate emphasis on cultural relativism, obscuring real biomedical differences. While pollution is in many ways a cultural construct, it is simultaneously an 'objective', quantifiable phenomenon that impacts negatively on human and ecological health. Waterborne or airborne pathogens are pollutants that can be measured in quantitative terms. This does not preclude the fact that the perception of the problems caused by the presence of disease vectors and pathogens differs from one group to the other, or that filth is used to draw or reaffirm social boundaries. Pollution, then, has two sides. It is a socially constructed phenomenon employed to reaffirm social order, as posited by Mary Douglas. We seek to remedy her overly constructivist inclinations by placing equal emphasis on pollution as a measurable condition affecting human well-being and environmental sustainability.

Globalisation and pollution

Douglas' work was based largely on 'primitive' societies and attempts to demonstrate the strong parallels between these and industrial societies. Critical processes of urbanisation and global change have altered the context of anthropology, but the concept of pollution remains as acute in the twenty-first century city. Concepts of pollution in cities are apparent in struggles over space and place, between groups differentiated on the basis of class, ethnicity or religion. Pollution is mediated by these same differentiations and can simultaneously reinforce urban divisions. Aesthetic and moral valuations, based on concepts of cleanliness and dirt, of purity and impurity, are constructed in the sociospatial arena that is the city. Especially in the context of globalisation – more specifically the ethnic diversification of cities, the increasingly contested power of the nation-state and the strengthening of local identities – social groups have a heightened tendency to perceive both their identities and access to resources as at risk. A dominant way of framing these threats is in terms of cultural pollution. As territorial borders appear to lose their salience or become increasingly porous, cultural borders are policed that much harder.

Mass migration, involuntary displacements and other territorial movements intensify anxieties with regard to pollution and the construction of physical and cultural boundaries. The fortification of cultural boundaries is accomplished by portraying outside influences as an invasive threat that will contaminate the 'pure' ethnonational entity. As Scanlan (2005: 182) notes, 'every act of differentiation produces garbage'. Ethnic groups, often new migrant groups but indigenous peoples as well (see Trnka, this volume), tend to be depicted as dirty and different. When the new presence of certain groups threatens existing ethnic configurations and social hierarchy, it may be tempting to portray this menace as one to the physical environment and public health. Defensive local or national identities are conveyed in environmental terms, while the protection of economic and territorial interests may be based on claims of (ethnic or national) purity and authenticity. Religious interpretations of pollution may intersect with these processes of identity formation, contrasting the pure, sacred and clean with the impure, profane and contaminated.

The mutually constitutive notions of cultural pollution and purity draw on ideas of a pre-existing, natural order that determines who and what belongs where. In this defining of the 'native' and the 'foreign', cultural identities become naturalised and humans are perceived as joined to a particular habitat. Belonging becomes a static concept that is inscribed in a specific territory and defined by a natural or ecological law (Olsen 1999; Comaroff and Comaroff 2001).[2] This geographical and cultural space must be protected from intrusive foreigners who will contaminate the 'natural' order. Invasive outsiders are perceived as harmful pollutants, besieging the territory and usurping its resources. Social distinctions are established by the 'native' group, who actively ascribe the intruders with alterity, whether in ethnic, linguistic or environmental terms. Changes in language and food are prominent examples of issues around which such debates revolve (Harrison 1999).

Cultural pollution is a key concept in nation-building processes; the imagined nation depends on ideas of ethnic or cultural homogeneity and leaves little room for blurred categories. The nation-state is envisioned, organically, as a body politic of varying robustness which is prone to, and

---

2. The specifically natural character of these people-place bonds is reflected in the use of horticultural metaphors describing 'rooted' identities, family 'trees and branches' and, of course, diaspora, which literally translates to 'spreading the seeds' (Ballinger 2004: 50). Such ecological imageries reveal the equation of social and environmental pollution as it is invoked by radical right wing environmentalists (Olsen 1999) and point to the intertwining of 'race' and nature as a terrain of power evident in cultural politics (Moore et al. 2003). Additionally, such usages, of course, hark back to the ecological terminology used by Chicago School urban sociologists.

must be protected against, pollution. The most extreme instance of how the concept of pollution is employed in militant national identities and their representations is the notion and practice of 'ethnic cleansing' – from the Holocaust to Rwanda and former Yugoslavia – in which deportation and genocide are posed as solutions to cultural pollution. Under the Nazi regime, cities such as Vienna or Warsaw from which the Jewish population had been forcefully removed would be pronounced *Judenrein*, clean of Jews (see Bauman 2002: 119–120). The purity associated with the homogeneous nation is manifested in a variety of spatial configurations. Malkki (1995), for instance, describes the narratives of purity and pollution as applied by Hutu refugees in Tanzania in order to legitimate claims to the nation. Cultural pollution also figures as a political rhetoric rejecting so-called western influences in non-western societies, expressed for instance in the concern over cityscapes transformed by the mushrooming of US fast food chains or 'McDonaldisation'. But this finds its parallel in 'autochthonous' objections to architectural signifiers of ethnic diversity in European cities, such as ethnic restaurants, mosques, halal butchers and phone houses.

The city itself is also imagined as a body politic and a corporal entity. Bodily metaphors are common in thinking of the city: flows and processes constitute an urban 'metabolism', certain areas are the 'beating heart', traffic and people 'pulsate' along urban streets, rivers or canals that function as the city's 'arteries'. This organism can be sick, wounded or polluted, or indeed robust and healthy (Harvey 2003; Goldberg 1993). The city itself, especially as unchecked urban sprawl, can take the shape of a cancerous growth, while neighbourhoods within a city are regarded as blighted and architectural objects are sores on the urban landscape.

The politics of public health

From the outset of urban research, dirt, filth and pollution have figured as prominent topics (cf. Chadwick 1842; Booth 1902–3). A considerable body of Victorian era literature was concerned with urban industrialisation and the associated living conditions of factory workers, who often resided in overcrowded quarters. Hygiene, sanitation and fear of contagion became important issues in city life. In a context of both rapid urban expansion and advances in medical science, urban overcrowding and filth were increasingly constructed as problematic through their association with disease. The nineteenth century was the backdrop for the rise of the sanitary reform movement, arising from concern for the urban poor but, at least as important, the economic need to ensure a healthy workforce. Infrastructural improvements – the provision of water and sanitation services – were combined with legal and administrative measures such as public health ordinances. Sanitation and public health reform expanded to a global movement which sought to combat health hazards but also cure social ills in European, American and colonial cities, based on a paradigm which associated poverty, pollution and disease (Strasser 1999). The combined eradication was to be achieved through combining technical and administrative measures with moral and educational strategies. The humanitarian and economic impulses that shaped such campaigns were accompanied by a strong moral imperative. If cleanliness is next to godliness, dirt is the devil. Dirt was, and is, often conflated with degeneracy. A physically dirty body, residence or public space is often associated with a certain moral decay. In this vein, sanitary reformers sought to instil civilisation and order in the lives they were saving from disease and poverty.

The civilising mission – driven by 'ideologies of cleanliness' (Gandy 2004) – had similar implications in cities throughout the world. Campaigns to eradicate diseases and cleanse cities of filth were often discriminatory in nature and reinforced existing social and ethnic hierarchies and power structures. Dirt and filth served as markers of racial and national distinction and had class and gender implications (Cohen 2005: xxvi). For instance, perceptions of pollution included connotations with sexuality and immorality, as gendered constructions of sexual deviance and 'disorderly' female bodies involved moral condemnation in terms of filth, dirt, and defilement (cf. Russo 1995; Bashford 1998). With regard to maintaining class distinctions within the urban arena, pollution and rituals of purification have been used in a variety of shifting ways. Odour for instance – extending into the social realm from a dominant discourse that focused on urban sanitation – took on significance in eighteenth and nineteenth century Paris, as a means of the deodorised bourgeoisie to distinguish themselves from the smelly masses (Corbin 1986). Similarly, in modern-day Buenos Aires, the middle-class – its socioeconomic position precarious due to neoliberal restructuring – differentiate themselves from the (ethnically distinct) urban poor, by framing the latter as a barbaric force that pollutes the city and threatens its modernity (Guano 2004). Chaplin (1999) makes a comparison between cities in contemporary India and mid-nineteenth century Britain. The politics of British sanitary reform, driven by middle-class fear of disease and social revolution, eventually led to environmental services being extended to the urban poor. The modern Indian middle-classes have less to be afraid of as modern medicine and civil engineering allow them to remove themselves from sanitary interdependency, while a large part of the population is excluded from access to basic urban services.

Colonial cities, particularly those in Africa, implemented a *cordon sanitaire* between indigenous and colonial sections of town in attempts to simultaneously curtail epidemics and impose racial delineations. Fear of infectious disease, not always equally grounded in medical fact, served as a rationale for the creation and later maintenance of racialised urban space within urban planning (Goldberg 1993: 48). As King (1990: 55) notes, 'the culture and class-specific *perception* of health hazards more than the actual health hazards themselves was instrumental in determining much colonial, urban-planning policy'. In the Philippines in the early twentieth century, public health reform enabled the medical production of colonial bodies and spaces. Grotesque, defecating Filipino bodies were contrasted with civilised, hygienic American ones. For American colonial health officers, human waste practices became the ordering principle by which to draw social and racial boundaries that validated US domination. This form of justification allowed in particular colonial control of urban public space, such as the marketplace and the fiesta (Anderson 1995). Racial, moral and sanitary discourse become intertwined, especially when residential segregation suggests maintainable ethno-spatial boundaries, for instance, in the case of Vancouver's Chinatown (Anderson 1991). In San Francisco, diseases such as tuberculosis and smallpox were used as political tools to construct physical and cultural boundaries and restrict spatial relations. Health policy determined social, physical and symbolic restructurings of the city, targeting the poor and ethnic minorities, specifically the Chinese community. Measures such as quarantine replicated the colonial *cordon sanitaire*, and testify to a continued construction of diseases as produced by place and categories of people, rather than by bacteria *per se* (Craddock 2000; Shah 2001).

Epidemics have often served as a validating context for the imposed ordering of public and private life in cities, with sick bodies either expelled from the urban environment in 'rituals of exclusion' or isolated and quarantined within 'disciplinary diagrams' that involve the division and control of urban space (Foucault 1977). Separating the pure and the impure involves the maintenance of spatial boundaries, ranging from the human skin as a barrier, to the isolation of patients in sanitoria and leper colonies, to defending the integrity of the national 'geobody' through immigration policy (Bashford 2004). Health concerns – and the need for information on which to base state intervention – lie at the root of early partitions and classification of urban space, including the census tract as an example of government-defined urban geography (Krieger 2006). Spatial management continues to be central to public health strategies and social medicine up to the present day, given the surveillance and environmental control involved.

Pollution and progress

While public health remains a strong pretext for restructuring urban space, tropes such as progress, civilisation and modernity are invoked with equal success. The civilising mission evident in both colonial and more recent sanitation and public health campaigns demonstrates how the absence or removal of urban pollution – however defined – is interpreted as a sign of progress, up into the postcolonial era. Sanitised, 'civilised' spaces figure prominently in ideologies of development and modernity. On the one hand, these beliefs are driving forces in processes of urbanisation and suburbanisation. Conversely, such ideologies are apparent in municipal policies ranging from slum clearance to the policing of public space.

Cities remain the loci of progress and modernity and the concept of global cities posits urban areas as sites where one finds the highest degree of order, logic, efficiency and the highest concentration of financial, political and cultural power. Such powerful, efficient, prestigious places cannot be reconciled with social or physical pollution. Where economic growth is linked to industrial activity and urbanisation, economic progress is generally accompanied by increased pollution within the city.[3] Yet, a society's progress towards 'civilisation', 'modernisation' or 'development' tends to be defined by the absence of – tangible, visible, smellable – pollution. Unobtrusive underground sewers that replace malodorous cesspits are seen as a mark of urban progress; and garbage collectors often come before dawn, in part to avoid daytime traffic, but presumably also to remove garbage and its disposal from plain sight and daily life. Modernisation is symbolised by cleanliness – the spaces of the global economy must be shiny and clean – but making the flipside of this prosperity and process go away calls for significant acts of conjure. A lot of 'dirty work', executed by hordes of inconspicuous cleaners, goes into removing and concealing the waste involved in contemporary production, consumption and social reproduction (Herod and Aguiar 2006).

As in Foucault's scheme, spatial strategies of urban control can involve separation (remove the pollutants from the city) or segmentation (divide, classify and regulate pollutants within the city) or a combination of the two. Until today, municipal governments throughout the world attempt to physically remove 'dirty', 'backward' or non-modern objects, people or entire neighbourhoods in the name of progress. Unplanned neighbourhoods or slums are seen as disfiguring the modern urban landscape and removed; street vendors are harassed for the sake of cleanliness and progress; homeless people removed. In 1999, a truckload of homeless people were transported from the Jamaican tourist town of Montego Bay, and abandoned in a remote area (Amnesty International 2001: 29–35). In a number of Indian cities, Mumbai included, authorities

---

3. This ecological degradation following economic expansion can be seen as the urban form of the 'second contradiction of capitalism', by which relations and forces of production and accumulation paradoxically destroy the social and material conditions of production on which they depend (O'Connor 1988).

rounded up beggars and homeless people on a nightly basis, transporting them out of the city. A 2003 news story reported plans by Thai authorities to remove thousands of homeless people from the streets of Bangkok in anticipation of a summit of world leaders. Cambodian beggars were repatriated, stray dogs were removed and government buildings renovated, as the city removed 'untidy activities' for the benefit of the 'orderliness and prestige of the country'. A high government official explained that 'we do not want our guests to see unpleasant scenes'.[4] In Brazilian cities, police have been notorious for the practice of rounding up and killing street children in 'one version of "urban renewal" ' (Scheper-Hughes 1993: 240).

Such examples of physical removal of un-modern and disturbing pollutants are supplemented by the more complex and sophisticated strategies to divide and regulate cities into modernity. The *Haussmannisation* of Paris in the nineteenth century is seen as emblematic of the project of modernity. Urban planner Baron Haussmann drastically rebuilt the city through widened boulevards, shopping arcades, public squares and monumental government buildings: a rational, modern architecture involving straight lines, efficiency and regulation. The ambition to create the ideal rational city involved displacing the poor from the city centre to the suburbs, reshaping Parisian architecture and public space for purposes of military control, capitalist advancement and bourgeois comfort. Of course, colonial governments and the South African apartheid state developed similar sophisticated planning mechanisms to maintain segregation and urban order in residential location and labour practices. Modernisation merges with pollution control as, in attaining the ideal of the city, 'rational organization must … repress all the physical, mental and political pollutions that would compromise it' (de Certeau 1984: 94).

In the twenty-first century, modernising urges and associated grand plans continue. Tomic et al. (2006) show how in Chile, neoliberal governments under Pinochet and his civilian successors made conscious efforts to conflate hygiene and cleanliness with modernity and development. In Santiago and other urban areas, 'sanitary landscapes' emerge as spaces of modernity; the government and the private sector maintain shopping malls, elite educational institutions and corporate skyscrapers as clean spaces emblematic of modernisation. Simultaneously, they establish clean, modern corridors of mobility – highways, streets, the train system – to link them. This spatial technique, not unique to Chile, results in the severing of connections with the 'dirty' spaces of alleged

4. Asian Economic News, 6 October 2003.

social and economic backwardness and exacerbates the urban fragmentation associated with neoliberal reform.

Urban order and security

The control exerted over urban space in the name of health care and progress points to the close relationship between pollution and urban order. Security is the sphere in which the connection between the two is perhaps most apparent. Pollution is associated with both symbolic and physical danger, in the form of violence, crime or health threats. Chaos, crime and violence are contrasted with order and safety in urban discourse that implicitly or explicitly draws on concepts of pollution. Cities in the popular imagination have often figured as dystopias, where pollution and turmoil reign. These chaotic, decadent, free-for-all spaces stand in contrast to the peaceful, unsullied character of rurality. Indeed, cities have always been depicted as having a weaker social and public order than rural areas, witnessed by individualisation, diversity and diminished social control. These factors may in fact be necessary to foster the freedom and creativity that make cities successful and attractive. Yet one of the paradoxes of the city is that both national and municipal governments have generally sought to counteract this disorder in efforts to establish and display their power. Owing to its central and symbolic position, the city is the site of many material manifestations of power – architecture, statues, parades and so on. Indeed, the more fluid character of the urban social order requires these manifestations as continuous assertions and demonstrations of power by those who wish to remain in control. In a time of global change and insecurity, urban policy discourse focuses increasingly on creating and maintaining urban order, in which, again, the social and the material are conflated.

The politics of urban order draw strongly on the issue of security, ridding the city of chaos, crime and violence. The concept of order connects morality, health and crime and is often used in reference to particular urban locations. Public behaviour deemed immoral by authorities can be suppressed in the name of safeguarding the public. Pollution is crucial in narratives of urban order and security. Avoiding or dispelling pollution involves ensuring that boundaries are not crossed, which in turn implies the need for literal and figurative policing of urban space and behaviour. Urban governments impose order on public space, in implicit or explicit attempts to create or maintain clean and safe cities. The measures meant to achieve urban security are diverse but include the organising, surveying and controlling of urban space and the elimination or segregation of urban elements that are conceptually polluting.

Garbage has become metaphor for laziness, moral dissolution and the abandonment of virtue. Those who live outside of visible social conventions and 'waste away' time, or their lives, are themselves characterised as (white) trash, wasters or scabs (Scanlan 2005). Prostitution, for instance, is often referred to in terms of pollution, defilement and sexual threat, and spatially, such activities are confined to red-light districts or expelled to marginal urban areas. Hubbard and Sanders (2003: 79) highlight how descriptions of red-light districts combine 'metaphors of sexual morality, environmental degradation, criminality and disease', while the identities of the sex workers are 'constructed through discourses of pollution and defilement'. They go on to demonstrate how spatial arrangements of deviance help to naturalise and cement the social order, notwithstanding tactics that resist dominant representations of urban space. This kind of moral geography, which involves the 'locating of impropriety', relies on collective constructions of social relations in public spaces (Dixon et al. 2006). Such shared constructions of place-behaviour bolster the dominant urban order and are employed by authorities in attempts to provide security.

Spatial grids of morality often become overlaid with class and ethnic divisions, as poor and ethnically distinct 'pollutants' are segregated and associated with danger. The ghettos formed by these divisions and exclusions become known as aggregates of poverty and deviance and are depicted as sources of potential contamination to other, untainted urban areas. Repressive policies that amount to the 'penalization of poverty' combine the enforcement of public order with the enforcement of the class order and ethnoracial hierarchies (Wacquant 2003). Urban design intended to improve security is often reliant on keeping out the raced or classed Other and maintaining purity through various spatial tactics. In general, such security strategies tend to limit freedom – of movement, expression or assembly – for some, while perhaps increasing it for others. Consequently, providing the security for some urban inhabitants will mean curtailing the liberty of others. The pollutants that threaten urban order can take on any number of forms and vary depending on the context: littering, urinating, smoking, spitting, loud music and graffiti may or may not be constructed as symbolic markers that threaten urban order.

As, in an age of global neoliberalism, cities become more polarised and the powers of municipal authorities are weakened, citizens have differential access to urban security based on their sociospatial position within the urban entity. Combined with declining trust in the police or social control, a preventive restructuring of urban space emerges, witnessed by the spread of gated communities and other instances of privatised public space and privatised governance. Cultures of control seek to eliminate risks by redistributing dangers throughout urban space (Franzén 2001; Low 2003). Paradoxically, security measures themselves involve the crossing of boundaries and the invasion of private spaces, for example, when police searches intrude on the integrity of the body or the private home, or when digital and camera surveillance constitute invasions of privacy (Staples 2000). The age of terrorism has heralded many new instances of restrictive measures promising increased security through an emphasis on order, backed by strategic 'fear management'. Cities are seen as obvious and vulnerable targets and as a response, urban space throughout the world is increasingly subject to mechanisms of surveillance and regulation. This strategy allows authorities to draw on the anxieties of citizens while validating their use of power in removing dangerous urban 'pollutants'. A small paradoxical way in which the link to material pollution is apparent is the removal of many rubbish bins in the centre of London, beginning with the IRA attacks of the 1970s, for fear of their potential as bomb receptacles.

Material pollution

Pollution and cultural value

In examining material forms of urban pollution, it is useful to make a distinction between the production and removal of garbage, sewage and other forms of waste. An analysis of the production of pollution requires definition of what objects or emissions constitute this category. Defining pollution implies a number of oppositions. The primary pair is that of purity and impurity as social constructions, described in detail above. However, pollution as waste also implies value and uselessness as central characteristics in defining what constitutes waste. Michael Thompson's *Rubbish Theory* (1979) addresses the latter form of categorisation, examining the relation between garbage and cultural value in an age of consumerism, where status is related not so much to what one possesses but to what one is able to discard. As a student of Mary Douglas, Thompson's concern is with cultural categorisation, though more specifically with objects[5] and their social processing. He sees first a categorisation of possessable objects as either valuable, valueless or negatively valued. He then distinguishes between transient and durable object categories. Transient objects have a limited life-span and decrease in value over that period, while durable objects can increase in value and ideally have an infinite life-span. However, these two types are accompanied by a third covert category of objects, namely that of rubbish: objects that are of zero and unchanging value. The different categories are, of course, socially constructed and enjoy porous boundaries; transient

---

5. Ultimately, the categories proposed in rubbish theory extend beyond objects to people and ideas as well.

objects slowly fade into rubbish but can then be transferred to the durable category. Following this categorisation, an object, for instance a vase, will lose value over time and will at a certain point be considered valueless rubbish. Yet the vase can shift from the rubbish category if it becomes revalued as an antique or a museum piece.

Value is a main determinant in the categorisation of what is garbage and what is not. The consumerism that has become endemic in many contemporary societies relates to this, in that accumulation goes hand in hand with disposal. Producers eschew the durable, preferring a system of 'planned product obsolescence' (Packard 1961) that ensures continued consumption and simultaneously waste production. Despite widespread awareness of the short and long term problems associated with visible and invisible pollution, and with management of the burgeoning mountains of waste, there appears to be what amounts to a 'conspiracy of blindness' (Thompson 1979), an unspoken agreement to collectively ignore certain forms of pollution. De Coverley et al. (2003) demonstrate how consumers are able to systematically disregard the garbage they produce. They found that the garbage bin, the bin men and socialisation against litter constitute three systems that allow people to avoid contemplating waste and their own role in its production. The garbage bin and the bin men obscure rubbish by swallowing it up and whisking it away, while opposition to litter – and, one might speculate, engaging in recycling activities – allows one to see oneself as a responsible citizen with regard to waste. Such mechanisms allow waste removal to remain 'back-stage' while supporting the consumerist nature of daily life.

Waste and stigma

A variety of 'technologies of expulsion' (Scanlan 2005: 122), from the most basic to the most advanced, exists in the field of waste removal. This practical business of removing waste – garbage and wastewater in particular – cannot be seen separately from the division of labour, cultural practice and gender constructions, and socioeconomic differentiation. Waste management and removal are generally seen as unpleasant activities. In everyday life they are widely perceived as male responsibilities, and professionally, the stigma attached to occupations related to waste seems universal. While this holds true for both formal and informal sector workers, the latter are generally subject to a larger degree of opprobrium. In many contexts, waste workers have a different ethnic background from the larger population. In India, garbage removal is often the domain of Dalits, or 'untouchables', in Muslim countries waste workers are often non-Muslims (Beall 2006). The occupational category tends to correlate with low socio-economic status, though the work itself may, in certain circumstances, be quite lucrative. A feedback loop of social reproduction maintains the socio-ethnic differentiation involved – 'dirty' jobs associated with the removal of waste are assigned to low status, ethnically differentiated groups and their association with pollution continues their distinction as low status Others.

The socio-cultural associations between physical, material pollution and certain groups of people have spatial consequences. The spaces in which people live, work and spend their leisure time are also categorised in terms of pollution and they reflect on the people who move in and through them. Polluted areas can suffer from what Drackner (2005) refers to as 'social contagion': polluted streets or neighbourhoods reflect on their residents who may, in certain cultural contexts, be seen as 'dirty' or 'nasty' people on account of their surroundings. This often entails some causal confusion. Poor and polluted neighbourhoods are classified as dirty because of the polluting, 'unhygienic' or 'asocial' poor people who live there.

Stigmatisation of the poor can be employed as a legitimation of their environmentally degraded urban areas. Rather than considering their unsanitary living and working conditions as a result of a weak socio-economic position, their 'nastiness' and concomitant social inferiority may be portrayed as the cause of their poverty. This sometimes morphs into 'blame the poor' discourse and policies. As often as not, the neighbourhoods are polluted because socially disadvantaged people do not receive environmental services and infrastructure such as solid waste collection and adequate sewage systems. Neighbourhood poverty often entails a lower level of the political and financial clout necessary to obtain – publicly or privately provided – environmental services or to fend off polluting industries. As Thompson (1979: 35) asserts, 'slums are socially determined … such physical, physiological, and economic considerations as poor living standards, lack of services and amenities, poor health, dampness, inadequate light, inadequate cooking facilities, overcrowding, high fire risk, whilst real enough are essentially the by-products of a concealed social process. They are the effects, not the cause.'

A proliferation of garbage is configured as a symbolic message, the urban 'text' of a dirty person, house, street or neighbourhood being read as signifying a lack of virtue. Garbage as an urban marker is used to distinguish urban segments and guide mobility. Small (2004: 102) speaks of the 'ecology of group differentiation', by which an area's spatial features become inextricably associated with class or ethnic features. This process reinforces differences between residents and nonresidents and spatialises boundary work, the construction of group differentiation and mutual exclusion discussed in the previous part of this introduction. In many cities, litter, graffiti and boarded-over, crumbling housing have become symbolic indicators of poverty, crime and violence. Environmental psychologists also find strong links between social and physical disorder, crime and fear of crime. These causal relationships are expressed in the so-called 'broken windows' thesis (Wilson and Kelling 1982). This theory posits that if a window in a building is broken and remains unrepaired, the other windows will soon be broken too, as the community and potential offenders interpret the non-repair – the disorder – as a sign that no one cares. Urban disorder is also manifest in 'standard' environmental problems, specifically garbage on the streets. Open sewers, substandard or abandoned housing, derelict cars and vandalised infrastructure are other conceivable environmental manifestations of urban disorder. However, as shown in the first part of this chapter, the perception of disorder is not only a matter of an objective level of cues in the environment. Rather, disorder is filtered by pre-existing ideas about certain groups and areas; a neighbourhood's racial, ethnic, and class composition shapes the perception of disorder (Sampson and Raudenbush 2004). Consequently, garbage appears to be dirtier and more visible when it is in an area occupied by a stigmatised group. The official neglect of such areas and their 'anti-social' tenants by 'slumologists' (Damer 1989) in municipal government can create self-fulfilling prophecies of environmental decay.

Urban political ecology and environmental justice

There are, then, various real and imagined associations between material pollution and marginalised and stigmatised urban groups, be they socio-economically, ethnically or otherwise differentiated. As noted above, when areas associated with particular groups are polluted, it is often because the inhabitants are denied environmental services and infrastructure. In addition, their marginal position means they are more likely to be the recipients of environmental 'bads', through their disproportionate exposure to industrial and traffic-related air pollution, proximity to (toxic) waste storage and disposal sites or employment in the most polluted and hazardous urban workplaces. A topical way of addressing this correlation between – and indeed, mutual constitution of – urban pollution and social inequality is through the theoretical lens of urban political ecology. Combining human ecology and political economy, political ecology studies human-environment relations in the context of politics and uneven power relations. It challenges apolitical studies of environmental change, critically examining dominant environmental narratives and exploring alternative socio-environmental arrangements (Robbins 2004: 12, cf. Keil 2003). Urban political ecology does this for the city, offering a critical understanding of relationships between urban power and pollution and the environmental implications of socio-economic, ethnic or gender inequalities. Discrimination on the basis of class, gender and ethnicity is linked to environmental degradation, while health and power differentials determine which groups of residents bear the brunt of urban pollution.

The most obvious division is that of class: the urban poor generally suffer most from exposure to pollution. In the past few decades, cities throughout the world have been submitted to neoliberal changes in the style of 'entrepreneurial' governance, characterised by a penchant for public-private partnerships in which local government focused on investment and economic development, and gave economic and political priority to the speculative construction of place over improving conditions within a specific territory (Harvey 2002). Despite the prominence of municipal policies, processes of urban privatisation – in environmental services, housing, security, education – and the emergence of gated communities in cities North and South expose governments' failure to provide citizens with a clean and safe environment. In the US, such processes have been exacerbated by suburbanisation and the concomitant flight of tax money from inner-cities, which result in both a strain on environmental infrastructure and services as urban sprawl and edge cities formed, and underinvestment and declines in infrastructure and services in the inner-city (Melosi 2000). Throughout the world, privatisation of basic services and of security, following neoliberal restructuring, results in cities where a safe and healthy environment is available at a price that not everyone can pay.

Spatialised urban divisions between rich and poor, resulting in and expressed by different levels of exposure to pollution, are compounded by gender inequalities. The gendered effects of environmental degradation in rural areas are well-documented, but urban women similarly suffer an unequal share of urban environmental problems. Given that in many cities throughout the world women have little political voice, they are disadvantaged in environmental decision-making, resulting in policies with a male bias. McGranahan et al. (2001: 130–156) demonstrate how, in the Ghanaian capital of Accra, micropolitics of power within the household and the neighbourhood result in greater environmental burdens and risks for women. A gendered division of urban labour means that household environmental problems such as air pollution from inadequate cooking and heating facilities affect cooks, caregivers and cleaners – predominantly female – the most. Moreover, the nature of labour in urban export-processing zones in low-wage countries, following global restructuring of production, mean that young women in particular are exposed to polluted and unhealthy workplaces (Doyal 2004). It becomes evident that urban divisions of power along gender lines find environmental expressions.

Socio-economic divisions often correlate with specific ethnic groups. Environmental racism is evident in the disproportionate concentrations of water, noise or air pollution and hazardous waste, especially when encountered in non-white neighbourhoods in predominantly white cities (Haughton 2004). Differential access to certain types of environmental facilities or services is one manner in which pollution becomes racialised. In Johannesburg, the legacy of apartheid is apparent in the highly uneven distributions of type of toilet, source of domestic water and energy source for cooking between African, Coloured, Indian and White groups (Beall et al. 2002: 155–6). In many cities in the United States, locally unwanted land uses (LULUs) – waste incinerators and toxic storage and disposal facilities – are disproportionately sited in or near African American or Latino residents (Pastor et al. 2001). Such discriminatory siting practices on the part of urban authorities – possible because of minorities' relative lack of political power – reveal the pervasiveness of environmental racism. While not necessarily an expression of malicious intent, 'white flight' to suburbs removed from older urban industrial zones exacerbates racialised environmental injustice (Pulido 2000).

Exposure of such ecological expressions of racism triggered collective action in the form of a social movement. In the 1980s, the environmental justice movement emerged as a branch of the North American environmental movement, redefining environmentalism to encompass poverty, inequity and the spatial distribution of environmental hazards. Environmental justice proved an effective frame for mobilising support for this specifically urban social movement. It focused on 'how discrimination results in humans harming each other, how racial minorities bear the brunt of the discrimination, and how discriminatory practices hasten the degradation of environments' as well as investigating 'corporate and governmental environmental behavior and the effects of those actions on the aggrieved communities' (Taylor 2000: 523).

Environmental movements and the politics of environmentalism

The environmental justice movement is one social movement specifically geared to address urban pollution and its relation to power and inequality. However, the larger North American environmental movement also displays a preoccupation with industrial pollution in particular. While the focus of the environmental movement has since shifted towards global issues such as climate change, pollution was initially the rallying issue, or collective action frame (Snow and Benford 1992), that enabled environment activists to mobilise on a large scale. Whether in terms of environmental justice for the environmentally disadvantaged urban poor, or in the context of middle-class suburbanites' NIMBY (not-in-my-back-yard) action, urban pollution features worldwide as a driver for community mobilisation and collective action (Evans 2002; Castells 1997: 110–33).[6]

Douglas and Wildavsky (1982) explain the emergence of environmentalism in the United States by focusing on fear of pollution,

---

6. Conversely, traditional conservationist discourses within environmentalism are also strongly invested in the 'purification' of nature (see e.g. Head and Muir 2006). Within such discourse, both 'nature out of place' (pests, exotic and genetically modified species) and 'non-nature' (humans, and particlary urban humans) are seen as pollutants that should preferably be removed from 'pure' or authentic nature (wilderness, endemic/indigenous species, etcetera).

arguing that environmental pollution in industrial societies is the functional equivalent of fear of ritual pollution in traditional societies. The function of 'modern' pollutants is similar in that they serve to protect the moral order. As in *Purity and Danger*, Mary Douglas concludes that environmental problems entail not only or primarily visible damage or specific health threats. Rather these environmental and technological risks, like dirt, are culturally constructed imageries related to purity, anxieties surrounding threats to the moral order. Environmentalism as a social movement must find new threats, new forms of pollution, to keep its activist members together. This kind of 'eschatological ecofatalism' (Beck 1992: 37) involves apocalyptic environmental narratives that posit activists as saviours (Hawkins and Muecke 2003).

This take on environmentalism has come under heavy critique, mainly as its strong constructionist character was seen to dispute the reality of environmental problems (Hannigan 2006: 110). However, the line of thought does point to a connection between pollution and the emergence of the risk society, associated with industrial and scientific development. This type of society is concerned not so much with the distribution of goods as with the distribution of (environmental) 'bads' (Beck 1992). This distribution of environmental bads, as noted previously, tends to work out to the disadvantage of those urban residents who wield the least power and often live and work in the most polluted parts of cities. Risk societies also tend to be accompanied by a generalised movement towards cultures of control, a tendency evident in the regulatory nature of many government strategies that aim to curb environmental risks.

As in all policy, power relations find expression in pollution control and management policies. Environmental policies, legislation and regulations can be seen as expressions of power, favouring the economic or social interests of specific parties over those of others. Equally, environmental movements generally display a political dimension. In Europe and the United States, environmentalism was entwined with other 'new social movements', including students, peace and women's movements (cf. Goodbody 2002), while contemporary environmentalist discourses may link to human rights struggles or indigenous movements. Environmentalists have often displayed an anti-establishment position and questioned established power relations by calling attention to the rights of future generations and socially marginalised groups (see Kerényi, this volume). However, environmentalism itself has become established and institutionalised in a variety of forms, lending the movement power in arenas ranging from local planning forums to global governance mechanisms. Moreover, the social movement has played a key role in terms of producing the environmental knowledge on which politics and policies are based. The articulation of environmental issues and 'eco-knowledge' within this range of institutional regimes can be viewed as discourses that shape citizens' understandings of the environment, thus affirming the power and knowledge of those institutions.

Following Foucault's concept of governmentality, as a discursive means of disciplining political subjects, these processes of instilling environmental consciousness and creating environmental subjects are described as 'environmentality' (Luke 1995; Agrawal 2005). As Jamison (2001: 17) alleges, 'an ecological consciousness … is in the process of being internalised in our cultures and our personalities'. Both governmental and non-governmental environmental organisations may be complicit in these discursive forms of environmentalist control, as they craft strategies that will raise environmental awareness and create environmentally conscious citizens. Discourses of urban pollution, then, also shape the way urban inhabitants see themselves and their surroundings, and influence how they think, speak, and act with regard to the urban environment. In some instances, urban actors will operate within a discourse that emphasises human-environment relations in terms of equity and justice, in other instances sanitation and morality will determine how actors define themselves in relation to the environment.

Garbage aesthetics

While pollution is repelling to most, and provokes reproving words and decisive action, it is appealing to others. Various forms of arts – poetry, cinema, painting, sculpture – have displayed a preoccupation with garbage. Many 'recycling artists' worldwide have transformed garbage – also known in this context as *objets trouvés*, or 'found objects' – into art. In 2001, Damien Hirst famously created an installation artwork, which consisted of empty beer bottles, coffee cups and discarded cigarette butts. Displayed in London's Eyestorm Gallery, a janitor failed to note that this was artistic garbage and swept it up. Gallery staff salvaged parts of the installation from rubbish bins and recreated it on the basis of photographs that had been taken earlier. A similar misunderstanding affected part of 'Recreation of First Public Demonstration of Auto-Destructive Art', a work by Gustav Metzger on display in London's Tate Britain gallery. The work featured a plastic garbage bag filled with paper and cardboard, which was also discarded by museum cleaners; it was subsequently replaced with a new bag. In art as in life, garbage relates to power struggles. In Brazil, the *cinema do lixo* or garbage cinema of the 1960s and 1970s, produced by the Undigrundi (Underground) movement, was framed with reference to local and international power relations, shocking bourgeois sensibilities and allegorising Brazil's marginal role as a Third World country (cf. Xavier 1997). Rubbish has also occupied a noteworthy place within literature. With regard to poetry, Haughton (2002) shows the centrality of garbage and its relation to margins and order in the work of Irish poet Derek

Mahon, akin to how Don DeLillo's American novel *Underworld* underlines the centrality of garbage as the shadow world created by modern life and consumerism. Early twentieth-century literary works often used garbage as pessimistic metaphors of decay and desolation, while later literature more frequently uses rubbish to critique the hyperconsumption and futility of affluent societies.

Conclusion

In conclusion, pollution means many things to many people. In this introduction, we have attempted to give an overview of themes relating to urban pollution, concentrating on cultural and material forms of pollution. We have examined how Mary Douglas' work on cultural pollution extends into the modern day context of globalisation and increasingly fluid cultural practices. Pollution is invoked as a reaction to insecurity and perceived cultural threats, or to bolster hegemonic orders, as witnessed by imperial and contemporary discourses on sanitation, civilisation, modernity and order. Cultural pollution is brought into play in urban space to establish or reinforce power relations, and this involves various forms of control of urban places and the people who inhabit them. The same interplay of power and pollution can be observed when studying material forms of pollution. Both the production and removal of waste involve expressions of power: influential actors determine what objects are considered valueless waste, less powerful actors end up responsible for the concrete disposal of this discarded matter. Within the city, the urban poor and other marginalised social groups bear the brunt of pollution, and social movements seek to address such environmental inequality but sometimes end up crafting their own exclusive regimes of environmental knowledge. Artists, finally, try to invert reality by turning garbage into art or using it as a social critique.

Structure of the book

Given the themes described in this introduction, studying urban pollution from a social science perspective appears to primarily concern practices of power in urban space, with a variety of discourses of pollution featuring in these practices. The contributions to this volume link pollution and environmental degradation to contemporary work in urban studies. They study how cultural pollution is reconfigured and figures in the (post)modern city, and how it intersects with space and power. The different chapters draw on fieldwork conducted in various cities around the globe, presenting a broad geographical range of varied cultural, natural and spatial contexts. The contributions include cases from traditional 'pollution studies' areas such as India and Indo-Fijians, as well as less familiar urban cases from 'industrialised areas' such as New Zealand and Central Europe. They explore the variety of cultural definitions and social constructions of nature, purity, cleanliness and pollution, and connect these to the spatialised workings of social differentiation and power in local urban arenas.

Following this introduction, the contributions draw both on cultural and material understandings of urban pollution. Some case studies focus explicitly on the mutual constitution of material and symbolic pollution; other chapters emphasise the specific meanings attributed to pollution in the context of urban and national relations between different ethnic, religious and socio-economic groups; and some take material pollution in cities as a starting point, indicating the inclusive and exclusive strategies to combat it, and the complex of power underlying waste production and removal in urban space.

Studying the social life of garbage in creating and countering narratives of social pollution, while pointing out how social distinctions do pollution 'work' on material objects, Eveline Dürr's contribution is based on the case of Auckland, New Zealand. Recent decades have seen an increase in migration from Asia that has significantly altered the demographic composition of the city. In the context of urban multiculturalism, identities are renegotiated in environmental terms. The perceived lack of environmental consciousness amongst Asian immigrants is employed in identity politics and nation-building strategies that contrast clean, green 'Kiwis' with 'dirty' ethnically distinct migrants. Damaris Lüthi implies a similar combination of symbolic and material categories in a study of religious definitions of cleanliness and how these inform polluting practices in Kottar, India. Drawing on religiously delineated dichotomies of public and private space, Kottar residents believe that neglecting personal hygiene and polluting indoor spaces will lead angry deities to punish the individual by inflicting disease or poverty. In contrast, polluting the outdoor, public environment is not associated with divine wrath and consequently is regarded as less hazardous.

The next three chapters privilege symbolic forms of pollution, linking them to urban negotiations of ethnicity, gender and class in contexts of contention and at times violence. Susanna Trnka examines Indo-Fijian perceptions of clean and dirty in relation to the urban and the jungle. Despite increasing environmental degradation, urban spaces are conceptualised as the essence of cleanliness through their association with wealth, modernity and development. This is related to politically contentious discourses of historical Indo-Fijian involvement in developing Fiji and clearing the 'jungle', which in turn is seen as wild, violent and uncivilised, and is associated with indigenous Fijians. Anouk de Koning describes contentious discourses of pollution of both urban spaces and the space of the gendered body in neoliberal Cairo, Egypt. She describes how young female professionals' spatial practices of mobility and consumption – including their presence in coffee shops, streets and public transport – are framed in terms of pollution. Class configurations and gender ideologies are renegotiated through the strategic movement of middle-class female bodies through urban space. Magnus Treiber studies similar processes in another context of urban social change. He demonstrates how the youth of Asmara, Eritrea differentiate between 'clean' and 'dirty' bars and hangouts, a distinction which reveals responses to the war-torn country's poverty and violence. Certain groups associated themselves with the 'clean' spaces, which symbolise safety, comfort, modernity and social exclusivity, while others adopt the dirt and danger of the older, unsanitised locales. Again, these distinctions between urban spaces map out in a gendered fashion on the space of the body.

The final three chapters examine the ways in which urban pollution actively shapes and is shaped by NGO campaigns and public policy. Starting from material pollution but illustrating its effectivity in shaping politics, Szabina Kerényi studies mobilisation around urban pollution in the Hungarian capital of Budapest. The Hungarian green movement is a grassroots movement, developed in opposition to the country's communist past but now splintered into a diversity of sub-sectors and actors. Pollution however, remains a central issue that can act as a crucial mobilising factor for the movement. Johanna Rolshoven's contribution examines Swiss, and more broadly European, policies that aim to increase control over public urban space, analysing the ideologies and power relations that underlie such policies. In practice, order, safety and cleanliness are achieved through the removal of unwanted persons, rather than garbage alone, disregarding the positive effects of chance encounters and a certain randomness in public space on urban liveability. Kathryn Scott, Angela Shaw and Christina Bava show the clash of government and resident discourses on the physical environment and urban order in an Auckland suburb, in an urban planning context. Low socioeconomic status, high rates of crime and a degraded physical environment made it the target of consecutive urban programmes. Official city-wide development strategies related to housing and urban design do not necessarily take into account local stakeholder definitions of well-being: resident and professional discourse and practice diverge on topics of pollution, urban order and sustainability.

These ethnographic examples presented in this volume illuminate the various ways in which urban pollution is conceptualised, by bringing together forms of cultural and material pollution and simultaneously stressing the fluidity and hybridity of these dynamic categories. They enrich our analytical approaches towards urban pollution and reveal the multiple ways in which it can be understood and addressed.

References

Agrawal, A. 2005. 'Environmentality: Community, Intimate Government, and the Making of Environmental Subjects in Kumaon, India', *Current Anthropology* 46 (2): 161–90.

Amnesty International. 2001. *Jamaica: Killings and Violence by Police: How Many More Victims?* Report No.: AMR 38.001.2001. London: Amnesty International Secretariat.

Anderson, K.J. 1991. *Vancouver's Chinatown: Racial Discourse in Canada, 1875–1980.* Montreal & Kingston: McGill-Queen's University Press.

Anderson, W. 1995. 'Excremental Colonialism: Public Health and the Poetics of Pollution', *Critical Inquiry* 21 (3): 640–69.

Aoyagi, K., P.J.M. Nas and J.W. Traphagan (eds) 1998. *Toward Sustainable Cities: Readings in the Anthropology of Urban Environments.* Leiden: Leiden Development Studies.

Ballinger, P. 2004. ' "Authentic Hybrids" in the Balkan Borderlands', *Current Anthropology* 45 (1): 31–60.

Bashford, A. 1998. *Purity and Pollution: Gender, Embodiment and Victorian Medicine.* London: Macmillan Press.

———— 2004. *Imperial Hygiene: A Critical History of Colonialism, Nationalism and Public Health.* New York: Palgrave Macmillan.

Bauman, Z. 2002. 'Modernity and the Holocaust' in *Genocide: An Anthropological Reader*, A.L. Hinton (ed.), pp. 110–33. Oxford: Blackwell.

Beall, J. 2006. 'Dealing with Dirt and the Disorder of Development: Managing Rubbish in Urban Pakistan', *Oxford Development Studies* 34 (1): 81–97.

Beall, J., O. Crankshaw and S. Parnell. 2002. *Uniting a Divided City: Governance and Social Exclusion in Johannesburg.* London: Earthscan.

Beck, U. 1992. *Risk Society: Towards a New Modernity.* London: Sage Publications.

Booth, C. (ed.) 1902–1903. *Life and Labour of the People in London.* 17 volumes. London: Macmillan.

Bullard, R.D. 2000. *Dumping in Dixie: Race, Class, and Environmental Quality.* Boulder: Westview Press.

Castells, M. 1997. *The Information Age: Economy, Society and Culture. Vol. II: The Power of Identity.* Oxford: Blackwell.

Chadwick, E. 1842. *Report on the Sanitary Condition of the Labouring Population of Great Britain.* Edinburgh: Edinburgh University Press.

Chaplin, S.E. 1999. 'Cities, Sewers and Poverty: India's Politics of Sanitation', *Environment and Urbanization* 11 (1): 145–58.

Checker, M. 2001. '"Like Nixon Coming to China": Finding Common Ground in a Multi-Ethnic Coalition for Environmental Justice', *Anthropological Quarterly* 74 (3): 135–46.

———— 2005. *Polluted Promises: Environmental Racism and the Search for Justice in a Southern Town.* New York and London: New York University Press.

Cohen, W.A. 2005. 'Introduction: Locating Filth' in *Filth: Dirt, Disgust, and Modern Life*, W.A Cohen and R. Johnson (eds), pp. vii–xxxvii. Minneapolis: University of Minnesota Press.

Comaroff, J. and J.L. Comaroff. 2001. 'Naturing the Nation: Aliens, Apocalypse, and the Postcolonial State', *Social Identities* 7 (2): 233–65.

Corbin, A. 1986. *The Foul and the Fragrant: Odor and the French Social Imagination.* Cambridge, Mass.: Harvard University Press.

Craddock, S. 2000. *City of Plagues: Disease, Poverty, and Deviance in San Francisco.* Minneapolis: University of Minnesota Press.

Damer, S. 1989. *From Moorepark to 'Wine Alley': The Rise and Fall of a Glasgow Housing Scheme.* Edinburgh: University of Edinburgh Press.

de Certeau, M. 1984. *The Practice of Everyday Life*, trans. S. Rendall. Berkeley, Los Angeles and London: University of California Press.

de Coverly, E., L. O'Malley and M. Patterson. 2003. *Hidden Mountain: The Social Avoidance of Waste.* Nottingham: International Centre for Corporate Social Responsibility. ICCSR Research Paper No. 08–2003.

Dixon, J., M. Levine and R. McAuley. 2006. 'Locating Impropriety: Street Drinking, Moral Order, and the Ideological Dilemma of Public Space', *Political Psychology* 27 (2): 187–206.

Douglas, M. 2002 [1966]. *Purity and Danger: An Analysis of Concept of Pollution and Taboo.* London: Routledge.

Douglas, M. and A. Wildavsky. 1982. *Risk and Culture: An Essay on the Selection of Technological and Environmental Dangers.* Berkeley: University of California Press.

Doyal, L. 2004. 'Women, Health and Global Restructuring: Setting the Scene', *Development* 47 (2): 18–23.

Drackner, M. 2005. 'What is Waste? To Whom? An Anthropological Perspective on Garbage', *Waste Management & Research* 23 (3): 175–81.

Evans, P. (ed.) 2002 Livable Cities? *Urban Struggles for Livelihood and Sustainability.* Berkeley: University of California Press.

Foucault, M. 1977. *Discipline and Punish: The Birth of the Prison*, trans. A. Sheridan. New York: Pantheon Books.

Franzén, M. 2001. Urban Order and the Preventive Restructuring of Space: The Operation of Border Controls in Micro Space, *The Sociological Review* 49 (2): 202–18.

Gandy, M. 2002. *Concrete and Clay: Reworking Nature in New York City.* Cambridge, MA: MIT Press.

Gandy, M. 2004. 'Rethinking Urban Metabolism: Water, Space and the Modern City', *City* 8 (3): 363–79.

George, T.S. 2001. *Minamata: Pollution and the Struggle for Democracy in Postwar Japan.* Cambridge: Harvard University Asia Center.

Gille, Z. 2007. *From the Cult of Waste to the Trash Heap of History: The Politics of Waste in Socialist and Post-Socialist Hungary.* Bloomington: Indiana University Press.

Goldberg, D.T. 1993. 'Polluting the Body Politic: Racist Discourse and Urban Location' in *Racism, the City, and the State*, M. Cross and M. Keith (eds), pp. 45–60. New York: Routledge.

Goodbody, A. (ed.) 2002. *The Culture of German Environmentalism: Anxieties, Visions, Realities*. Oxford: Berghahn Books.

Guano, E. 2004. 'The Denial of Citizenship: "Barbaric" Buenos Aires and the Middle-Class Imaginary', *City and Society* 16 (1): 69–97.

Hajer, M.A. 1995. *The Politics of Environmental Discourse: Ecological Modernization and the Policy Process*. Oxford: Oxford University Press.

Hall, S. (ed.) 1997. *Representation: Cultural Representations and Signifying Practices*. London: Sage.

Hannigan, J. 2006. *Environmental Sociology*, 2nd edn. London and New York: Routledge.

Harrison, S. 1999. 'Cultural Boundaries', *Anthropology Today* 15 (5): 10–13.

Harvey, D. 2002 [1989]. 'From Managerialism to Entrepreneurialism: The Transformation of Urban Governance in Late Capitalism' in *The Blackwell City Reader*, G. Bridge and S. Watson (eds), pp. 456–63. Oxford: Blackwell.

———— 2003. 'The City as Body Politic' in *Wounded Cities: Destruction and Reconstruction in a Globalized* World, J. Schneider and I. Susser (eds), pp. 25–44. Oxford and New York: Berg.

Haughton, G. 2004. 'Environmental Justice and the Sustainable City' in *The City Cultures Reader*, M. Miles, T. Hall and I. Borden (eds), pp. 461–74. New York: Routledge.

Haughton, H. 2002. ' "The Bright Garbage on the Incoming Wave": Rubbish in the Poetry of Derek Mahon', *Textual Practice* 16 (2): 323–43.

Hawkins, G. 2005. *The Ethics of Waste: How We Relate to Rubbish*. Lanham, MD: Rowman & Littlefield.

Hawkins, G. and S. Muecke, (eds) 2003. *Culture and Waste: The Creation and Destruction of Value*. Lanham: Rowman & Littlefield.

Herod, A. and L.L.M. Aguiar, 2006. 'Introduction: Cleaners and the Dirty Work of Neoliberalism', *Antipode* 38 (3): 425–34.

Head, L. and P. Muir. 2006. 'Suburban life and the boundaries of nature: resilience and rupture in Australian backyard gardens', *Transactions of the Institute of British Geographers* 31 (4): 505–24.

Heynen, N., M. Kaika and E. Swyngedouw, (eds) 2006. *In the Nature of Cities: Urban Political Ecology and the Politics of Urban Metabolism*. London: Routledge.

Hubbard, P. and T. Sanders. 2003. 'Making Space for Sex Work: Female Street Prostitution and the Production of Urban Space', *International Journal of Urban and Regional Research*, 27 (1): 75–89.

Inda, J.X. and R. Rosaldo. 2008 [2002]. 'Tracking Global Flows' in *The Anthropology of Globalization: A Reader*, J.X. Inda and R. Rosaldo (eds), pp. 3–46. Malden: Blackwell.

Jamison, A. 2001. *The Making of Green Knowledge: Environmental Politics and Green Transformation*. Cambridge: Cambridge University Press.

Kaika, M. 2005. *City of Flows: Modernity, Nature and the City*. London and New York: Routledge.

Keil, R. 2003. 'Urban Political Ecology', *Urban Geography* 24 (8): 723–38.

King, A.D. 1990. *Urbanism, Colonialism, and the World-Economy: Cultural and Spatial Foundations of the World Urban System*. London and New York: Routledge.

Krieger, N. 2006. 'A Century of Census Tracts: Health & the Body Politic (1906–2006)', *Journal of Urban Health* 83 (3): 355–61.

Latour, B. 1993. *We Have Never Been Modern*. Cambridge, MA: Harvard University Press.

Law, J. 1999. 'After ANT: Complexity, Naming and Topology' in *Actor Network Theory and After*, J. Law and J. Hassard (eds), pp. 1–14. Oxford: Blackwell.

Low, S. 2003. *Behind the Gates: Life, Security and the Pursuit of Happiness in Fortress America*. New York and London: Routledge.

Luke, T.W. 1995. 'On Environmentality: Geo-Power and Eco-Knowledge in the Discourses of Contemporary Environmentalism', *Cultural Critique* 31: 57–81.

Malkki, L.H. 1995. *Purity and Exile: Violence, Memory, and National Cosmology among Hutu Refugees in Tanzania*. Chicago: University of Chicago Press.

McGranahan, G., P. Jacobi, J. Songsore, C. Surjadi and M. Kjellén. 2001. *The Citizens at Risk: From Urban Sanitation to Sustainable Cities*. London: Earthscan.

McKean, M.A. 1981. *Environmental Protest and Citizen Politics in Japan*. Berkeley: University of California Press London.

Melosi, M.V. 2000. *Sanitary City: Urban Infrastructure in America from Colonial Times to the Present*. Baltimore: Johns Hopkins University Press.

Moore, D.S., J. Kosek and A. Pandian. 2003. 'Introduction: The Cultural Politics of Race and Nature: Terrains of Power and Practice' in *Race, Nature, and the Politics of Difference*, Donald S. Moore, Jake Kosek and Anand Pandian (eds), pp. 1–70. Durham and London: Duke University Press.

Nguyen, V.-K. and K. Peschard. 2003. 'Anthropology, Inequality, and Disease: A Review', *Annual Review of Anthropology* 32: 447–74.

O'Connor, J. 1988. 'Capitalism, Nature, Socialism: An Introduction', *Capitalism, Nature, Socialism* 1 (1): 11–38.

Obrist, B., M. Tanner and T. Harpham. 2003. 'Engaging Anthropology in Urban Hralth Research: Issues and Prospects', *Anthropology & Medicine* 10 (3): 361–71.

Olsen, J. 1999. *Nature and Nationalism: Right-Wing Ecology and the Politics of Identity in Contemporary Germany*. New York: St. Martin's Press.

Packard, V. 1961. *The Waste Makers*. London: Longman.

Pastor, M., J. Sadd and J. Hipp. 2001. 'Which Came First? Toxic Facilities, Minority Move-In and Environmental Justice', *Journal of Urban Affairs* 23 (1): 1–21.

Pellow, D.N. 2002. *Garbage Wars: The Struggle for Environmental Justice in Chicago*. Cambridge, MA: MIT Press.

Pulido, L. 2000. 'Rethinking Environmental Racism: White Privilege and Urban Development in Southern California', *Annals of the Association of American Geographers* 90 (1): 12–40.

Robbins, P. 2004. *Political Ecology: A Critical Introduction*. Oxford: Blackwell.

Russo, M. 1995. *The Female Grotesque: Risk, Excess, and Modernity*. New York: Routledge.

Sampson, R.J., and S.W. Raudenbush. 2004. 'Seeing Disorder: Neighbourhood Stigma and the Social Construction of "Broken Windows" ', *Social Psychology Quarterly* 67 (4): 319–42.

Scanlan, J. 2005. *On Garbage*. London: Reaktion Books.

Schell, L. M. and M. Denham. 2003. 'Environmental Pollution in Urban Environments and Human Biology', *Annual Review of Anthropology* 32: 111–34.

Scheper-Hughes, N. 1993. *Death Without Weeping: The Violence of Everyday Life in Brazil*. Berkeley and Los Angeles: University of California Press.

Shah, N. 2001. *Contagious Divides: Epidemics and Race in San Francisco's Chinatown*. Berkeley and Los Angeles: University of California Press.

Small, M.L. 2004. *Villa Victoria: The Transformation of Social Capital in a Boston Barrio*. Chicago: University of Chicago Press.

Snow, D.A. and R.D. Benford. 1992. 'Master Frames and Cycles of Protest' in *Frontiers in Social Movement Theory*, A.D. Morris and C.M. Mueller (eds), pp. 133–55. New Haven: Yale University Press.

Staples, W.G. 2000. *Everyday Surveillance: Vigilance and Visibility in Postmodern Life*. Lanham: Rowman and Littlefield.

Strasser, S. 1999. *Waste and Want: A Social History of Trash*. New York: Metropolitan Books.

Swyngedouw, E. 2004. *Social Power and the Urbanization of Water: Flows of Power*. Oxford: Oxford University Press.

Taylor, D.E. 2000. 'The Rise of the Environmental Justice Paradigm: Injustice Framing and the Social Construction of Environmental Discourses', *American Behavioral Scientist* 43 (4): 508–80.

Thompson, M. 1979. *Rubbish Theory: The Creation and Destruction of Value*. Oxford: Oxford University Press.

Tomic, P., R. Trumper and R.H. Dattwyler. 2006. 'Manufacturing Modernity: Cleaning, Dirt, and Neoliberalism in Chile', *Antipode* 38 (3): 508–29.

Wacquant, L. 2003. 'Toward a Dictatorship Over the Poor? Notes on the Penalization of Poverty in Brazil', *Punishment and Society* 5 (2): 197–205.

Wilson, J.Q. and G.L. Kelling. 1982. 'The Police and Neighbourhood Safety: Broken Windows', *The Atlantic Monthly* 127: 29–38.

Xavier, I. 1997. *Allegories of Underdevelopment: Aesthetics and Politics in Modern Brazilian Cinema*. Minneapolis: University of Minnesota Press.

CHAPTER 2

'Tidy Kiwis/Dirty Asians': Cultural Pollution and Migration in Auckland, New Zealand

EVELINE DÜRR

Introduction

As Asian migration[1] to Pacific Rim countries like New Zealand has grown enormously in volume over the last decades, Asian migrants have become more visible in these societies, especially through impacts on demographic patterns, residential structure and intercultural relationships (Skeldon 2000; Li 2006). Asian migrants are not new to ex-British colonies in the Pacific Rim, but political and economic conditions in the destination countries and in Asian 'homelands' are markedly different now than in the past. These changes are also evident in migratory patterns and migrants' socio-economic characteristics. While in the past the great majority of the migrants were part of the unskilled workforce, they are now increasingly well-educated, asset-rich and professionally trained (Li 2006: 9). Their preferred destinations are large metropolitan areas providing favourable conditions for entrepreneurs and investors. Unlike their predecessors, skilled and financially potent migrants choose to settle in affluent neighbourhoods. Tensions often emerge between the local residents and the new migrants as their arrival contributes not only to local ethnic diversity but also to the subsequent conversion of

1. Following Skeldon's study (2000: 369) discussing migration in the Asian and Pacific region, I exclude West Asia (also the Middle East) and Central Asia when I refer to 'Asia' in this article. In the early 1990s, up to half a million immigrants a year, predominately Chinese and Indian, were received in the US, Canada and Australia alone (Skeldon 2000: 370).

these suburbs as a consequence of new housing styles, business activities and cultural practices. Thus, contemporary studies of Asian migration to Pacific Rim cities highlight critical issues such as the transformation of space, settlement patterns, economic restructuring, policy making, citizenship and integration (Hu-DeHart 1999; Mitchell 2004; Anderson and Lee 2005). The same issues have surfaced in New Zealand and are addressed in numerous studies (Ip 1995; Lidgard 1996; Ip and Pang 2005; Bedford 2005; Ho and Bedford 2006).

In this article, I shift the focus to perceptions of Asian migrants and especially scrutinise the ways in which they are culturally conceptualised as aggravating pollution in New Zealand. In contrast to earlier narratives on 'dirty Asians' referring to filth, disease and loose morals, contemporary perceptions are more concerned with Asians' ignorance of, and indifference towards, the natural environment. While discourses stigmatising Asian immigrants as 'polluting others' have emerged also in other national contexts (Mitchell 2004: 182), they have a particular relevance in New Zealand, where the majestic landscape, its endemic flora and fauna and natural 'purity' contribute to the country's uniqueness and are significant sources of national pride and identity (Bell 1996: 46–7). I argue that perceptions of Asian migrants in New Zealand, which sometimes find expression in a specific set of environmental discourses, are tied into New Zealand's self-perception and international reputation as a 'clean', 'green' and environmentally friendly country. I am particularly interested in Pākehā's[2] subjectivities and perceptions of urban migrants' cultural practices and environmental attitudes. As the hegemonic group in New Zealand's society, they once defined themselves in terms of race, as essentially 'white' and 'British' (Belich 2001: 118). Now their identity construction entails an ideal environmental ethos. In this vein, I examine the discursive intersection between national identity, migration and cultural pollution. The research findings are based on ethnographic methods

2. The label Pākehā is contested and has multiple meanings. According to Spoonley's (1993: 57) definition it is related to power: 'New Zealanders of a European background, whose cultural values and behaviour have been primarily formed from the experience of being a member of the dominant group of New Zealand.' This definition includes individuals who might not apply the term Pākehā to themselves. A more recent observation (Webster 2001: 15) shows that the term Pākehā is also used by individuals to imply a definition of not being Māori. Others refer to the colonisation process and the recognition of biculturalism (Spoonley 2005: 102). There is no agreed definition of the term Pākehā and its meaning needs to be explored in the specific context of its use. In this study, I use Pākehā to refer to New Zealanders who perceive themselves as non-Māori and as descendants of British settlers. Because I focus on Pākehā perspectives in this article, I refer to 'New Zealand' instead of Aotearoa New Zealand.

and indepth narrative interviews conducted with immigrants from various Asian countries and with Pākehā and Asian community stakeholders in Auckland in 2005, 2006 and 2007. Analysis of these individuals' accounts shows that the radical changes in New Zealand's cultural composition are presented using concepts of littering, dirt and pollution, which are transferred to the social realm and linked to cultural attributes of new immigrants. I also point to the reverberating effects of these perceptions, discourses and representations by showing how they are accommodated and counterbalanced by Asian migrants' agency.

In New Zealand as elsewhere, the perception of Asian migrants, in particular Chinese, has transformed in intriguing ways during the course of their migration history. Covering extremes, these perceptions ranged from the 'yellow peril', conveying a disease-ridden, inferior group in the nineteenth century to a hard working, successful and disciplined 'model minority' in the 1960s, to an economically thriving, transnational bridge-building community on the modern-day Pacific Rim (Hu-DeHart 1999: 8). These narratives, repeatedly shared in different national contexts, reflect the ambiguity ascribed to this highly visible, physically distinct migratory group which continues to be widely perceived as 'foreign' (Hu-DeHart 1999: 13). This oscillating perception reflects specific historical circumstances in the origin and destination countries of Asian migrants and is shaped by an Orientalist construction and dissemination of a particular 'Asian' image. In New Zealand, resurfacing discourses on Asians as 'polluting others' reflect uncertainty in terms of national identity and the country's positioning in the global order. These discursive representations are not just symbolic struggles but also linked to power and access to resources.

Pollution and contamination are associated with alterity and serve to establish social distinctions between the native and the foreign (Douglas 1966). The binary of 'tidy Kiwi[3]/dirty Asian' does very specific work in New Zealand by generating and reinforcing ideals about New Zealand's identity and representation. Narratives on migration that entail fear of waste and environmental concerns serve as rhetorical warnings that New Zealand's national self-image is exposed to dramatic changes – and under threat of being polluted. Based on Mary Douglas' approach (1966), I will show how otherness is mediated in environmental terms and juxtaposed to 'clean' Kiwi values. This dichotomy also underlies Said's (1978) process

3. Kiwi *(Apterygidae)* is a flightless bird, unique to New Zealand, and the colloquial term for New Zealand nationals.

of Orientalism by representing and discursively constructing insuperable differences between 'self' and 'other'. Notably, this perceived dichotomy ignores the dynamics of cultural and national boundaries which are blurred and renegotiated according to changing contexts and interests (Bhabha 1994). It also disregards contested claims and internal hierarchies amongst specific groups by constructing them discursively as homogenous cultural entities, in this case as 'Asians'. However, I will demonstrate that these group members also apply categorisations of 'clean' and 'dirty' in order to mark social distinctions between themselves. This shows that 'culture' or what is perceived as 'the other' is not a pre-existing, static entity, but rather a construction informed by specific interaction patterns and interests. In this vein, postcolonial approaches point to a dynamic understanding of culture, as a constantly changing process in which meanings are continually negotiated and renegotiated between actors and framed by global conditions (Bhabha 1994; Appadurai 1996; Hall 1997; Inda and Rosaldo 2008). Dichotomist notions of 'self' and 'other' are reviewed and emphasis is placed on the dissolution of rigid boundaries and on transgression between cultural groups which were once perceived as separate. 'Self' and 'other' are rather seen as interrelated categories which are co-constitutive. Following these theoretical lines, I posit that 'polluting Asians' actually reassure 'tidy Kiwis' and strengthen their national identity as 'clean' – and in more recent terminology 'environmentally friendly'.

The natural environment as a New Zealand icon dates back to colonial times, when it was conceptualised as an ideal Arcadia in order to attract new settlers and investors to the remote and marginal islands (Fairburn 1989: 20). To date, New Zealand's scenery is an integral part of the country's representation and plays a key role in its national branding in the internationally competitive tourist industry. Its remoteness, scenic beauty and low population density are portrayed as unique features, promising undiluted and pristine nature in a contaminated and overcrowded world (Bell 1996). Recent film and media publicity add to this positive international reception of New Zealand's landscape. Thus, New Zealand's natural environment constitutes a nationally and internationally recognised asset (Dürr 2007, 2008). Environmental and ecological awareness, however, are more recent features in New Zealand's branding. The '100% Pure New Zealand' global campaign, which suggested that these notions are idiosyncratic to New Zealand, was invented in the late 1990s in order to position New Zealand favourably in the global tourist industry (McClure 2004: 285).

Also, indigenous Ma⁻ ori feel a spiritual relationship with the environment and see themselves as custodians of the land (Smith 2004). This finds expression in New Zealand's image in the outside world and has political relevance inside the officially bicultural[4] society, which is based on an idea of equal relationship between indigenous Ma⁻ ori and Pa⁻ keha⁻ , as articulated in the Treaty of Waitangi signed in 1840 by Ma⁻ ori chiefs and the Crown.[5] Unlike Ma⁻ ori, Asian New Zealanders are hardly included in New Zealand's national and international representation and their position in New Zealand's social matrix is still under debate. This is framed by the perceived tension between a bicultural versus a multicultural definition of New Zealand's society. Māori attitudes towards Asian immigrants have hardened in recent years (Gendall et al. 2007: 26, 30). They are concerned that Asian immigration challenges their particular status as indigenous peoples of New Zealand (*tangata whenua*) and dilutes the recognition of the Treaty of Waitangi, which is a key document and political tool in the relationship and identity formations of both Ma⁻ ori and Pa⁻ keha⁻ . Ma⁻ ori concerns in this matter reach beyond the symbolic appreciation of their status as indigenous peoples and are also nurtured by a perceived threat to their privileged access to natural resources and political power as promised by the Treaty. However, there are also voices advocating overcoming the binary definition of New Zealand's society while still accepting Treaty obligations (Ward and Lin 2006: 168).

The politics of identities are always tied into the wider national ambit and require a close examination of the historical and contemporary economic and social frame. In this vein, I first discuss the historical conditions shaping New Zealand's immigration policies. I will then

4. Božić-Vrbančić (2003: 295) points out that use of the term biculturalism in New Zealand policy demonstrates that the government does not define biculturalism as a relationship solely between Pākehā and Māori but also other cultures: 'we are one nation, two peoples and many cultures'. I use the term in this article to point to the Pākehā and Māori cultural heritage.

5. On 6 February 1840, representatives of the British government and around 520 Māori *rangatira* (chiefs) signed a treaty at Waitangi. In three articles, this document addresses sovereignty and access to land and legal rights. However, until the twentieth century, the Treaty was either ignored or interpreted to advantage the European population. It gained new importance in the context of Māori resurgence, when the Treaty of Waitangi Tribunal was established by the Treaty of Waitangi Act in 1975 to make recommendations regarding unsolved Treaty grievances (see Stokes 1992; Durie 1998; Brookfield 2006).

outline more recent anti-immigrant tendencies in the social ambience and their impact on the wider perceptions of Asian migrants. I draw particular attention to public discourses on migration, identity and environmental issues. These discourses contribute to the image of Asian migrants as 'polluting other', producer of 'foreign waste' and as an 'environmental threat' as well as a threat to a self-image of environmentally friendly and 'tidy Kiwis'. The locus of this empirical research is Auckland, New Zealand's gateway city, where Asian migrants are especially present and their high visibility in the cityscape raises debates on racial prejudice and ethnic tension. The significant and rapid modification of Auckland's city centre in terms of cultural composition and built environment provides an excellent lens to analyse these processes and to draw general conclusions.

Framing migration policies and politics

Migration and settlement patterns of Asian migrants are similar in the four major immigrant receiving Pacific Rim countries, the USA, Canada, Australia and New Zealand (Li 2006: 2), but remain mediated by the national context and local conditions. New Zealand differs in several regards from other ex-British colonies. Even though concern was expressed about its low population density, New Zealand practised discriminatory policies towards immigrants from so called 'non-traditional source countries' longer than others (Ip 2003a: 339). It was the last Pacific Rim country to alter its racially based immigration policy, a change made in 1987. It also had proportionally fewer immigrants than other immigrant countries, but even today it has a much higher indigenous population segment (14 percent) than the USA, Australia or Canada (ranging from 1.5 to 3.5 percent).[6]

In comparison with other white settler colonies, New Zealand's ties to Britain were particularly strong and enduring, even after the decolonisation process in the early twentieth century. As a European country and British outpost in the South Pacific, many Pākehā still thought

6. See http://www.stats.govt.nz/census/2006–census-data/quickstats-about-culture-identity/quickstats-about-culture-and-identity.htm,
   http://www.library.ubc.ca/xwi7xwa/stats.htm,
   http://www.census.gov/population/www/socdemo/race/indian.html,
   http://www.abs.gov.au/ausstats/abs@.nsf/productsbytitle/B0B7B5B83FE0CDABCA25722E001A39AA?OpenDocument, retrieved 5 August 2007.

of themselves as members of the British nation (Belich 2001: 118). Conducive to this identity pattern was the fact that New Zealand was one of the most ethnically homogenous white settler societies until the end of World War II (Ward and Lin 2006: 156). In 1948, the British Nationality and New Zealand Citizenship Act prepared the way for the status of New Zealand rather than British citizens (McMillan 2004: 277). However, this prospect received little enthusiasm in New Zealand and independent citizenship was introduced only with the Citizenship Act in 1977 (Spoonley and Macpherson 2004: 179).[7]

New Zealand has both a colonial and a national history of receiving migrants, mainly from Great Britain and Ireland. A range of restrictions based on a colonial model limited the influx of Chinese, Indians and Croatians, mainly from Dalmatia (Spoonley et al. 2004: 109) and racist ideologies and stereotypes were used to justify strict immigration rules. In the late nineteenth century, immigration challenged the racial purity of New Zealand's imagined British society, and particular groups were targeted. Distinctions were made between 'pure white' and 'dirty white', to classify the Croats, who worked predominantly in the Kauri gum industry (Božić-Vrbančić 2003: 304).

Early Chinese immigrants to Otago in the South Island, who arrived as gold miners at the invitation of the Dunedin Chamber of Commerce in 1866, were first welcomed as hardy labourers (Ip 1995: 162), but as they soon expanded their economic activities into laundry businesses and market gardening, their productivity became perceived as an economic threat. By the 1870s, Chinese migrants were subject to discrimination, social exclusion and stereotyping (Božić-Vrbančić 2003: 305). Their situation worsened after the economic crisis in 1881 with the imposition of a poll tax on Chinese immigrants, followed by further tax increases and restrictions on Chinese immigration. Common depictions in the media portrayed them as unclean, unhygienic, contractors of infectious diseases, living in filth and stench, and associated with immoral behaviour, including opium use, bargaining and gambling (Ip and Murphy 2005: 19–25). These representations corresponded to Victorian campaigns that

7. The then Minister of Internal Affairs, W.E. Parry, expressed his sentiments about the new status. He felt that New Zealand's government should not have initiated this change in citizenship status, but should have retained the status quo (McMillan 2004: 277). Despite this resentment, the Citizenship Act was introduced in 1977 and took effect on 1 January 1978 (McMillan 2004: 279).

sought to cleanse cities in the British home country, intertwining poverty, rubbish and contagious diseases. Nineteenth and early twentieth-century sanitary reforms were often violently discriminatory and based on moralising, middle-class values and imperial hygiene (Strasser 1999: 136; Cohen 2005: xx). These practices swept to the colonies, where nationalism and segregative ambitions informed governance strategies expressed in immigration restrictions and subjectivities on foreign bodies and contagion. Cleanliness and health issues were perceived as both mission and duty, necessary to manage race relations and ensure whiteness (Bashford 2004: 1; see also Bashford 1998; Anderson 1991: 82ff.). In New Zealand, this overt discrimination towards Chinese immigrants reached its peak in the 1920s (Spoonley and Trlin 2004: 24).

After World War II, the colonial ties to Great Britain were weakened, but discriminatory state legislation continued. In 1951, Chinese had to fulfil more criteria for citizenship than applicants from other countries (Ip and Pang 2005: 179). Racially based laws were not repealed until 1964 (Munshi 1998: 104). Subsequently, immigration became more diversified and Pacific Peoples[8] transformed New Zealand's cultural composition. However, growing economic tensions and the oil crisis in 1973 created a climate of social competition which contributed to discrimination against Pacific Peoples.

The liberal and non-discriminatory reformulation of the Immigration Act in 1987 marked a new area of national migration policies. Under the act, the New Zealand Government aimed to attract skilled and asset-rich immigrants, capable of enhancing entrepreneurial capacity in the country. This caused an unexpectedly high influx of migrants from Asian countries. Between 1990 and 1996 migrants came mostly from Hong Kong, Taiwan and South Korea. In 1996, Taiwan (5634 immigrants in total) outstripped the UK (5371 immigrants) as the biggest single source country for the first time (Munshi 1998: 98). In the late 1990s, migrants from India and China dominated the migration flow (Bedford 2005: 146; Spoonley 2005: 105). In a relatively short period of time, so-called Asian immigrants overtook Pacific Peoples as the third largest demographic group within New

---

8. The term Pacific Islanders is gradually being replaced by Pacific Peoples or as in census reporting by Pasifika in order to recognise that the majority of individuals of Pacific descent are no longer born and raised in their island homelands, but in other cultural contexts (see Macpherson 2004: 139). Some population groups from Pacific Islands, such as Niue or Cook Islands, are represented by greater populations in New Zealand than in their country of origin (Bell 1996: 7).

Zealand after Māori and Pākehā New Zealanders. As the fastest growing group, in 2006 they represented nine percent of the national population and are expected to comprise fifteen percent in 2021.[9]

The significant diversity of the new Asian immigrant groups is homogenised in dominant public discourse, which classifies them simply as 'Asians'. This essentialising label conceals the wide range of Asian cultures, ignores their divergent historical experiences and hinders the emergence of an adequate intercultural dialogue. By flattening all differences between them, Orientalist, racialist and monolithic notions of 'Asians' are constructed, describing them as foreign, external and unassimilationist.

New Zealand's relatively recent orientation towards Asia is mainly a result of economic pressure and revised political conditions. The country lost its most important trading partner when Britain eventually became a full member of the European Economic Community in 1973 (Spoonley and Macpherson 2004: 179). This event marked a watershed in the decolonisation process of New Zealand. Māori resurgence, immigration from the Pacific Islands and an increasingly fragile relationship to Britain caused uncertainty in terms of identity and belonging (Belich 2001: 425). In addition, during the 1980s, policy officials and market analysts identified Asian markets as engines for growth and initiated stronger economic linkages with Asia. In 1995, forty percent of New Zealand's exports were bound for Asian countries as opposed to only seventeen percent in 1970 (Bell 1996: 186). In 1989, New Zealand's new fee-paying student policy led to the opening of English Language Schools, which were attended by a large number of students from China, Japan and Korea. This resulted in a billion-dollar business for New Zealand (Ip and Murphy 2005: 147). New Zealand joined the lucrative export tertiary education market in 2000, attracting 120,000 international students in 2004 nationwide, mostly of Asian origin (Ip and Murphy 2005: 36).[10]

9. Statistics New Zealand, http://www.stats.govt.nz/analytical-reports/dem-trends-05/default.htm, retrieved 17 October 2006 and http://www.stats.govt.nz/census/2006–census-data/quickstats-about-culture-identity/quickstats-about-culture-and-identity.htm?page=para015Master, retrieved 15 October 2007.
10. It is estimated that the export education sector contributes NZ$700 million to Auckland city's economy, or 2 percent of the GDP (see Auckland City Council 2004a: 3; Informetrics 2003: 8–9). Since 2003 however, adverse publicity in China about New Zealand's resentment towards new migrants, lax behaviour and lack of supervision in schools led to a decline of this lucrative business (Ip and Murphy 2005: 156).

Even though economic figures and current migration flows demonstrate the entanglement of the two regions, within New Zealand the perceived social relationship to Asia remains ambivalent. Geographically, New Zealand has always been much closer to Asia than to Europe, but not in terms of historical networks and cultural linkages. New Zealand's recent repositioning in the global economy, its reorientation towards Asia or even tentative identification as part of Asia, along with neoliberal tendencies, has manifold consequences. While it is conducive to an increasing engagement with Asian popular culture and practices, like sports, arts, literature, cuisine, religion or festivals (Johnson and Moloughney 2006), it fuels emotional debates and anxiety in terms of national identity and self-perception.

Resentments towards 'Asians': Representations and discourses

In the mid 1990s, some of the nineteenth century panic of the 'yellow peril' resurfaced. Reporting by the press was stereotypical, with a tendency to focus on negative aspects of Asian immigrants, pointing to rising property values, driving habits, pressure on the local infrastructure and tensions in schools created by the Asian migrants' presence (Lidgard 1996: 3, 44; Vasil and Yoon 1996: 24). Newspaper articles emphasised the invasion narrative by referring to an 'Inv-Asian', while television series used labels such as 'Asia Down Under' (Spoonley and Trlin 2004: 57).

Anti-Asian resentments were linked to environmental issues and used in political rhetoric during the 1996 election campaign, when New Zealand's image as nuclear-free, pristine and pure was said to be threatened by initiatives to introduce genetically engineered food. This could affect and possibly contaminate the natural ecosystem, which is a significant feature of New Zealand's national and international representation. Conservative political forces transferred this possible scenario to the social realm and used it as a metaphor to describe the future of New Zealand's society. They argued that continuing Asian migration to New Zealand would constitute a similar pollution threat to the country by culturally and racially contaminating New Zealand's society with alien elements (Ip and Murphy 2005: 154).

Representatives of the emerging Māori Party articulated comparable concerns, intertwining anti-immigration sentiments with fear of environmental degradation. Asian immigrants were blamed for the decline in numbers of fish and shellfish near the cities and represented as a threat to New Zealand's ecosystem (Ip 2003b: 246; see also Chen 1993: 6). Environmental harm and ecological damage were perceived as a result of Asian immigrants' culture and as a proof of their otherness. Coming from dirty and overcrowded cities, they were portrayed as unable to appreciate green and clean nature and New Zealand's natural assets. This debate was played out in the public media, where newspaper articles posited that 'Asians are raping New Zealand's coastlines' (Ip 2003b: 246).

These statements are challenged by quantitative findings when Asian migrants were asked to list their motives for migrating to New Zealand. Rather than asserting economic advantages for their migration, one third of respondents to this survey mentioned general lifestyle, environmental advantages, clean and green environment or climate as their primary reasons for migrating (Friesen and Ip 1997: 6; see also Lidgard 1996: 23; Beal 2001: 39; Chui 2004: 120). Nevertheless, limiting immigration in order to prevent overburdening and overexploitation of the environment became a popular claim in the political rhetoric and public perception.

Non-natives were portrayed as dangerous intruders menacing New Zealand's natural beauty and international status. Hence, the call for protecting and caring for the natural environment justified social exclusion, created otherness and strengthened New Zealanders' self-perception as 'clean'.

In the early 2000s, New Zealand benefited immensely from migration. The construction industry in Auckland was booming, the export education industry fuelled overseas earnings and the city's skilled labour workforce grew considerably (Bedford 2005: 144). This drew public attention to beneficial aspects of the relationship to Asia and the relevance of Asian migrants to the future prosperity of New Zealand. Asians' input could counterbalance New Zealand's aging workforce, declining fertility rate and brain drain. In this vein, media reporting became more differentiated towards migration[11] and politics after the 2002 election endorsed a culturally diversified society. However, tendencies to discriminate against Asians, in particular Chinese, persist and are especially evident in Auckland, the country's gateway city attracting the overwhelming majority of new migrants. Opinion surveys from 2002 show that anti-Asian sentiments in Auckland are stronger than in the rest of the country.

---

11. Newspaper articles discussed the incentives for migration to New Zealand and included detailed information on the source countries. In addition to economic or military necessities, environmental issues, lifestyle choices and advancement of children's education in an English-speaking country were portrayed as significant factors in migrants' decision-making processes. Other motivations included references to New Zealand's international reputation as a safe place and healthy environment promising an escape from poor living conditions and often extremely competitive educational systems in Asian countries (*The New Zealand Herald*, 26 October 2002, 17 April 2006 and 18 April 2006).

Among Auckland respondents, 54 percent feel that there are too many immigrants from Asia, compared to 31 percent to 44 percent in other parts of New Zealand (Ho and Bedford 2006: 230). Aucklanders' attitudes towards immigrants are best seen as ambivalent. A survey in 2003 shows that 48 percent feel that immigration has contributed to more crime and violence, but the same survey found that 46 percent think that immigration is good for Auckland (Crothers 2005: 13, 14). A survey from 2006 confirms that negative attitudes towards Asians are particularly present in Auckland and that the majority of respondents had heard people in New Zealand make racist remarks about immigrants (Gendall et al. 2007: 11, 14, 23, 24).

I will now show how these tendencies are to some extent reflected in specific narrative accounts on Asian migrants. While earlier perceptions focussed on matters of hygiene and contagion, intertwined with racial purity and imperialism, contemporary discourses tend to address environmental concerns and national identity. Equally important are moral implications, which accompany these visions. Targeting gambling and opium addiction in the past, emphasis is now placed on environmental ethics, the preservation of the environment for future generations or claims to the intrinsic values of native flora and fauna. This shows that a particular set of discourses on 'polluting others' has re-emerged, but it is bound by a new context, experience and vocabulary. In accordance with dominant concerns in the wider society, the attributes ascribed to Asian migrants shifted from 'infected' and 'contagious' to 'environmentally harmful' and 'ecologically irresponsible'. These discourses produce a range of counter-discourses and activities. While some voices in the Asian community protest discrimination and reject stereotyping, others appropriate these discourses into their self-perception and national identity construction.

Multicultural urbanity and reformulations of identities

Auckland is New Zealand's largest metropolitan region with over 1.3 million inhabitants. The Central Business District (CBD) is the country's largest centre of higher education where 70 percent of all tertiary students in the Auckland region attend classes (Auckland City Council 2004b).

The tertiary education institutions contribute to the city's multicultural flair. In 2002, nearly 20,000 foreign students were enrolled, using the various facilities in this district.[12] A large majority of these students are of

12. The number of foreign fee paying students in New Zealand in 2001–2002 was 88,000 (See Auckland City Council 2004a: 3; Informetrics 2003: 1, 8, 9).

Asian origin and they shape the appearance of the student community in the streets. Further changes occurred because of the district's sharp residential growth in recent years. From 1991 to 2001, the population increased from 1500 to 8977, of which 27 percent were students.[13] In 2006, the estimated population of the CBD had almost doubled and comprised 17,937 residents. Another aspect contributing to the visibility of Asians in the city's centre is the increasing number of overseas visitors.[14] About one third of New Zealand's tourists are from Asian countries. These recent and rapid developments have led to a specific ethnic composition in this district, which differs considerably from the rest of the Auckland region and the country. Compared to the Auckland region, it has proportionately more Asian residents (47 percent compared to 18 percent) and proportionately less Māori, Pacific Peoples and New Zealand Europeans.[15]

Figure 2.1. View of Auckland's Central Business District (CBD).

13. See Auckland City Council 2004a: 6.
14. Although precise figures are not available, it is mirrored in the significant increase in accommodation. Between 1996 and 2002 the guest night capacity increased from 50,000 of over 200,000 per month (See Auckland City Council 2004a: 4).
15. Census 2006, Statistics New Zealand. Detailed information and statistical data on the Chinese population in Auckland are provided by Ho and Bedford (2006).

Figure 2.2. Pedestrians and street signs on Queen Street in Auckland.

The main boulevard of this downtown area, Queen Street, has been increasingly dominated by international students and tourists from Asia. This finds expression in the built environment and visual layout of the streetscape. New stores selling inexpensive items opened to attend to the students' needs and restaurants and takeaways cater to this new constituency. Street signs and advertisements are increasingly written in Korean, Chinese and Japanese in order to provide directions to students and foreign visitors. In a very short period of time, the city centre has acquired a new face symbolising significant change rather than continuity. As a consequence, some local residents feel as if they are surrounded or even dominated by foreigners. Anxieties, disorientation, disorder and uncertainty replace familiarity and add to the impression that the city centre is under siege and invaded by otherness. This feeling is expressed by Anthony,[16] a Pākehā long term resident in the city's centre:

16. All names are pseudonyms to guarantee confidentiality.

The city centre is only newly multicultural. Most of Aucklanders walk down Queen Street and go: 'My god, where did all these Chinese, Japanese, Koreans come from?' or they would actually say 'Where did all "these Asians" come from'. And it's a hell of a shock if anyone from Christchurch, Palmerston North or Hamilton come into Queen Street. They will get a hell of a shock. They would imagine they are on holiday in Singapore, and this has only happened in the last ten years. ... Then came the buying passports initiative by the government. If you had a business and if you invested a million dollars you're in, you had a passport. That and of course in that stage, 1997, or when did Hong Kong go to China? In 1999, yeah, almost all the Hong Kong Chinese, 'oh my god, the commies are coming I want at least the option to leave the country before it goes bad.' The option was a New Zealand passport. So some of them moved over here, got children. Okay, it's a great place to stay, but all the Pākehās were going: 'Where the hell do these people come from?' And that's happened in the last ten years, so still people are not used to the idea that Auckland is a multicultural town. ... It's all it is, it is a physical impression, there may be Serbians, there may be English there may be Croatians out there, but you don't see them, but the Korean, the Chinese, the Japanese they look so different, it is very obvious.

The Auckland City Council is aware of the significant changes to the city centre and has allocated NZ $23.4 million[17] to the upgrading of the streetscape. It aims for a high quality urban environment, which includes the reduction of pollution and improving inner-city cleanliness.[18] Queen Street is used by around 50,000 pedestrians daily.[19] It is swept every night and flushed with water five times a week. The footpaths are scrubbed twice a year. Also, there are ten people cleaning the street on a daily basis, picking up litter and emptying the rubbish bins. In spite of all these efforts, business owners and residents still complain about dirt and untidiness. As the cause for the ongoing pollution, they often point towards the strong presence of Asian students in the streets. They perceive 'Asian' cultural practices, such as eating habits or spitting, as pollution and signs of alienness.[20] These stereotypes are also reinforced by the media, which label

17. In early 2007, the exchange rate was NZ$1.00 = €0.54.
18. The Auckland City Council's Queen Street upgrade project is contested and divergent interests need to be considered. While pedestrian advocacy groups support reducing the volumes of traffic, businesses feared this will result in a cut-down of clients. Emotional debates also arose over the question whether foreign or endemic plants and trees are more appropriate to decorate Queen Street.
19. See Auckland City Council 2005b.
20. In surveys carried out by the Auckland City Council some participants differentiate between Asian groups and perceive the Chinese as worst polluters: 'Japanese and Koreans are not that bad, but Chinese are the worst...' (See Auckland City Council 2002).

Figure 2.3. Cleaning up Queen Street.

Asian students as 'by far the biggest litterers' and identify chopsticks, noodle and rice packets as clear indicators of 'Asian' rubbish.[21] These comments represent Asians as insensitive to environmental issues and as waste producers because of particular cultural practices – regardless of the fact that many non-Asians have adopted Asian eating habits.

Joanne, a Pākehā woman who has worked in the CBD for decades, argues along the lines that Asian eating habits contribute to pollution because fast food and takeaways produce disposable rubbish. In her view, this 'throw-away culture' is an Asian characteristic and part of a 'throw-away mentality'. She interprets this behaviour as the result of unreflective consumerism and a lack of environmental awareness, which in turn attracts shops that cater to this specific constituency by selling cheap and disposable items. She criticises the rise of this pollution pattern and explains it through Asian immigration to New Zealand:

21. *The New Zealand Herald*, 24 December 2003, 26 December 2003 and 16 June 2004.

New Zealanders perhaps aren't so ready to eat in public or to walk down the street eating, you know what I mean, that's a cultural difference. ... What I am saying is if you see these people [Asian students] eating out of containers on the run, out of takeaway disposable containers, then you sort of connect that disposability with them and with pollution. ... So you might see a lot of disposable containers and the same sort of goods, throw-away goods, which come through those cheap stores, you know, the two-dollar-shop or the plastic goods. They're comical things, funny things, that you also perceive as throw-away commodities. You are actually generating pollution by bringing in those sorts of goods as well, goods that weren't available before and really aren't essential items, you know what I mean? You trace it back to [the] source they are actually abusing a lot of resources.

Joanne entangles environmental carelessness and pollution with Asian culture, which she sees as menacing civilised life and modern ideas of sustainability. Her statement entails a moral component, implying wrong-doing by aggravating pollution instead of environmental care and waste prevention. Her concerns are further fuelled by recent reporting in the press on accidents polluting the environment in China and Chinese imports containing hazardous substances.[22] The recall of Chinese toys with a toxic amount of lead, food scandals, poisoned toothpaste and clothing alarmed the wider public and gave rise to anxieties regarding health and safety issues. She posits that:

New Zealanders actually do care for the environment, it is our land and future as well, and we want a healthy future for our children, you know what I mean? That's a cultural issue here, and maybe educational as well. We try to avoid chemical fertilisers and pesticides and they [the Asians] don't care. It's all about profit. Maybe they [Asian migrants] will dominate our economy. Soon we are exposed to contaminated ingredients and all the additives - all those Chinese-made ingredients.

This statement expresses fear of a powerful Asian economy polluting undiluted New Zealand and its future generations. It also shows the perception of China's recklessness and posits Chinese culture as profit-seeking while lacking in ethical responsibility – which is juxtaposed to New Zealand's integrity and considerateness. This stereotype reinforces otherness and contrasts strongly with New Zealand's national and international image. By referring to 'culture' and 'education' as main issues associated with Asians' polluting cultural practices, they are

22. *The New Zealand Herald*, 23 August 2007, 9 September 2007, 21 September 2007.

portrayed as unlikely to adapt to New Zealand's environmentally friendly and therefore morally superior society.

'Asian' migrants' responses: Purifying public images

These discourses impact on Asian migrants' identity and agency. Recognising these stereotypes, a group of Asian students developed strategies to purify their public image and counterbalance these perceptions. A young Korean language student founded an international volunteer group that gathered to pick up rubbish on Saturday afternoons on Queen Street.[23] He advertised in several free Asian student magazines and recruited around twenty members from different East Asian countries, mainly Japan, Korea and China. Equipped with long grippers, huge black rubbish bags and special t-shirts, they were easy to distinguish from other pedestrians on Queen Street. In interviews with the local newspaper, the group leader stated that he had formed this group to challenge the litterbug label for Asians and to demonstrate that international students care about New Zealand and the environment.[24]

This initiative was featured positively in the press and Auckland's mayor applauded the group, presenting them as role models for their environmental concern. However, the group's effort to publicly conform to local 'Kiwi' values and to acknowledge the existing order is not born simply out of the deeper insight that Asian migrants are indeed less 'clean' than their New Zealand hosts. Some students joined the group because it provided an opportunity to socialise, to meet new friends or to practice language skills. Other students would use this activity as a reference in their home country, where volunteer work is common amongst young people. In contrast to the public perception, their main motive was not necessarily 'to clean up Asian students' image in the public' or to counter the 'dirty Asian' stereotype, as it was interpreted in the newspapers and proudly stated by the group's leader and reiterated by the mayor. In fact, most group members considered themselves and their country of origin to be, in general, even cleaner than New Zealand and did not see any necessity to change their environmental behaviour. They acknowledge New Zealand's image as 'green' – which might have been an incentive for them to come to New Zealand in the first place – but not as particularly 'clean'. Korean and Japanese volunteer group members, for instance, are strongly convinced that their countries are much cleaner than

23. The Korean student was inspired by Japanese students, who had set up a similar group. The group was founded in January 2004 and operated for around 18 months, until the leading members went back to their country of origin when their student or work visa expired.
24. *The New Zealand Herald*, 16 August 2004.

New Zealand. They point to pollution education in their schools and to the rigid systems, including prohibitions against littering, that keep their cities clean. They also assume that New Zealand is not really clean because 'it is not highly developed and industrialised compared to other nations', as one Japanese student expressed it. He elaborated further on the differences between Japan and New Zealand:

> Many Asian people think that New Zealand is very, very clean and a good place to be, for instance they see the very good scenery and the beautiful country. I think that the clean image in New Zealand comes from nature, not from care about rubbish. … Auckland is quite green, like nuclear-free, but if you go to side streets or back streets, you will find lots and lots of rubbish, bins, cans, so it is not that clean. … I think that Japan is even cleaner than New Zealand. … I think it is the way people are thinking. In Japan, yes, some people actually do throw rubbish and stuff, but it is not normal, it is unusual, it should not be done - that sort of stuff. But I think that more people are dropping stuff after eating ice cream or after lunching in New Zealand. For us, for Japanese people, it is very bad to throw rubbish away, it is very dirty and polluted and we are actually encouraged in schools not to throw away things. We are very clean. We are also told by the teacher not to do this.

The students create categories of social distinction not just between their group and New Zealand, but also amongst themselves by differentiating levels of cleanliness according to nationalities. While attitudes towards the environment are related to questions of integration, assimilation and national identity in the public discourse, similar conceptual categories are articulated amongst the group's members in order to mark otherness. A female Japanese student, who joined the group primarily for social reasons, asserts that the toilets, takeaways, restaurants and, of course, the streets are far cleaner in Japan than in New Zealand. She is not too concerned about the negative stereotyping of Asians in New Zealand either. Speaking about discrimination against Asian migrants in Auckland, she stated that she personally never really felt discriminated against. As she explained, she is Japanese by origin and not Chinese – and therefore obviously very different. She suggested that Chinese migrants are more exposed to discrimination, because they are surely dirtier than Japanese migrants. This would be evident in Chinese flats, which are far dirtier than Japanese ones:

> In China, many people just don't care for rubbish, they just throw away, and if you go to big cities or big towns, you will see lots of people just throwing away stuff, and nobody cares. I think that Chinese people are less educated. In my opinion, they are not so interested in picking up rubbish, they just don't care. We got just one, only one Chinese was

group member. In Japan, we are educated not to throw away rubbish; we have strict policies in our cities unlike less-developed countries.

In her view, the reasons for these differences are rooted in China's one-child policy. This results in only-child, selfish, spoiled, loud and dirty individuals, whereas Japanese education produces modest, quiet, shy and timid individuals. The Japanese are clean, because they are educated, which she implicitly links with supremacy. In contrast to the Chinese, she perceives Koreans to be almost as clean and strong as Japanese, albeit too nationalistic. In her view, cleanliness is an indicator of a good education and civilised behaviour. In this case, again, categories of dirt and environmental behaviour mark and reinforce cultural boundaries and subjective social positions. This does not only involve divergent values or perceptions, but, equally, power relations and status that are negotiated symbolically in environmental discourses and social classifications of clean and dirty (Argyrou 1997: 160, 167). It also shows that categorisations of clean and dirty are used to mark social distinctions within a group of 'Asian' migrants that is perceived as homogenous and monolithic by the dominant society and discursively constructed as such in the public media.

Unlike the Asian students, other Asian community members have appropriated and accommodated negative stereotypes into their identity constructions and are eager to counter the 'dirty Asian' label. In cooperation with the Auckland City Council, a Chinese Conservation Education Trust was founded in 2002. One of its aims is 'to educate' Auckland's Chinese community regarding environmental issues and to stimulate awareness for environmental conservation. Yung, a Chinese member of this trust who migrated to New Zealand in the mid 1990s, is dedicated to this community work primarily in order to improve the image of Chinese as polluters amongst the urban public, but also because of his own strong environmental ethics. After his arrival in New Zealand, he became involved in environmental issues and changed his attitude towards the environment significantly. In his own words, he became 'educated' in this regard and is now passionately committed to environmental protection. Education is central to his approach towards the Chinese community. This reflects the Auckland City Council strategy, which focuses on waste education as the principal element in its strategic plan to improve environmental behaviour in the city.[25] It is also linked to the public

25. Political and civil authorities are responsible for implementing a regulatory policy to control pollution which entails governance implications. In 2004, the city launched a campaign with the slogan 'Come on, be a Tidy Kiwi', which echoed the efforts of the 1970s campaign, 'Be a Tidy Kiwi.' Litter educators and compliance officers were sent out and issued instant fines of up to NZ$ 100 (See Auckland City Council 2005a). In 2004, Aucklanders dropped more litter per capita in the CBD every day than their counterparts in Sydney which is regarded as Australia's dirtiest city in terms of litter (*The New Zealand Herald*, 18 June 2004).

misperception that Chinese migrants are less educated and therefore more likely to pollute. These views had a significant impact on Yung, who identifies major differences between Chinese and New Zealand environmental perceptions. He classifies the Chinese attitudes as selfish and ignorant towards both the environment and future generations because of the overexploitation of nature:

> What is clean and what is dirty in China, in Hong Kong and in New Zealand, is a totally different thing. ... Mainstream New Zealand is talking about us in the news saying that Asians are doing the bad thing, you know, like over-harvesting the shellfish on the beach, and over-harvesting in fishing, and you know. And there is a lot of negative image, particular of Asia and Chinese. ... There is this kind of people who come from wherever in Asia and they are not really concerned about the limits. They are not aware of how many shellfish they can pick on the beach and they try to pick as many as possible, even though some people do recognise it is illegal. ... Most Kiwis do some gardening, they have grass. And this is not the Chinese way. It is as much as possible concrete, because they have very different values and they think there is no maintenance. You have grass and you need to mow the lawn. No grass - no problem! And it is the same with any concept for conservation and protection of endangered species. Chinese are not really concerned with that, but for Kiwis this is a typical concern. ... And that is the objective of the trust; how do we educate the Chinese community in this country to protect the environment and to do the conservation, in order to keep our life forever, for our grand-grand-grand-grandchildren? That is the concept.

Yung has adopted dominant discourses and environmentally-termed cultural distinctions, transforming himself from 'an uneducated, careless Chinese to a tidy, educated and ethical 'yellow Kiwi',' as he refers to himself. In the public discourse, incorporating environmental values constitutes a process of individual disciplining, enculturation and virtue-adding (Hawkings 2001: 12f.). Failing to embrace environmental care is seen as backward, uneducated and morally problematic or even unethical and uncivilised, and certainly resistant to dominant values. Perceived improvident polluters are considered to actually harm the environment, in the process fouling the country's international reputation and identity marker as well.

It is interesting to note that concepts of nature and human-environment interactions have changed enormously in New Zealand in the last decades and continue to take on new meanings (Pawson and Brooking 2002). Whereas, similar to most early settler colonies, dominating, mastering and taming nature were signs of imperial power, civilisation and achievement, often associated with male identities, the focus has more recently shifted towards a mutual dependency or even responsibility towards nature and human beings. This altered concept of nature which is embedded in globalised discourses on climate change and environmental awareness entails affection and aesthetics that require modified environmental ethics and also a concern for future generations.

Conclusion

A significant influx of migrants from Asian countries, particularly visible in urban centres, poses a challenge to the construction of a bicultural, but dominantly European nation in the South Pacific. Although links to Asia play a major role in the contemporary economy, and Asian communities have been present in New Zealand since the nineteenth century, they are only beginning to be considered as integral parts of the imagined nation. Their increasing presence adds to the complexity of nation-building processes and forces the re-articulation of identity politics. From this perspective, the Asian migration flow is contaminating New Zealand's self-perception and requires a revised definition of the country's nationhood and cultural composition.

The discursive classification of Asian migrants as polluting others links to notions of them as a morally backward, unethical and subversive group, disturbing the social order and hindering national advancement. These representations also entail a moralising righteousness and justified rejection of otherness, and of those perceived as indifferent towards the environment or even as a threat to national treasures by aggravating pollution. Littering as morally inferior behaviour is attributed to foreigners, concomitantly asserting New Zealanders' self-assessments as advanced, clean and rightful. This process reflects the mutual construction and entanglement of otherness and self which are perceived as fundamentally different categories. As a marker of distinction between the native and the foreign, litterers must still accommodate to dominant values in order to become fully accepted members of the society, with a visible commitment to modernity.

Public discourses and prejudice affect identity formations and impact on social classifications by creating a language of exclusion and disapprobation. While the nineteenth-century discourse was framed by Victorian hygiene and racialised sanitary notions, popular and political imaginaries about immigrants are now situated in a new context of moralising environmentalism and globalised understandings of pollution control. In New Zealand, the role of these hegemonic discourses is situated in a bicultural social context which is challenged by recent ideas on and realities of multiculturalism and plurality. The emerging tensions also contest New Zealand's self-image as a tolerant, inclusive and non-racist society.

Asian migrants respond to their stereotyping as litterers and 'dirty others' in various ways. Some transient Asian students may be eager to purify their image by publicly displaying their environmental care, even though they perceive themselves and their countries as clean or even cleaner in comparison to New Zealand. In contrast, some members of the resident Chinese community seem to adjust to dominant values and expectations by appropriating these discourses into their identity formation and modifying their self-perception. This is tied into urban governance strategies of the Auckland's City and Regional Councils, which try to improve pollution control through education and environmental awareness-raising. The discourses on dirty Asians are not based primarily on actual, measurable pollution, but constitute cultural constructions and classifications of cleanliness, dirt and environmental behaviour as the result of specific social conditions. They reach far beyond ecological concerns and represent both a symbolic and material struggle over social positioning and national identity, but also over privileged access to resources and power.

References

Anderson, K.J. 1991. *Vancouver's Chinatown. Racial Discourse in Canada, 1875–1980*. Montreal: McGill-Queen's University Press.

Anderson, W.W. and R.G. Lee. 2005. *Displacements and Diasporas. Asians in the Americas*. New Brunswick: Rutgers University Press.

Appadurai, A. 1996. *Modernity at Large. Cultural Dimensions of Globalization*. Minneapolis, Minn.: University of Minnesota Press.

Argyrou, V. 1997. ' "Keep Cyprus Clean": Littering, Pollution, and Otherness', *Cultural Anthropology* 12 (2): 159–178.

Auckland City Council. 2002. *Multi-Dwellings Research: Qualitative Research*. Auckland: Auckland City, September/October 2002.

———— 2004a. *The Economy of Auckland's CBD*. Auckland: Auckland City.

————2004b. *Auckland's CBD Into the Future Strategy*. http://www.aucklandcity.govt.nz/council/documents/cbdstrategy/default.asp, retrieved 10 October 2006.

————2005a. *Auckland City Waste Education Strategy*. 21 July 2005.

———— 2005b. *The Vision for Queen Street*.

Bashford, A. 1998. *Purity and Pollution: Gender, Embodiment and Victorian Medicine*. London: Macmillan Press.

————2004. Imperial Hygiene: *A Critical History of Colonialism, Nationalism and Public Health*. New York: Palgrave Macmillan.

Beal, T. 2001. 'Taiwanese Business Migration to Australia and New Zealand' in *Re-examining Chinese Transnationalism in Australia-New Zealand*, M. Ip (ed.), pp. 25–44. Centre for the Study of the Southern Chinese Diaspora, Division of Pacific and Asian History, RSPAS, The Australian National University.

Bedford, R. 2005. 'International Migration and Globalization: The Transformation of New Zealand's Migration System since the mid-1980s' in *Sovereignty Under Siege? Globalisation and New Zealand*, R. Patman and C. Rudd (eds), pp. 129–55. Aldershot: Ashgate.

Belich, J. 2001. *Paradise Reforged: A History of New Zealanders from the 1880s to the Year 2000*. Auckland: Allen Lane and Penguin.

Bell, C. 1996. *Inventing New Zealand: Everyday Myths of Pakeha Identity*. Auckland: Penguin Books.

Bhabha, H.K. 1994. *The Location of Culture*. London: Routledge.

Božić-Vrbančić, S. 2003. 'One Nation, Two Peoples, Many Cultures: Exhibiting Identity at Te Papa Tonarewa', *Journal of the Polynesian Society* 112 (3): 295–313.

Brookfield, F.M. 2006. *Waitangi and Indigenous Rights: Revolution, Law and Legitimation. Auckland*: Auckland University Press.

Chen, M. 1993. 'Discrimination, Law, and Being a Chinese Immigrant Woman in New Zealand', *Women's Studies Journal* 9 (2): 1–29.

Chui, R. 2004. 'Auckland's 'Economic Immigrants' form Asia' in *Almighty Auckland?*, I. Cater, D. Craig and S. Matthewman (eds), pp. 111–34. Palmerston North: Dunmore Press.

Cohen, W.A. 2005. 'Introduction: Locating *Filth*' in *Filth: Dirt, Disgust, and Modern Life*, W.A. Cohen and R. Johnson (eds), pp. vii–xxxvii. Minneapolis: University of Minnesota Press.

Crothers, C. 2005. *Aucklanders' Attitudes to Auckland's Growth and Environment*. Working paper in Communication Research, vol. 2, Institute of Culture, Discourse and Communication, Auckland University of Technology, Auckland.

Douglas, M. 1966. *Purity and Danger: An Analysis of Concepts of Pollution and Taboo*. London: Routledge.

Durie, M.H. 1998. *Te mana, te kāwanatanga: The Politics of Māori Self-Determination*. Auckland: Oxford University Press.

Dürr, E. 2007. 'Arcadia in the Antipodes: Tourists' Reflections on New Zealand as Nature Experience', *SITES, A Journal of Social Anthropology and Cultural Studies, Special Issue: Mobility, Migration and Multi-culturalism in New Zealand*, 4 (2): 57–82.

————2008. 'Reinforcing Cultural Hegemony: Pākehā Perceptions of Brand New Zealand', *Journal of New Zealand Studies, Special Issue: Watching the Kiwis*, 6–7: 59–76.

Fairburn, M. 1989. *The Ideal Society and Its Enemies. The Foundations of Modern New Zealand Society 1850–1900*. Auckland: Auckland University Press.

Fleras, A. and P. Spoonley. 1999. *Recalling Aotearoa: Indigenous Politics and Ethnic Relations in New Zealand*. Auckland: Oxford University Press.

Friesen, W. and M. Ip. 1997. 'New Chinese New Zealanders: Profile of a Transnational Community in Auckland', in *East Asian New Zealanders:*

Research on New Migrants, W. Friesen, M. Ip, E. Ho, R. Bedford and J. Goodwin (eds), pp. 3–19. Albany, N.Z.: Asia-Pacific Migration Research Network.

Gendall, P., P. Spoonley and A. Trlin. 2007. *The Attitudes of New Zealanders to Immigrants and Immigration: 2003 and 2006 Compared*, Occasional Publication No. 17. Palmerston North: New Settlers Programme, Massey University.

Hall, S. (ed.) 1997. *Representation: Cultural Representations and Signifying Practices*. London: Sage.

Hawkins, G. 2001. 'Plastic Bags: Living with Rubbish', *International Journal of Cultural Studies* 4 (1): 5–23.

Ho, E. and R. Bedford. 2006. 'The Chinese in Auckland: Changing Profiles in a More Diverse Society', in *From Urban Enclave to Ethnic Suburb*, W. Li (ed.), pp. 203–230. Honolulu: University of Hawai'i Press.

Hu-DeHart, E. (ed.) 1999. *Across the Pacific. Asian Americans and Globalization*. Philadelphia: Temple University Press.

Informetrics. 2003. *International Students and Their Impact on Auckland City*. December 2003.

Inda, X.J. and R. Rosaldo. 2008 [2002]. 'Tracking Global Flows', in *The Anthropology of Globalization. A Reader*, J.X. Inda and R. Rosaldo (eds), pp. 3–46. Malden: Blackwell.

Ip, M. 1995. 'Chinese New Zealanders: Old Settlers and New Immigrants' in *Immigration and National Identity in New Zealand: One People, Two Peoples, Many Peoples?* S. William Greif (ed.), pp. 161–99. Palmerston North, NZ: Dunmore Press.

———2003a. *'Chinese Immigration and Transnationals in New Zealand. A Fortress Opened'*, in *Chinese Diaspora: Space, Place, Mobility, and Identity*, L.J.C. Ma and C. Cartier (eds), pp. 339–58. Boston: Rowman and Littlefield.

———2003b. 'Maori-Chinese Encounters: Indigine-Immigrant Interaction in New Zealand', *Asian Studies Review* 27 (2): 227–52.

Ip, M. and N. Murphy. 2005. *Aliens at My Table: Asians as New Zealanders See Them*. Auckland: Penguin Books.

Ip, M. and D. Pang 2005. 'New Zealand Chinese Identity: Sojourners, Model Minority and Multiple Identities', in *New Zealand Identities. Departures and Destinations*. In: H.J. Liu, T. McCreanor, T. McIntosh and T. Teaiwa (eds), pp. 174–89. Wellington: Victoria University Press.

Johnson, H. and B. Moloughney. 2006. 'Introduction: Asia in the Making of Multicultural New Zealand' in *Asia in the Making of New Zealand*, H. Johnson and B. Moloughney (eds), pp. 1–10. Auckland: Auckland University Press.

Li, W. 2006. 'Asian Immigration and Community in the Pacific Rim', in *From Urban Enclave to Ethnics Suburb. New Asian Communities in Pacific Rim Countries*, W. Li (ed.), pp. 1–22. Honolulu: University of Hawai'i Press.

Lidgard, J. 1996. *East Asian Migration to Aotearoa/New Zealand: Perspectives of Some New Arrivals*. Hamilton, N.Z.: Population Studies Centre, University of Waikato.

Macpherson, C. 2004. 'From Pacific Islanders to Pacific People and Beyond' in *Tangata tangata: The Changing Ethnic Contours of New Zealand*, P. Spoonley, D.G. Pearson and C. Macpherson (eds), pp. 135–56. Southbank, Vic.; Thomson/Dunmore Press.

McClure, M. 2004. *The Wonder Country. Making New Zealand Tourism*. Auckland: Auckland University Press.

McMillan, K. 2004. 'Developing Citizens. Subjects, Aliens and Citizens in New Zealand since 1840' in *Tangata tangata: The Changing Ethnic Contours of New Zealand*, P. Spoonley, D.G. Pearson and C. Macpherson (eds), pp. 267–89. Southbank, Vic.; Thomson/Dunmore Press.

Mitchell, K. 2004. *Crossing the Neoliberal Line: Pacific Rim Migration and the Metropolis*. Philadelphia: Temple University Press.

Munshi, D. 1998. 'Media, Politics, and the Asianisation of a Polarised Immigration Debate in New Zealand', *Australian Journal of Communication* 25 (1): 97–110.

Pawson, E. and T. Brooking. 2002. *Environmental Histories of New Zealand*. Oxford: Oxford University Press.

Said, E. 1978. *Orientalism*. New York: Pantheon Books.

Skeldon, R. 2000. 'Trends in International Migration in the Asian and Pacific Region', *International Social Sciences Journal* 52 (165): 369–382.

Smith, A. 2004. 'A Maori Sense of Place? Taranaki Waiata Tangi and Feelings for Place'. *New Zealand Geographer* 60: 12–17.

Spoonley, P. 1993. *Racism and Ethnicity*, revised edn. Auckland: Oxford University Press.

————2005. 'Becoming Pakeha: Majority Group Identity in a Globalising World' in *Sovereignty Under Siege? Globalisation and New Zealand*, R. Patman and C. Rudd (eds), pp. 97–110. Aldershot: Ashgate.

Spoonley, P. and C. Macpherson. 2004. 'Transnational New Zealand. Immigrants and Cross-border Connections and Activities' in *Tangata tangata: The Changing Ethnic Contours of New Zealand*, P. Spoonley, D.G. Pearson and C. Macpherson (eds), pp. 175–94. Southbank, Vic.; Thomson/Dunmore Press.

Spoonley, P., D.G. Pearson and C. Macpherson (eds). 2004. *Tangata tangata: The Changing Ethnic Contours of New Zealand*. Southbank, Vic.: Thomson/Dunmore Press.

Spoonley, P. and A. Trlin. 2004. *Immigration, Immigrants and the Media: Making Sense of Multicultural New Zealand*. Palmerston North, NZ: New Settlers Programme, Massey University.

Strasser, S. 1999. *Waste and Want: A Social History of Trash*. New York: Metropolitan Books.

Stokes, E. 1992. 'The Treaty of Waitangi and the Waitangi Tribunal: Maori Claims in New Zealand', *Applied Geography* 12: 176–191.

The New Zealand Herald.

Vasil, Raj and H.K. Yoon 1996. *New Zealanders of Asian Origin*. Institute of Policy Studies: Victoria University of Wellington.

Ward, C. and E.-Y. Lin 2005. 'Immigration, Acculturation and National Identity', in: *New Zealand Identities. Departures and Destinations*. H.J. Liu, T. McCreanor, T. McIntosh and T. Teaiwa (eds), pp. 155–73. Wellington: Victoria University Press.

Webster, A. 2001. *Spiral of Values*. Hawera: Alpha Publications.

CHAPTER 3

Private Cleanliness, Public Mess: Purity, Pollution and Space in Kottar, South India

DAMARIS LÜTHI

Introduction

Historical differences in concepts of hygiene illustrate that changing concepts of cleanliness relate to changing images of the body and changing ideas about health and wellbeing. The 'rationality' of 'hygienic' practices is continuously redefined in line with changed insights and discourses. For example, ideas of health and hygiene have been in constant flux in Europe and North America (e.g. Illi and Steiner 1997; Vigarello 1985; Williams 1991). The French historian Georges Vigarello (1985) relates these processes to changing images of the body, its envelopes and its environment. Medieval concern with cleanliness, for example, was limited to the visible parts of the body. In the sixteenth century, cleanliness was not seen as related to washing and the body was 'cleaned' by rubbing it with a dry cloth. Bathing was seen as dangerous because water could enter the body and transmit diseases. However, by the end of the eighteenth century people believed that cold water would reinforce and consolidate the body's hidden powers. Only towards the end of the nineteenth century did the concept of the microbe become accepted, and was washing seen as a defence against ill-health. Expanding urban populations, the associated growth of squalid slums, and a series of epidemics – particularly cholera and typhoid – led to sanitary reforms such as public baths for the poor, along with improvements in water supply, sewage, waste collection and the provision of public parks and playgrounds.

In today's India, environmental squalor strikes me and other – both foreign and native – observers as a salient feature of cities and towns that stands in surprising contrast to often meticulously clean private settings. My outsider's view is rooted in having grown up in Switzerland, where public sanitation is quite controlled, following the nineteenth century epidemic-fuelled development of waste and potable water systems and the moralisation of cleanliness into a persistent cross-class concern. In India, other historical and cultural processes have resulted in a different situation of public and private hygiene. Thus, my intention is certainly not to suggest that Indian ideas and practices have undergone a parallel development as outlined above. Nor would it be fair to see hygienic practices as the achievement of an evolutionary Western 'civilising process' of increasing needs and constraints (Elias 1982), with a somewhat 'primitive' South Asia trailing behind. To the contrary, throughout much of their history, Indians have been far more concerned with matters of purity than Europeans (Orenstein 1965, 1968; Leslie 1989). Similarly, prior to colonialism Africans had their own systems of hygiene, and cleanliness formed part of the language of ethnic rivalry (Burke 1996: 17 ff.).

Attitudes to bodily emissions and threats to the boundaries of the body may reveal much about attitudes towards social boundaries (Das 1976, 1977, 1985), as is evident in the Indian concept of caste. Im/purity concepts in relation to the morphology of caste are a long-established interest of scholars working on South Asia.[1] In his highly influential and controversial structuralist approach, Louis Dumont (1966) proclaimed ritual ideas of purity and pollution to be the fundamental idea underlying the caste system, encompassing all other concepts. His theory was contested by Marriott (1976, 1989) and Marriott and Inden (1977), who proposed an equally all-embracing idea underlying a pan-Indian caste system, based on the concept of coded substances which manifest status by the extent of transactions they enable between castes. Apart from such abstract discussions on the relevance of the so-called 'ritual' values of purity and pollution for the caste system, there are hardly any reflections on how daily physical practices relating to 'hygiene' could be linked with the im/purity concepts underlying the caste system. There is a certain impression that biological dirt could play a role in ideas of impurity, but most scholars assume that hygienic concepts must differ fundamentally from ideas related to 'ritual' purity, though they concede that they sometimes overlap.[2] My study of ordinary hygienic practices among

---

1. E.g., Burghart (1978); Dirks (1989); Dumont (1966); Hutton (1963); Moffatt (1979); Srinivas (1952); Stevenson (1954).
2. Dumont (1966; 1971: 75); Parry (1991); Ryan (1980); Srinivas (1952; 1976).

average residents of Kottar found that hygienic and so-called ritual notions of purity and impurity are closely related. Yet, the basic concepts of purity and hygiene are closer to orthodox ideas of im/purity as formulated in the Dharmashastras, the South Asian sacred law texts that have served as a guide for behaviour rules for two thousand years (Orenstein 1965, 1968; Leslie 1989), than to germ theories of dirt. Most of the body's waste products are considered polluting, and those of persons belonging to castes lower than one's own are more so.

A common aspect of worldwide ideas about im/purity is that dirt is seen as deviance and danger (Douglas 1966). However, the type of danger represented by impurity in specific historical, social and cultural contexts remains open. In Kottar, the danger of dirt is that it provokes the wrath of deities, who may punish with misfortune such as poverty or disease. The basic reason for avoiding impurity is, then, its incompatibility with sacredness, as the pollution of sacred realms is not permitted. Consequently, impurities are avoided and removed from the body and from private and sacred spaces.

Reflections on the reasons for public squalor in India

A number of scholars have reflected on the reasons for public pollution in India and its social and historical dimensions. Milner (1987), for example, argued that the pollution of the Indian environment was the result of treating dirt as 'primarily social, rather than physical' – social cleanliness and group order being more important than physical cleanliness – and that this idea of cleanliness did not harmonise with a Western germ theory of disease. According to Milner, social purity is inexpandable, and pure persons entail impure ones. Hence, orthodox members of the upper caste reject modern public sanitation systems, because such improvement towards increased purity would raise the status of the lower castes, and thereby become a threat to their position.

Gupta (2000: 23ff.) also argues that it is the caste system that is resistant to notions of public health and hygiene. However, he sees the persistence of outside squalor in cleansing mechanisms that are socially and physically based, which tolerate impurities in public places, but not inside of bodies and private spaces. This pan-South Asian cultural concept, he argues, is grounded in the idea that people of different castes are naturally dissimilar, because they consist of different substances, and that the invasion of the body by substances produced by other castes should be avoided. Bodily emissions are seen as polluting and should be eliminated, and anything entering the body must be controlled. Likewise, impurities are not tolerated inside a house and must be removed in the same way that secretions are expelled from the body. The reason for the persistence of outside pollution in spite of a specialised Sweeper caste, he contends, is that their task is primarily to remove the dirt from the houses and neighbourhoods of dominant castes.

Rosin (2000) argues that inhabitants of the Indian subcontinent consider dust in the streets, which is used as a cleansing agent, as processed dirt and thus clean. Traffic, through its churning, is seen as inducing a purifying transformative process, which corresponds to ideas of traditional South Asian philosophy as well as ethnographic and Indological findings.

Kaviraj (1997) interprets environmental pollution as a result of lower-class protest. He claims that in Calcutta traditional habits related to the environment were guided by the orthodox dichotomies *apan/par* ('own'/'others', 'self'/'not self'), and *ghare/baire* ('home inside'/'street i.e. world outside'), with the inhospitable outside considered beyond control. He argues that during colonial times the Indian elites absorbed the Western idea of public space as worthy of protection, which led to the creation of 'maidans', parks and other open spaces in bigger cities, superimposing the new concept on the traditional dichotomy. The marked squalor of public spaces today is to be seen as a subtle expression of class protest by the lower orders, who have turned the parks into slums.

Conversely, Harriss-White (1998) explains outside mess as the result of a lack of coordination and inconsistency of public and private efforts dealing with the sanitary infrastructure. Moreover, she claims that the contrast of private cleanliness and public chaos is the result of space being gendered: the domestic area, dominated by females, is clean, whereas public spaces are under male control and impure.

Alley (2002) explains the pollution of the river Ganges by pointing to the dominance of the idea of the river's sacredness and the insufficient sanitary infrastructure and other measures of waste control. Banaras Hindu residents make a distinction between ritual impurity – referring to physical uncleanness but also to the impurity of cosmos, soul and heart – and material dirtiness – referring to conditions of material uncleanliness but also to the moral degeneracy of humankind. Divine power is seen as overruling profane material forces. But although dirt, *gandagi*, does not alter Ganga's purity, it is understood by religious experts that dirtiness should be kept away from the sacred river and other places of worship. On the other hand Ganga, like a good mother, is seen as forgiving human dirtiness. However, the citizens recognize that wastewater is a force they must come to understand and control, even if sacred purity transcends it.

Historical research (Arnold 1993; Prashad 2001; da Silva Gracias 1994) has shown that political, conceptual and practical obstacles in India prevented the implementation of sanitary reforms, along with an insufficient adaptation of modern technology to the Indian context. For example, the necessity of improving public sanitation was discussed in

South Indian medical circles as early as in the 1850s, followed by the appointment of sanitary commissioners. Yet, the army, police and railways absorbed most of the funds under the colonial regime, leaving little for other divisions. Moreover, Indian indigenous people were considered to have a 'special fondness for dirt' (Prashad 2001: 115 ff.). In the end, there were a few sanitary interventions, mostly restricted to major cities and military camps, and there only in the more affluent quarters and neighbourhoods. However, where it was implemented, modern sanitation had a remarkable effect on the health of the population (Arnold 1989: 277; Crook 1989: 292). According to Prashad (2001), the continuous reluctance of the authorities in India to finance modern public sanitation systems results in the persistent occupational role of the traditional Sweepers, thought to go hand in hand with a lack of public cleanliness due to their poor performance.

My own research,[3] based on an interest in the relationship between ordinary everyday hygiene and so-called ritual notions of purity and impurity, confirms many of these interpretations. However, in Kottar, the urban social context in which I conducted my fieldwork, concepts of hygiene, cleanliness and purity all included a physical dimension.

Kottar is a part of the South Indian town of Nagercoil, which lies in the southernmost tip of Tamil Nadu, 18 kilometres north-west of Cape Comorin and close to the Kerala border. With a population of 189,482 (1991) it is one of the nine largest urban centres in Tamil Nadu. The town is the headquarters and commercial centre of the Kanyakumari district. Nagercoil ('snake temple') in the past used to be a small temple town with a temple dedicated to the snake-god Nagaraja and was a smaller settlement than nearby Kottar. Kottar was formerly an important business centre and on old maps is indicated as an independent place with this name. Nowadays it forms an integrated administrative and structural whole with Nagercoil to its west, which has given the name to the new structure. Kottar was moreover the missionary St. Xavier's domicile with a big church, which still exists today. A narrow but very busy arterial road divides Kottar into two and connects it with Nagercoil centre via a formerly uninhabited area, now filled with school buildings, the police headquarters and the government hospital. There is the *Pazhayar* river in the north-east, the *Parakkai* sewer as its tributary and the *Anandanar* channel on the western and southern side.

---

3. This chapter draws on the author's PhD dissertation (Lüthi 1999). A short version of this paper was presented at the 2001 IUAES Intercongress, and a German version was published subsequently (Lüthi 2004).

In Kottar, certain defilements and purities were considered specifically strong and were distinguished clearly from ordinary everyday un/cleanliness, but all im/purities were thought to have a physical dimension. Standard public pollution was both the result of the validity of traditional concepts of cleanliness incongruent with a germ theory of impurity and danger (shared equally among high, middle and low-caste Hindus and Catholic Christians[4]), as well as the reluctance of the educated municipality to finance the construction of modern sanitary infrastructure such as underground sewage works.

The findings of this study are based on sixteen months of fieldwork in 1995–1996, relying on the standard anthropological techniques of participant observation and unstructured interviewing, though I also conducted a household survey of the four castes with which I worked. I also mapped the neighbourhood, collected data on styles of domestic architecture, and followed the annual ritual cycle. I did my research in a mixed neighbourhood with Hindus of several different castes as well as Christians and Muslims, and with old residents as well as people who had recently moved there from elsewhere.[5]

Bodily impurities and personal hygiene in Kottar

The normal state of both the female and male body is considered slightly impure (Tam. *alukku*).[6] After bathing it is clean for no more than two hours, before it is thought to be stained again due to sweating and impure surroundings. The body is divided vertically and horizontally into pure and impure sites (cf. Malamoud 1989: 82–83; Orenstein 1968: 123; Srinivas 1976: 264). The parts above the waist are deemed purer than those below, and the right hand purer than the left. The interior of the body has neutral organs and impure cavities, for example the alimentary and respiratory tracts, which are the sites of foul saliva, phlegm and faeces. Digestion is thought to separate the food into clean blood and squalid refuse. Most products of the body are considered defiling, but breast-milk, tears and

---

4. South Indian Catholics share many concepts and habits with the Hindus (see for example Mosse 1994).
5. My research mostly focused on four different castes, the high-caste and class Cettis, the middle-caste (and both lower middle class or poor) Vaniya Cettiar, the middle-caste but lower-class Saurashtra, and the low-caste (and wealthy, middle or lower-class) Catholic Paravar. In terms of religious affiliation, attention was mainly on Hindus, but included Catholics, whose habits tend to overlap.
6. Cf. Srinivas (1952: 108; 1976: 190); Harper (1964: 152–153); Barnett (1976: 143).

semen are clean, although the dry residue in the corner of the eyes and emitted semen are seen as impure. Head hair is considered precious, while hair on intimate parts of the body including armpits is found repellent and is therefore shaved. Owing to the presence of such waste, all the bodily orifices are deemed impure (Tam. *acinkam* or *aruveruppu*), as are the left hand that cleanses such places, and the feet, due to their constant contact with the dirty ground. The left hand is, therefore, taboo as an eating-tool and inauspicious when used to hand over things. The lips, continuously stained by saliva, should not touch the cup or glass while drinking. After eating, a plate is deemed defiled by the saliva of the eater, and the person washing it becomes polluted. To avoid polluting another person, an eater often prefers to wash his or her own plate. Similarly, to lick the back of a stamp with saliva to stick it on a letter is considered unacceptably polluting to the postal clerk and the recipient. 'People scold the person: "How can I take the envelope from you, are you literate or illiterate?" ', my field assistant tried to explain.

Due to the worries about impurities produced by their bodies, people follow a careful procedure of personal hygiene. For example, in the morning they first clean their mouth to prevent the foul dry saliva that has accumulated inside the mouth during sleep from being swallowed and thereby polluting the body. For most people this is followed by the 'morning duties', comprising of defecation, bathing and changing into clean clothes. On the whole, bathing with water – which consists of rinsing the whole body with water from a bucket – is considered the most all-inclusive purifying activity, even without the use of soap, though the body is normally soaped. It is a precondition for temple visits or attending ritual events, as only clean bodies are tolerable to the deities (cf. Fuller 1979). Asked what would happen if one visited the temple without having bathed, it was explained to me that this was *pavam* (Tam. 'sinful', 'poor') and would be punished by the gods with minor ill-health or other misfortune.

Orthodox people prefer to eat breakfast only after bathing, to reduce the risk of polluting the food with their own physical impurities. Food is easily defiled through physical contact – for example, during the cooking process the cook's bodily emissions, especially saliva, is believed to fall into the food and pollute it. Raw food is considered less susceptible to defilement, as it has not been processed by any cook. Furthermore, once the food is served it becomes contaminated by the eater's own saliva. Sharing the food on one's plate with someone else is, therefore, unthinkable. Only inferiors find such 'leftovers', called 'saliva-food', acceptable: a wife might accept it from her husband, or a small child from its mother. Eating leftover food and thereby accepting defilement demonstrates subordination. Another central aspect is the intrinsic im/purity of food. A vegetarian diet, for example, is considered purer than a diet comprising meat or alcohol, which are both seen as defiling. Best are the products of 'divine' origin, such as water from holy waters, or the products of the holy cow as the embodiment of the goddess Lakshmi, such as milk, yoghurt and butter.

While under normal circumstances the purifying measure of a bath is considered sufficient for visiting a temple, attending a house ritual or a festival, or participating in a pilgrimage, this is not enough in cases of more severe pollution (called Tam. *tittu*) during menstruation, after childbirth or upon death. This would again be *pavam* and annoy the gods. Whereas 'normal' blood is considered only slightly impure, the uterine discharge during menstruation and delivery is considered extremely defiling, and the loss of the uyir ('breath of life') at death makes the entire body very impure and polluting. *Tittu* bodies are incompatible with the divine, even after bathing, until the end of the physical discharge or decay.

Apart from waiting for the end of the physical process, common measures taken against *tittu* pollution are seclusion and more thorough cleansing efforts. *Tittu* persons remain separate from persons in a normal state of im/purity, and even more so from those in a particularly pure and/or sacred state, such as babies, or people who follow a religious fast, or who are possessed by a deity. At the end of a *tittu* period the clothes are not washed at home, as is normally the case, but given to the washing caste for thorough cleansing. After childbirth and death the entire house is whitewashed, and a priest sprays *pañcagavya*, a cleansing mixture of the divine substances of the cow – milk, yoghurt, butter, cow dung and cow urine – and sometimes Ganga-water, towards all the polluted spaces as well as giving a mouthful of this to the house dwellers to drink.

Bodily waste was considered specifically unclean by my Kottar informants if it emerged from the body of a person belonging to a caste lower than them. Apparently, people have specific innate degrees of impurity. It was explained to me that these are the outcome of present and past *pavam*, and are influenced by their occupation. For example Sweepers, Barbers or Washer-people, who are at the lowest end of the caste system and who are in constant touch with impurities such as faeces, cadavers, disconnected hair and uterine blood, are considered severely and perpetually stained. 'We give the clothes by the feet, and they cleanse them by the hands', explained one Cetti informant. Similarly, unlike in Zimbabwe (Burke 1996: 32), white foreigners, generally called 'Americans' or 'English' by my informants, were considered dirty and stinking. In spite of my more than regular bathing habits in the heat, Kottar residents kept asking my field assistant whether my hygienic habits were as non-existent as those of other foreigners.

There are also bodies or physical states that are considered specifically pure. Babies, for example, from the end of birth-pollution until they are one year old, are considered pure. Their excreta are not deemed impure and are hence tolerated on clothes and floors without immediate cleansing. Other persons deemed pure and divine are patients suffering from chickenpox or measles, which are inflicted by goddesses. *Camiyatis* (Tam. 'god-dancers') who are periodically possessed by a deity and who then act as diviners, are also considered pure.

A person's caste conforms to the innate im/purity of the body and, correspondingly, the higher the status the more pure i.e. vegetarian the choice of diet. The lower the caste, the more reduced is its ambition to perfect the purity of the body, and hence the more meat features as an integral part of the diet. Meals prepared by lower castes are, therefore, considered defiling for upper castes. Conversely, food prepared by upper castes is considered acceptable to all the lower castes, and the *prasada* (Skt. symbolic [food] leftovers of the deities) given to devotees in temples, for example a mixture of raw fruits offered to a deity and blessed by him or her, is so divine that it is suitable for all.

Ultimately, then, for ordinary people in Kottar the concepts relating to hygiene, dirt and pollution, contiguous with practice described in other ethnographies, and similar to what was observed by Rosin (2000), seem closer to orthodox shastric ideas of cleanliness and purity – of which the main goal was the avoidance of pollution in order to achieve moksha (liberation) or spiritual power (Orenstein 1968: 115) – than to a pathogenic microbial idea of danger in dirt. The concept of dirt as a carrier of germs was not used as an explanation for cleansing measures or health hazards connected with pollution. This does not automatically imply that the dominance of this discourse among both the local higher and lower castes has a long tradition. Ultimately, in contrast to what Burke (1996), for example, observed in Zimbabwe, where ideas on hygiene were dominated by the colonial discourse and today are still influenced by foreign concepts, ideas and practices of hygiene and purity in Kottar have mostly indigenous orthodox roots.

Impurity and the organisation of private environments

To a certain extent, the metaphor of the body is applied to private homes in Kottar, as is common in Hindu approaches to the house, the temple and the world.[7] In ritual concepts, for example, the perfect square represents the ideal body, and the main shrine in the temple is associated with a womb.[8] In the house, the divine body of Shiva, or the demon Vastupurusa, are imagined as forming the ground plan (Beck 1976). Kottar residents make a division into pure and impure areas of their homes that resemble the way in which they map their bodies. They display a comparable preoccupation with the evacuation of waste and the prevention of impurities from intruding their private spaces. This is evident, for

7. Beck (1976); Daniel (1984); Eck (1998: 175 ff.); Kramrisch (1976).
8. Beck (1976: 238); Kramrisch (1976: 27).

example, in the clear differentiation of a clean front with a respectable façade, and an impure and neglected rear, where the most unclean waste of the house, such as sewage from toilets, leaves the compound.

The traditional house of a wealthy high-caste family is an almost square structure surrounding an open courtyard[9] (see Fig. 3.1). Similar house structures were proposed by the *Mayamata*, an architectural treatise written between the ninth and twelfth century.[10] This discourse reserved the square form with a central courtyard for the highest castes and deities (*Mayamata* 1985: xlii), whereas the lower orders were only allowed to use rectangular house shapes without interior courtyards (see Fig. 3.2). Traditional buildings for wealthy joint families were large structures with several courtyards (see Fig. 3.3).[11] In Kottar, all three types are found, though big houses with more than one courtyard are rare.

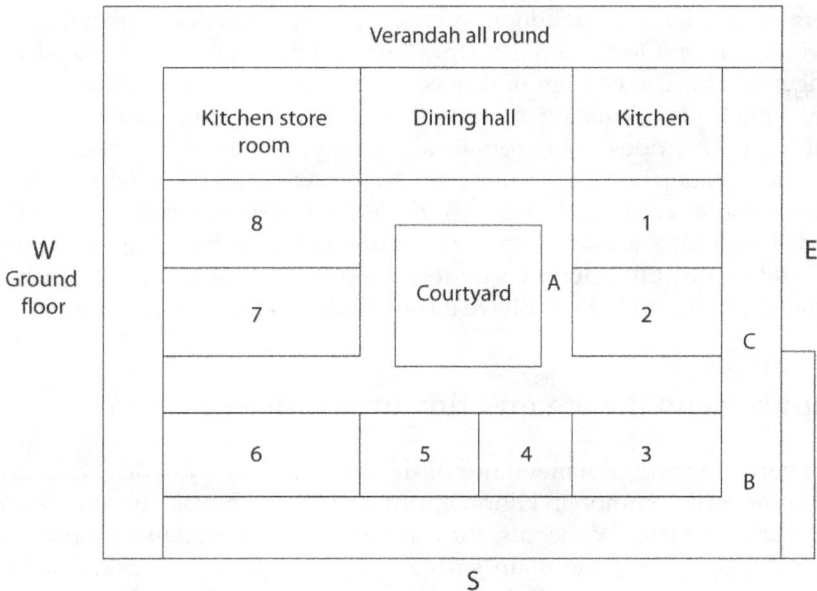

Figure 3.1. Traditional upper caste house.

9. Similar to the traditional Nayar house (Moore 1989: 176; Thurston 1909: 362) in the former Travancore area, which includes the south of Tamil Nadu.
10. This discourse on architecture for 'immortals or mortals' (*Mayamata* 1985: iii) represents an architectural school well known throughout South India. Monuments influenced by this school cover a period of fifteen centuries and a large part of the Indian peninsula.
11. *Mayamata* (1985: 230); Moore (1989: 171).

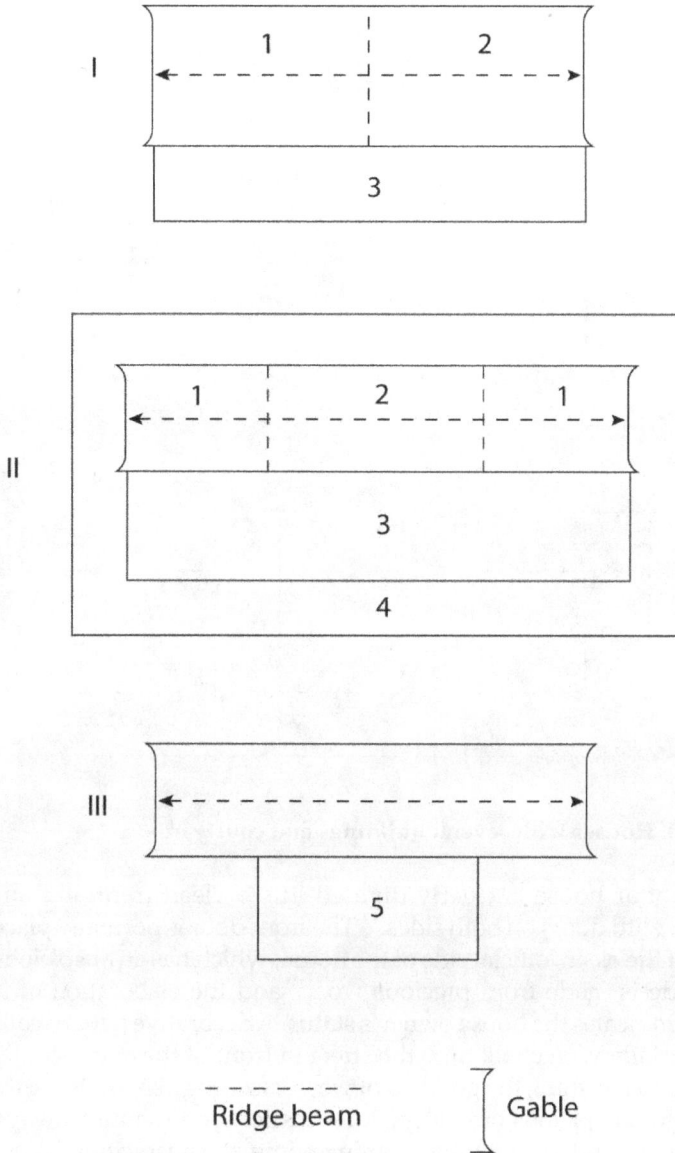

Figure 3.2. Houses with a single main building.

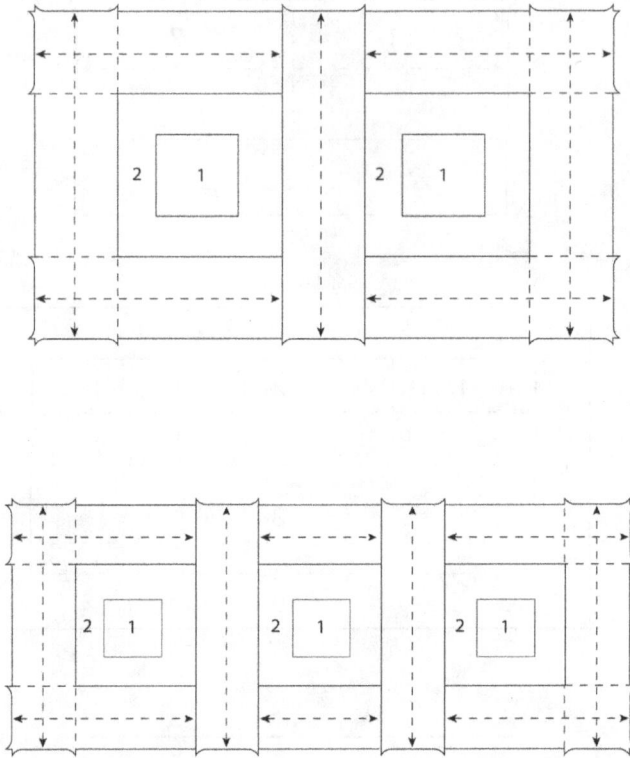

Figure 3.3. Houses with several buildings and courtyards.

The Kottar house is clearly divided into a clean front and an impure backside, with doors on both sides.[12] The front door is normally placed in the middle of the clean, official side of the house, which has an auspicious façade. The façade is made from precious wood, and the elaboration of its wood carvings indicates the house owner's status. A decorative pattern called *kolam* is drawn daily with chalk onto the street in front of the entrance steps as an invitation to Lakshmi, the goddess of wealth (see Fig. 3.4). To leave the house, whether for auspicious or inauspicious missions, one should always use the propitious front door. Yet when coming home, the auspicious front entrance must only be used if one is returning from a visit with an auspicious character. This includes, for instance, visiting a woman who has given birth recently, despite its defiling aspect, but excludes a condolence call after a death. Upon returning from such a visit, which is both inauspicious and defiling, one must use the back door and bathe before entering.

12. Cf. Reiniche (1981: 25) for the house in nearby Tirunelveli.

Figure 3.4. Women drawing *kolams* in front of the house entrance.

The front door opens onto a small veranda or lobby. Next to this is the main room, which is adjacent to or includes the courtyard. The main room is considered auspicious and is the most important place for propitious functions, such as rituals connected with engagements or marriages, and even the dead bodies of house members are usually laid out there. Further inside are a *puja* (worship) room, a storeroom, a kitchen and a room for eating. The *puja* room, which must be kept clean, i.e. pure, should be separated from the kitchen by at least one room, as the representations of the deities must be protected from the impurities emanating during food preparation. The kitchen, too, is a place that should be protected from pollution, although nowadays the rules are relaxed in most non-orthodox households. While in high-caste houses menstruating women are not allowed to enter the kitchen or even the house, in almost all middle or lower-caste households the women do the cooking even during their impure days. The kitchen is normally hidden in the house interior, near or at its rear, to protect it both from pollution and the Evil Eye. According to my lower-caste informants, before hospital births became compulsory, many women even gave birth in the kitchen so as to escape the Evil Eye. The person doing the cooking should face east in the auspicious direction of the gods, hence the hearth is placed accordingly.[13]

13. Dumont (1986: 70); Moore (1989: 174); Reiniche (1981).

At the periphery of the house compound, near the back door, stands the latrine cabin (*kakkus*). With the exception of new houses, most toilets are outside, as people feel that their presence inside would make the whole place too polluted and stinking (cf. Searle-Chatterjee 1981: 93; Vatuk 1972). The place for bathing is deemed less problematic and is tolerated closer to the house, though it is often close to the latrine.

The more open spaces of the veranda, courtyard and backyard are a sort of transitional areas between inside and outside zones. Visitors are received on the veranda and in orthodox households are not invited inside the house. In high-caste traditional households menstruating household members are exiled there. The backyard hosts sanitary facilities, livestock, larger rubbish and the compost. Household waste is generally first swept into the courtyard before being disposed of outside.

Nowadays, most old, traditional houses have been divided up among siblings, rather than being shared as a joint family compound. As a result, long, narrow tunnels, separated by walls and consisting of a chain of connecting small rooms, extend from the front street to the backyard (Fig. 3.5). Apart from the reduced size, the arrangement of the rooms and sites is the same as in the full-sized structure. Moreover, new houses have a similar organisation of rooms, as do the houses of the poor and lower castes, which emulate, on a smaller scale, the spatial arrangements of the higher castes and the wealthier.[14] Modern houses generally feature a small fenced garden at their entrance, and the front door opens directly onto the covered main room without courtyard. The kitchen and *puja*-room are almost always tucked away farther into the interior, behind the main room. Sometimes there are inside bathrooms attached to bedrooms or inside toilets, but these are tolerable because new houses often have septic tanks instead of open gutters.

Instead of a *puja*-room, the houses of the poor have a *puja*-site with shutters in the main room. The main room sometimes serves as a workplace for handicrafts such as weaving. Most poor people do not have latrines and instead frequent open gutters, public toilets or the fields at the town periphery (cf. Lynch 1969).

Dealing with waste

Ideally, the private home should be *cuttam* (Tam. 'clean'), hence impure matter is disposed of or kept outside. Private spaces are cleansed regularly, and people say that a tidy house attracts the deities, who bring fortune. In particular Lakshmi, the goddess of wealth, is expected to visit and inspect at the twilight times of dawn or dusk (cf. Leslie 1989: 59).

14. For old modest houses in the region see Iyer (1981, II: 9) and Mateer (1991: 52), for more recent ones Dumont (1986: 69 ff.) and Reiniche (1981; medium size structures).

N

Latrine

(uncovered)

Bathroom

Hearth

Kitchen

Dining hall

Puja-room | Store room

W

E

Living room

Study room

Part of open
courtyard

Front door
Veranda

S

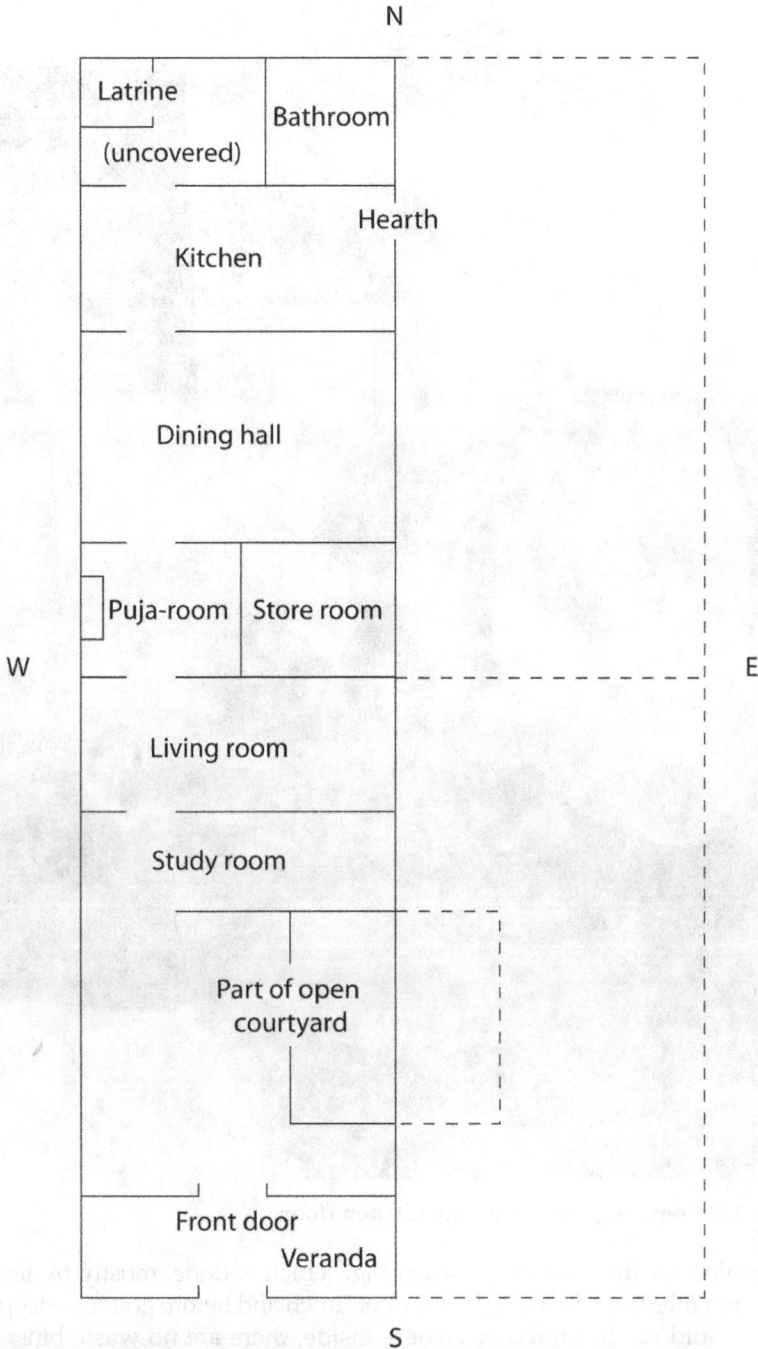

Figure 3.5. Traditional upper caste house divided.

Figure 3.6. Preparing a snack on the kitchen floor.

Cleaning means, first of all, sweeping, which is done, mostly by female household members, at dawn, dusk, after lunch and before going to sleep. As waste should not be stored anywhere inside, there are no waste bins, and rubbish is simply dropped onto the floor to be swept later, or thrown over the compound wall. The main technique is to sweep the dust and waste from one room to the next and then move it into the courtyard, the street or the gutter. Many women use the same broom for the floor, table and counters, just as all these surfaces serve equally for preparing food, eating, sitting, sleeping and working (see Fig. 3.6). Larger pieces of garbage are either thrown outside into the open gutter or placed on a heap in front of or at the back of the house (Fig. 3.7 and Fig. 3.8). Waste must be visible rather than covered by bags, as this is interpreted by neighbours as a sign that very polluting *tittu* refuse had to be covered up, and that by coming close to the bag one would be seriously polluted. Consequently, the only way for women to get rid of used sanitary towels, which would be clearly visible if disposed of in the gutters or on the open heaps, is to burn them in the small hearth in the bathing-place next to many latrines. The house floors are also washed regularly by first scrubbing the floors with water or soap water, and then sweeping the fluid toward a small outlet in the wall, or towards the door, to be brushed outside. Mud floors are always cleansed with cow-dung water, a method which was very common in the past when there were no concrete floors (cf. Dubois 1985: 153; Leslie 1989: 59). In orthodox households the place where a menstruating woman has slept or where a lower-caste person has eaten is still cleansed with cow-dung water after the person leaves.

Figure 3.7. Garbage heaps in front of houses.

As impurities in general should not enter the house, certain habits and materials are only allowed in the peripheral spaces. It is fine, for example, to spit on the floor, dispose of nose mucus or to clean fish on the veranda, in the courtyard or in the backyard, but this is not allowed inside the house. Shoes must be left on the veranda before entering. The toilet and bathing water of the house flows through open gutters to the gutter bordering the back lane, while kitchen water flows to the gutter bordering the front lane (Fig. 3.7 and Fig. 3.8).

Figure 3.8. Back street with open gutter.

To a certain extent, house-cleaning is done in line with sacred timings and spaces (cf. Kaviraj 1997: 98), analogous to cleaning efforts focused on the body. The entire house is swept regularly at dusk and dawn, as this is the time when goddess Lakshmi is said to visit, especially on the sacred days Tuesday and Friday. After sweeping before sunrise the women draw a *kolam* in front of the entrance to please Lakshmi, and most high-caste women draw another *kolam* at dusk. In most households, the floors are washed once a week before sacred Friday, but many women scrub the purest rooms of the house, the kitchen and the puja room, daily. Moreover, the houses are washed on new and full moon days before the ancestors are worshipped, as well as on the first day of the Tamil month, and before festivities.

In connection with specifically severe physical pollution during a woman's menstruation, after childbirth or after a death, parts of or the whole house are considered seriously polluted (*tittu*). There are additional measures against such defilement such as the seclusion of certain household members and/or the purification by a Brahmin priest. In orthodox, mostly higher-caste, households, therefore, a woman must stay apart from the rest of the house in a separate room or on the veranda. This does not work at childbirth and death, when the entire household is considered polluted for some time. This requires a certain lapse of time and the purification of the house by a Brahmin priest, who sprays *pañcagavva*, a mixture of the products of the sacred cow, and gives the household members a sip to drink. Those who cannot afford a priest, among them many poor higher-caste families, purify the house on their own with water to which some add turmeric. Moreover, after a birth or a death, a house is generally whitewashed.

Access to houses

Access to homes is restricted in order to protect them from pollution. In particular, the *puja*-room or site and the kitchen must be guarded. A menstruating household member, especially if it is her first period, must not enter the *puja*-room, as she would defile the representations of the deities. In orthodox high-caste households, she is not even allowed to enter the house or to touch her children and must live and sleep on the veranda or in a separate room. During my fieldwork, on crossing the doorstep of a high-caste Cetti house, my assistant normally shouted loudly 'I am clean' to indicate that she was not in a dangerously polluting state. Persons belonging to lower castes than the household members are not normally allowed to enter the house except to do certain work. They are received on the veranda or in the entrance room.[15] My high-caste Vellalar neighbours were very surprised to see that the Brahman family invited me and my low-caste assistant inside their house. In the past, our informants told us, the low castes, for example a Sweeper who came for toilet cleaning

15. E.g., Moore (1989: 178); Reiniche (1981: 24); Srinivas (1952: 74).

or a washerwoman picking up the dirty clothes, were only allowed to come as close as the rear of the house. Servants entered only as far as the entrance room and carried their own plates with them for eating.

Members of higher castes prefer not to visit the homes of lower-caste people, as such houses are thought to be 'naturally' unclean and thus not very welcoming. Moreover, the homes of poor people, even if they belong to high castes, are also routinely considered dirty, to the extent that their caste status is brought in doubt. Conversely, if people are known as educated and well-off, their houses are often considered automatically clean.

The tactics of handling the im/purity of private space are not only similar to practices relating to the body; they express the social meaning of im/purity. Access to the house is restricted for impure household members as well as for lower castes, and the homes of the poor tend to be considered naturally less clean. This means that in today's Kottar context the cleanliness and im/purity concept is applied not only in the conceptualization of caste, as polluting occupations and life styles are associated with low-caste status, but in the case of class as well, as the uneducated and poor are also marked as impure.

The neighbourhood and outside world

Dichotomies similar to those applying to private space pertain to the outside world. In any Kottar town neighbourhood, entire rows of houses are divided into clean and respectable fronts and uncared-for backs. The facades face presentable mud and sometimes paved streets, lined by narrow open gutters, whereas the passages at the back are full of grimy waste, often appearing as mere extensions of the open sewers there (see Fig. 3.8). Kottar inhabitants have various concepts pertaining to outside space. For example, they distinguish between 'good', clean streets and neighbourhoods, which are high-lying and/or central as well as high-caste and high-class, and 'bad', unclean sites, which are generally low-lying, peripheral, polluted and inhabited by the lower castes and classes. In each neighbourhood there are sacred sites, such as temples, which are considered specifically pure. In fact, this perception corresponds closely to the reality of Kottar's shared space, which is similar to what has been documented in recent ethnographies.[16] Formerly, each Kottar caste used to share the same street or neighbourhood, a history which is still expressed today in caste-specific street and neighbourhood names, such as 'Cetti Street'. Certain castes, such as the Cetti or Saurashtra, still dominate specific streets today, but in general strict separation is dissolving. Instead, former caste neighbourhoods are now

16. See, e.g., Béteille (1965); Deliège (1992: 169, 170; 1995: 304); Dumont (1966: 173); Lynch (1969: 169); Moffatt (1979: 64 ff.); Searle-Chatterjee (1981); Srinivas (1952: 27).

gradually converting into representations of class. Traditional high-caste streets such as the one formerly inhabited only by Brahmin families, for example, are now dominated by wealthy middle castes, such as the Vellalar, who have gradually bought up the old houses and constructed new ones as well. In contrast, the lower castes and classes live on the urban periphery, in the most polluted neighbourhoods with hardly any public infrastructure. Impoverished middle-caste families live in the slum area near the river and in unauthorised 'colonies' along arterial roads, and the lowest-caste and class Kuluvan and Cakkiliar live in the '*kakkus* area' ('latrine site') along the *Parakkai* sewer. In the past, I was told, persons belonging to low castes were forbidden to enter the streets of higher castes, or were only allowed to do so barefoot and bareheaded. Today, with the more mixed neighbourhoods, people reluctantly accept that contacts with other castes are unavoidable, and some even find it unproblematic. The low-caste Paravar fishing people now have access to Cetti Street, although they are only allowed to sell fish at the rear doors, and the low-caste Nadar boldly walk through the neighbourhood of the higher-caste Saurashtra, though these complain about this loss of respect.

People use the term *ur* to describe both the place they inhabit and the place of origin of their caste (cf. Daniel 1984: 63 ff.), and they use the expression *gramam* for 'village' or 'neighbourhood'. According to high-caste informants, this idea was especially evident in the past, when it manifested itself in 'real' *gramams* with a temple and high-caste streets in the centre, and the lower-caste neighbourhoods and *ceris* situated farther out. This reflects that the idea and practice of public space shared by members of a similar status of im/purity in a concentric fashion is old. Generally, the perception and organisation of Kottar neighbourhoods is evocative of South Asian orthodox concepts pertaining to the outside. According to Zimmermann (1987: 101), throughout Sanskrit literature the term *gramya* ('domesticated') was opposed to *aranya* ('wild'). In Vedic and Brahman India the term *grama* described a social concentration of people, in contrast to *aranya*, the forest outside (Malamoud 1976: 4; Zimmermann 1987: 102). In later texts, the expression was used for the description of an artificial environment in contrast to the earth as primary site (Lewandowski 1977: 185; *Mayamata* 1985: viii, 26). According to old architectural treatises (*Mayamata* 1985), *gramas* are divided into concentric zones (see Fig. 3.9; ibid.: xiii, 27; Kramrisch 1976: 42). A temple or an altar with a sanctum (*garbhagrha* i.e. 'womb' room) had to be installed at its centre.[17] The street encircling the middle of the settlement was called *brahmavithi* and was seen as its navel (*Mayamata* 1985: 28). Caste (*varna*) as

17. Beck (1976: 238); Kramrisch (1976: 27); Malamoud (1989: 84); *Mayamata* (1985: 28); O'Flaherty (1980: 20).

well as economic hierarchy were incorporated into the architectural plan, with the highest and wealthiest communities near the centre, and the lowest orders at the periphery.[18] The outskirts also featured the cremation site, and even farther outside the inferior cemetery (*Mayamata* 1985: 31–34). Similar town structures were promulgated in later history (Hofmeister 1980; Lewandowski 1977: 194). Moreover, the Indian landscape is perceived in a similarly concentric way (Eck 1998).

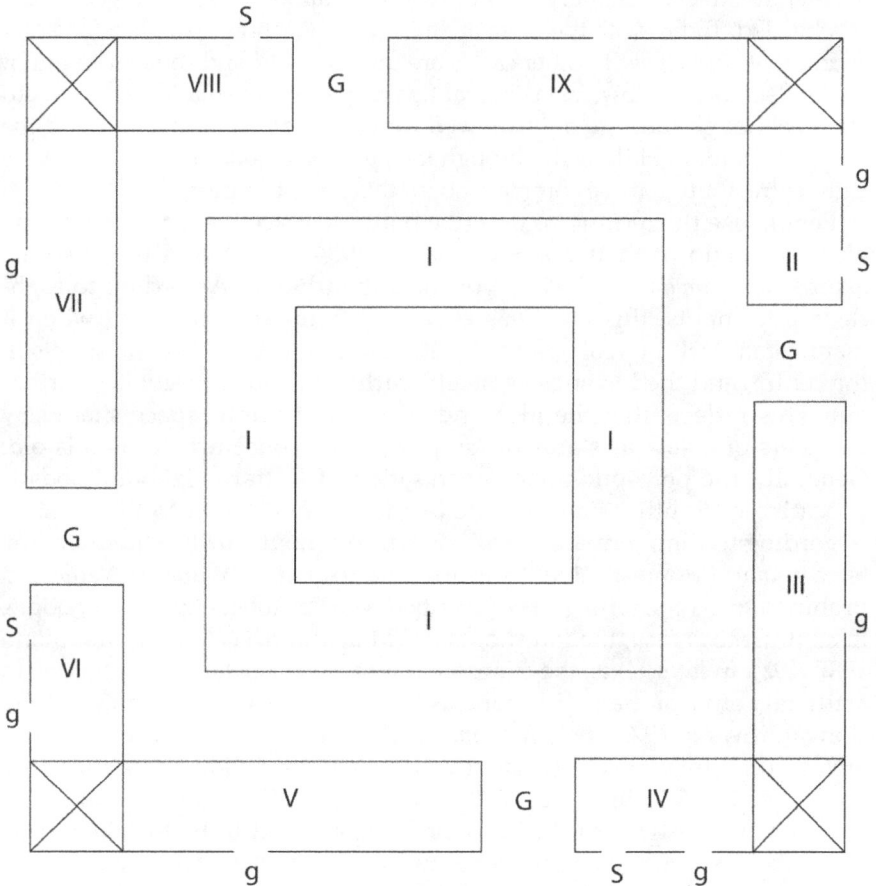

Figure 3.9. Traditional town layout.

---

18. *Mayamata* (1985: xliii). Cf. Guilmoto et al. (1990: 195); Hofmeister (1980: 105); Lewandowski (1977: 189, 192).

Polluting the outside

The perception of the outside world as concentric circles, with the purest areas in the middle and the most polluted ones at the periphery, is reflected in the way Kottar residents relate to it in their practical everyday life. Outside of private and sacred zones like temples, they have no interest in cleanliness. Their interest in cleanliness stops at the doorsteps of private homes, and the habits related to the outside define it as an irrelevant rubbish dump. As noted above, people simply throw household waste outside, and when people move through the neighbourhood and town, they drop any waste as they walk, and spit and throw nasal mucus on the ground. Poor people without private latrines prefer to relieve themselves in open gutters, parks or fields, rather than using the few public toilets, which are considered too dirty. Consequently, Kottar's streets are filled with scattered heaps of rubbish, and open areas are littered with waste that is blown around by the wind or dragged from the heaps by animals or toddlers. The open gutters are filled with a sluggish grey-brown liquid, which finds its way around plastic and other solid matter into the larger collecting sewer (see Fig. 3.10) proceeding to the *Pazhayar* river at the periphery. During the monsoon the sewers overflow, and people wade barefoot through this lethal sauce.

Like private homes and especially their *puja*-rooms, temples and other sacred sites are protected from pollution. As noted above, one is not allowed to visit a temple if one is not clean. People therefore bathe and eat vegetarian food before such a visit, and shirts and shoes, considered impure, must be left outside. Menstruating women are considered too impure for temple visits for at least three days. Once a year, before the representation of a temple deity is processed around the neighbourhood, the streets are carefully swept.

In spite of the ban on the pollution of deities, sacred waters such as certain rivers or ponds are often contaminated, as they are receptacles of untreated sewage. Similar to the view Hindus of Banaras hold on the sacred Ganga (Alley 2002), such sacred waters are seen as possessing powerful purifying, healing and other forces, irrespective of the presence of germs, and bathing in them is thus considered beneficial.

The concept of 'public space' signifying areas open to a wide public considered worthy of protection, and whose upkeep is thought to have an impact on physical wellbeing, was absent among my informants. In colonial India, the idea of 'public space', which had emerged in the West by the eighteenth century (Sennett 1974), had led to the creation of parks and other public spaces in bigger cities (Kaviraj 1997: 87; Lewandowski 1977). In Kottar, this concept was manifest in the existence of eight parks. However, these were obviously not used in the way they had been conceptualised, as all of these spaces were full of foul-smelling waste and faecal matter. The municipal health officer was the only informant expressing a view of a different use, explaining that these parks were originally meant for 'passive recreation'.

There are organised cleansing efforts focusing on the outside represented by Sweepers. The majority of them belong to the very low Chakkiliar caste and are employed by the municipality. They occasionally turn up to sweep, clean the public toilets and pick up waste from the open gutters and heaps. Waste is transported to 90 sub-deposits, and from there on to a big disposal site outside town. Lowest-caste Kuluvan Scavengers search the waste-heaps for specific things, which they sell to retail stores. In spite of such efforts, the Kottar public environment is constantly polluted, a fact the town authorities attribute to a shortage of Sweepers.

The public sanitation system is archaic. It consists of open gutters and sewers and no treatment facilities, while the drinking-water supply

Figure 3.10. Collecting sewer.

consists of street corner taps that provide water only irregularly. The town authorities are not interested in any improvement, and there is no political pressure towards this goal. The only action against outside pollution during my fieldwork was a protest against a sub-deposit near a Hindu temple by nearby residents; they requested that the deposit be moved to the mosque. The municipal health officer argued that the town did not have the funds to improve the sanitary system, and that health problems could easily be treated with medication. 'It would cost twenty crores, and it would damage the entire road system', he moaned. 'Open gutters have the big advantage that they can easily be de-blocked from solid materials'.

While, then, cleanliness in connection with private homes and temples is thought to have a positive effect on the goodwill of the deities, and bathing in sacred waters is considered beneficial irrespective of the presence of microbes, most Kottar people do not perceive the pollution of the outside world as worrying because it is not considered to have an influence on personal wellbeing. Most informants did not see a connection between pollution and health hazards.

Conclusion

In the context of Kottar, private cleanliness and outside pollution are the result of a specific scheme of hygiene and purity which is closer to a shastric understanding of purity and the organisation of space than to a microbial theory. In this scheme, bodily exudations of lower castes are considered impure, while emissions of the cow as divine being are deemed pure and sacred. Similar to Banaras (Alley 2002), Kottar residents use different terms for 'ordinary' un-cleanliness and more serious defilement (*tittu*), but in view of the frequent absence of ritual acts in connection with such states, I think that the English term of 'ritual' defilement is not justified. Rather than being an accurate translation, it seems to express the helplessness of scholars in the face of habits that do not fit in with scientific ideas of cleanliness. In Kottar, the concept of purity and impurity, similar to a scientific understanding, clearly relates to the physical qualities of the material world and not to immaterial aspects. It is thus not in itself 'social' (Milner 1987), which does not exclude a significant social 'impact' in the form of caste and class segregation, as contact with lower-caste substances is seen as more dangerous than with those of higher castes. Nor is environmental pollution the result of gendered space (Harriss-White 1998), as there is no difference in how men and women deal with im/purity related to private and public space. However, in contrast to a dominant scientific understanding, in Kottar, the danger of impurities is not conceptualised in the form of health hazards caused by microbes, but in terms of provoking the gods, who might then bring misfortune in the form of disease and poverty. Outside of private and sacred spaces there is, therefore, no danger connected with impurity, and as a result, pollution of the outside is deemed irrelevant. Unlike in Banaras, where the residents recognised that river pollution was a force they had to understand and control, even if sacred purity transcended it (Alley 2002), Kottar citizens were thus indifferent towards environmental pollution. In combination with the reluctance of the public authorities to improve the sanitary infrastructure, from the point of view of a scientific understanding this perpetuates environmental squalor and hence danger.

References

Alley, K.D. 2002. *On the Banks of the Ganga: When Wastewater Meets a Sacred River*. Ann Arbor: University of Michigan Press.
————1994. 'Ganga and Gandagi: Interpretations of Pollution and Waste in Benaras', *Ethnology* 33 (2): 127–45.
Arnold, D. 1993. *Colonizing the Body: State Medicine and Epidemic Disease in Nineteenth Century India*. Berkeley: University of California Press.
Barnett, S. 1976. 'Coconuts and Gold: Relational Identity in a South Indian Caste', Contributions to Indian Sociology (N.S.) 10 (1): 133–56.
Beck, B.E.F. 1976. 'The Symbolic Merger of Body, Space and Cosmos in Hindu Tamil Nadu', *Contributions to Indian Sociology* (N.S.) 10: 213–43.
Béteille, A. 1965. *Caste, Class and Power*. Berkeley and Los Angeles: University of California Press.
Burghart, R. 1978. 'Hierarchical Models of the Hindu Social System', *Man* (N.S.) 13: 519–36.
Burke, T. 1996. *Lifebuoy Men, Lux Women: Commodification, Consumption, and Cleanliness in Modern Zimbabwe*. London: Leicester University Press.
Crook, N. 1989. 'On the Comparative Historical Perspective: India, Europe, the Far East' in *India's Historical Demography: Studies in Famine, Disease and Society*, T. Dyson (ed.), pp. 285–96. London: Curzon Press.
da Silva Gracias, F. 1994. *Health and Hygiene in Colonial Goa 1510–1961*. New Delhi: Concept.
Daniel, E.V. 1984. *Fluid Signs: Being a Person the Tamil Way*. Berkeley: University of California Press.
Das, Veena. 1976. 'The Uses of Liminality: Society and Cosmos in Hinduism', *Contributions to In¬dian So¬ciology* 10 (2): 245–63.
————1985. 'Paradigms of Body Symbolism: An Analysis of Selected Themes in Hindu Cul¬ture' in *Indian Religion*, R. Burghart and A. Cantlie (eds), pp. 180–207. London: Centre of South Asian Stu¬d¬ies, SOAS.
————1992 [1977]. *Structure and Cognition: Aspects of Hindu Caste and Ri¬tual*. Delhi: Oxford Uni¬ver¬sity Press.
Deliège, R. 1992. 'Replication and Consensus: Untouchability, Caste and Ideology in India', *Man* (N.S.) 27: 155–73.

———— 1995. *Les intouchables en Inde: Des castes d'exclus*. Paris: Imago.

Dirks, N.B. 1989. 'The Original Caste: Power, History and Hierarchy in South Asia', *Contributions to Indian Sociology* (n.s.) 23 (1): 59–77.

Douglas, M. 1966. *Purity and Danger: An Analysis of the Concepts of Pollution and Taboo*. London: Routledge and Kegan Paul.

Dubois, A.J.A. 1985 [1906]. *Hindu Manners, Customs and Ceremonies*. Oxford: Oxford University Press.

Dumont, L. 1966. *homo hierarchicus: Le système des castes et ses implications*. Paris: Editions Gallimard.

———— 1971. 'On Putative Hierarchy and Some Allergies to It', *Contributions to Indian sociology* (N.S.) 5: 58–78.

———— 1986. *A South Indian Subcaste*. Delhi: Oxford University Press.

Eck, D.L. 1998. 'The Imagined Landscape: Patterns in the Construction of Hindu Sacred Geography', *Contribution to Indian Sociology* 32 (2): 165–87.

Eichinger Ferro-Luzzi, G. 1974. 'Women's Pollution Periods in Tamilnad (India)', *Anthropos* 69: 8–161.

Elias, N. 1982. *The Civilizing Process*. Oxford: Blackwell.

Fuller, C.J. 1979. 'Gods, Priests and Purity: On the Relation Between Hinduism and the Caste System', *Man* 14: 459–76.

Guilmoto, C., M.-L. Reiniche and P. Pichard. 1990. *Tiruvannamalai: Un lieu saint Sivaite du Sud de l' Inde 5: La ville*. Paris: Ecole Française d'Extrême Orient.

Gupta, D. 2000. *Mistaken Modernity: India between the Worlds*. New Delhi: HarperCollins.

Harper, E.B. 1964. 'Ritual Pollution as an Integrator of Caste and Religion', *Journal of Asian Studies* 23: 151–97.

Harriss-White, B. 1998. 'Rural Infrastructure, Urban Civic Services and the Micro Politics of Governance'. Workshop paper, *The Anthropology of the Indian State*. London: London School of Economics, 9 May.

Hofmeister, B. 1980. *Die Stadtstruktur*. Darmstadt: wb.

Hutton, J.H. 1963 [1946]. *Caste in India: Its Nature, Functions and Origins*. Cambridge: Cambridge University Press.

Illi, M. and H.-R. Steiner. 1987. *Von der Schissgruob zur modernen Stadtentwässerung*. Zürich: Verlag NZZ.

Iyer, A.K. 1981 [1912]. *The Tribes and Castes of Cochin*, 3 vols. New Delhi: Cosmo.

Kaviraj, S. 1997. 'Filth and the Public Sphere: Concepts and Practices about Space in Calcutta', *Public Culture* 10 (1): 83–113.

Kramrisch, S. 1976 [1946]. *The Hindu Temple*, 2 vols. Delhi: Motilal Banarsidass.

Leslie, J.I. 1989. *The Perfect Wife: The Orthodox Hindu Woman According to the Stridharmapaddhati of Tryambakayajvan*. Delhi: Oxford University Press.

Lewandowski, S.J. 1977. 'Changing Form and Function in the Ceremonial and the Colonial Port City in India: An Historical Analysis of Madurai and Madras', *Modern Asian Studies*, 11 (2): 183–212.

Lüthi, D. 1998. 'The Kottar Body: Polished Refuse', *Rebus* 12&13: 69–82.

──────1999. *Washing off Sin: Cleanliness in Kottar, South India*. Ph.D. diss., University of Berne.

──────2001. 'Erklärungsmodelle für Erkrankungen und Strategien zur Gesundheitserhaltung im tamilischen Kottar (Südindien)', *Curare* 24: 9–18.

──────2004. 'Private Reinlichkeit, öffentliches Chaos: Un/reinheit und Raum im südindisch-tamilischen Kottar', *Zeitschrift für Ethnologie* 129: 1–31.

Lynch, O.M. 1969. *The Politics of Untouchability: Social Mobility and Social Change in a City of India*. New York: Columbia University Press.

McGilvray, D.B. 1982. 'Sexual Power and Fertility in Sri Lanka: Batticaloa Tamils and Moors' in *Ethnography of Fertility and Birth*, C.P. MacCormack (ed.), pp. 25–73. London: Academic Press.

Madan, T.N. 1987. *Non-Renunciation: Themes and Interpretations of Hindu Culture*. Oxford: Oxford University Press.

Malamoud, C. 1976. 'Village et forêt dans l'idéologie de l'Inde brâhmanique', *Archives Européennes de Sociologie* 17: 3–20.

──────1989. 'Indian Speculations about the Sex of the Sacrifice' in *Fragments of a History of the Human Body*, M. Feher (ed.), pp. 74–103. New York: Zone.

Marriott, M. 1976. 'Hindu Transactions: Diversity without Dualism' in *Transaction and meaning*, B. Kapferer (ed.), pp. 109–42. Phi¬ladelphia: Institute for the Study of Human Issues.

──────1989. 'Constructing an Indian Ethnosociology', Contributions to Indian Sociology (N.S.) 23 (1): 1–39.

Marriott, M. and R.B. Inden. 1977. 'Toward an Ethnosociology of South Asian Caste Systems' in *The New Wind: Changing Identities in South Asia*, K. David (ed.), pp. 227–38. The Hague: Mouton Publishers.

Mateer, S. 1991 [1870]. *The Land of Charity: A Descriptive Account of Travancore and Its People*. New Delhi: AES.

Mayamata: An Indian Treatise on Housing, Architecture and Iconography (trans. Bruno Dagens). 1985. New Delhi: Sitaram Bhartia Institute of Scientific Research.

Milner, M. 1987. 'Dirt and Development in India', Virginia Quarterly Review 63: 54–71.

Mines, D.P. 1989. 'Hindu Periods of Death "Impurity" ', Contributions to Indian Sociology 23 (1): 103–30.

Moffatt, M. 1979. *An Untouchable Community in South India: Structure and Consensus*. Princeton: Princeton University Press.

Moore, M.A. 1989. 'The Kerala House as a Hindu Cosmos', *Contributions to Indian Sociology* (N.S.) 23 (1): 169–202.

Mosse, D. 1994. 'Replication and Consensus among Indian Untouchable (Harijan) Castes', *Man* 29: 457–60.

O'Flaherty, W.D. 1980. *Women, Androgynes and Other Mythical Beasts*. Chicago: Chicago University Press.

Orenstein, H. 1965. 'The Structure of Hindu Caste Values: A Preliminary Study of Hierarchy and Ritual Defilement', *Ethnology* 4: 1–15.

————1968. 'Toward a Grammar of Defilement in Hindu Sacred Law' in M. Singer and B.S. Cohn (eds), *Structure and Change in Indian Society*, pp. 115–31. Chicago: Aldine Publishing Co.

Parry, J.P. 1989. 'The End of the Body' in *Fragments of a History of the Human Body*, M. Feher (ed.), pp. 490–517. New York: Zone.

————1991. 'The Hindu Lexicographer? A Note on Auspiciousness and Purity', *Contributions to Indian Sociology*, 25 (2): 267–85.

Prashad, V. 2001. 'The Technology of Sanitation in Colonial Delhi', *Modern Asian Studies* 35 (1): 113–55.

Reiniche, M.-L. 1981. 'La maison au Tirunelveli', *Bulletin de l'Ecole Française d'Extrême Orient* 70: 21–57.

Rosin, Th.R. 2000. 'Wind, Traffic and Dust: The Recycling of Wastes', *Contributions to Indian Sociology* (n.s.) 34 (3): 361–408.

Ryan, K.S. 1980. *Pollution in Practice: Ritual, Structure and Change in Tamil Sri Lanka*. Ph. D. diss., Cornell University.

Searle-Chatterjee, M. 1981. *Reversible Sex Roles: The Special Case of Benares Sweepers*. Oxford: Pergamon Press.

Sennett, R. 1974. *The Fall of Public Man*. New York and London: Norton.

Srinivas, M.N. 1952. *Religion and Society among the Coorgs of South India*. Oxford: Clarendon Press.

————1976. *The Remembered Village*. Delhi: Oxford University Press.

Stevenson, H.N.C. 1954. 'Status Evaluation in the Hindu Caste System', *Journal of the Royal Anthropological Institute*, 84 (1–2): 45–65.

Stork, H. 1992 [1991]. 'Mothering Rituals in Tamilnadu: Some Magico-Religious Beliefs' in *Roles and Rituals for Hindu Women*, J. Leslie (ed.), pp. 89–105. Delhi: Motilal Banarsidass.

Thurston, E. 1909. *Castes and Tribes of Southern India*. Madras: Government Press.

Vatuk, S. 1972. *Kinship and Urbanization*: White Collar Migrants in North India. Berkeley: University of California Press.

Vidyarnava, R.B.S.C. 1979 [1918]. *The Daily Practice of the Hindus: Containing the Morning and Midday Duties*. Delhi: Oriental Books Reprint.

Vigarello, G. 1985. *Le propre et le sale: L'hygiène du corps depuis le Moyen Age*. Paris: Editions du Seuil.

Williams, M.T. 1991. *Washing 'the Great Unwashed': Public Baths in Urban America, 1840–1920*. Columbus: Ohio State University Press.

Yalman, N. 1963. 'On the Purity of Women in the Castes of Ceylon and Malabar', *Journal of the Royal Anthropological Institute* 93 (1): 25–58.

Zimmermann, F. 1987 [1982]. *The Jungle and the Aroma of Meats*. Berkeley: University of California Press.

CHAPTER 4

The Jungle and the City: Perceptions of the Urban among Indo-Fijians in Suva, Fiji

Susanna Trnka

The city of Suva is located on the southeast side of Viti Levu, Fiji's largest island. With a population of over 167,000 and a downtown packed with bars, nightclubs, internet cafés and ethnic restaurants, Suva is, as tourist guidebooks like to point out, 'the most cosmopolitan city in the South Pacific' (Bienstock 2003: 406). It is also a city plagued by increasing levels of crime, contagious disease and environmental hazards. This chapter examines how Indo-Fijians, Fiji's second largest cultural group and roughly thirty nine percent of Suva's population, perceive of the City in opposition to the Jungle.[1] Mindful of the complex cultural understandings of 'clean' versus 'unclean' which for many Indo-Fijians shapes their identity as Hindus, I suggest how Indo-Fijian perspectives of urban spaces posit urban 'development' in relation to fears of an encroaching unruly 'jungle'. I do so by probing two moments of crisis, the destruction of parts of Suva during the May 2000 coup and the accidental burning of the Lami rubbish dump in July 2005, to demonstrate how urban spaces not only represent prosperity and progress, but can also be sites of intense distress.

---

1. Approximately another fifty one percent of the population is indigenous Fijian. The remaining ten percent are Asian, European and other Pacific Islanders. These figures are from 1996. In the last ten years the city's population has grown, but the Fiji Islands Bureau of Statistics is unable to provide more recent information on Suva's population than that of the 1996 census (Fiji Islands Bureau of Statistics, personal communication).

My analysis focuses on Indo-Fijians, the majority of whom are Hindus for whom the cultural categories of purity, impurity, cleanliness and pollution shape religious practice, community life and religious and ethnic identity.[2] In a politically contentious environment marked by three purportedly 'anti-Indian' political coups in the past twenty years,[3] assertions of Indo-Fijian rights have, moreover, increasingly invoked the importance of Indo-Fijian labour in the economic development and urbanisation of Fiji (Trnka 2002, 2005, 2008; Kelly 1988b, 1998). In local terminology, the Indian contribution to the development of the modern nation is depicted through the imagery of clearing away the 'wild' jungle and transforming it into a clean, developed and economically prosperous terrain. Urban spaces, in particular, are seen as representing a highly desirable way of life that is widely considered to be more modern, advanced and 'civilised', even though city living is also recognised as being subject to severe problems including disease, poverty, violent crime and environmental crises. Recent economic downturns, government mismanagement and increasing internal migration from rural to urban areas have further compounded these problems. At the same time, there is a depletion of professionals and skilled trades people as structural inadequacies and political turbulence encourage migration overseas.

Within this context, this chapter considers how the City can be conceptualised as intrinsically 'clean' despite widespread awareness of and concern over its polluted state. In doing so, my aim is to draw together insights from two bodies of scholarly literature. The first consists of anthropological examinations of cultural perceptions of purity and impurity, particularly as associated with religious and ethnic identity (e.g. Appadurai 1998, 2006; Aretxaga 1995; Jackson 2002; Malkki 1995; Mbembe 2003; Pedersen 2002; Reinhart 1990; Rouse and Hoskins 2004; Valeri 1990, 2000). Much of this work is grounded in but also critical of Mary Douglas' classic analysis of purity and pollution (Douglas 2005). The second body of scholarship critiques colonial and post-colonial perceptions of the innate inter-relationships between 'race' and place, in particular, assumptions

---

2. See Brown (1978, 1981); Gill (1988); Jayawardena (1971); Kelly (1988a); Trnka (2002, 2004, 2005).
3. Fiji's fourth and, to date, most recent coup, which occurred in December 2006, is a notable exception. It was not accompanied by anti-Indian sentiment. In fact, coup leader Commodore Frank Bainimarama attempted to justify his takeover on the grounds that the racist policies of the previous government were part of his motivation in forcing it out of power. Given the military's crackdown on open political debate, it is too soon to assess the long term responses of Fiji's populace to Bainimarama's actions, though some have suggested that the events following 2006 might further entrench communal sentiment. See, for example, Madraiwiwi (2007).

about the shared characteristics of 'wild' landscapes and the indigenous inhabitants who occupy them (Birtles 1997; Chatterjee 2001; Comaroff and Comaroff 1991; Taussig 1987). By means of a detailed examination of one ethnographic case, i.e. the City as viewed by Indo-Fijians in Suva, I intend to demonstrate how current political and economic crises combined with the enduring legacies of colonial rule have created an ethnically-marked terrain. Based on historical research, interviews, and on-going ethnographic engagement with residents of Suva and surrounding areas, initially over the course of two years of intensive fieldwork (1999–2000) and later as part of follow-up research in 2005 and 2006, I examine how the City is invested with symbolic meanings that configure both the actions and imaginations of contemporary post-colonial urban residents with respect to urban 'cleanliness'.

The city of Suva

It is difficult to determine the exact boundaries of the city of Suva. It is bordered to the south by the ocean, but on all other sides the city is flanked by sprawling peri-urban settlements. Indeed, the 1996 census notes that while the population of the city proper is 77,000, there are another 90,000 peri-urban residents. Nineteen kilometres away from Suva is another urban hub, Nausori Town, with a population of over 5,000 and close to 16,000 peri-urban residents. Because of the proximity between the two urban centres, the area is commonly referred to as 'the Suva-Nausori corridor'.

Suva is Fiji's centre of economic, political and cultural life. Not only does it boast a bustling downtown business district, it is also the seat of government and the home of the Secretariat of the South Pacific Forum, various NGOs and the University of the South Pacific, which serves students from twelve nations across the Pacific. Suva also offers the best health care, employment opportunities and educational services in Fiji.

It is thus no surprise that Suva is highly regarded for offering the most cosmopolitan lifestyle in Fiji. Both urban Indo-Fijians and those for whom a trip to Suva is a rare treat speak of the city as the epitome of commerce and consumer culture, emphasising the city's modernity, wealth and convenience. Of special note are the greater reliability of running water and electricity as well as the availability of globalised forms of consumer culture in the capital. One family I met in the farming area outside of Labasa, on Fiji's second largest island of Vanua Levu, about an hour away from Suva by plane, had memorialised their only trip to Suva in their family photo album through images of themselves standing outside of Suva's McDonalds, the Village Six movie theatre and the then newly built American grocery store, Cost-U-Less.

People's enthusiasm over Suva leads them to sometimes overplay the city's distinctions. After eight months of living in the centre of Suva, I moved into an area just outside of Nausori Town which appeared to me to be just like one of Suva's peri-urban neighbourhoods. Complete with paved roads, running water and electricity, the neighbourhood was quite developed. The bulk of its residents, moreover, supported themselves through non-agricultural labour, many of them commuting daily to downtown Suva. But Suva residents remarked upon the lack of amenities I would face living outside of the city and warned me of problems such as potential water shortages (something I had frequently experienced during my stay in the city centre). I was even more surprised when local Nausori residents also commented upon how different their life was from life in the city. I was not sure what they were referring to when they kept speaking of 'the village', until I realised I was now living in one. 'Do you know that people in Nausori say they live in a village?' I asked one of my Suva friends. 'Of course', he replied, 'they have cows there'. His comment underscores the assumption that any area that has agriculture or animal husbandry, even if it is nominal, is distinctly un-urban.[4]

But the permeability of the urban and the agricultural are clearly observable even in 'developed' areas such as the capital. In addition to the cafés and business offices, a variety of domestic and wild animal life exists in the city. People cultivate crops in the minute green spaces between the city's apartment blocks. Suva's fruit trees are regularly harvested and subsistence fishing takes place off of Suva Harbour. It is possible to encounter stray pigs running through inner-city neighbourhoods. Such elements of city living are, however, generally overlooked in order to emphasise the modernity of urban life, as opposed to that of less 'developed' areas such as outlying villages.

While Suva's modernity and distinction are articulated with pride, there are, however, moments when fears abound over the fragility of both the city and Fiji's claims to being cosmopolitan. One of these moments occurred when the city's downtown and the Parliament complex were destroyed during the political coup of May 2000.

A political overthrow and fears of encroaching jungle

On the morning of 19 May 2000, Fiji underwent its third, and to date most violent, political coup. The largely unknown businessman George Speight declared the 'return' of Fiji to indigenous Fijians by taking over the

---

4. A second factor that differentiates cities from peri-urban 'villages' is their settlement patterns and the resulting social ties between residents (see Trnka 2004).

Parliamentary Complex in Suva and holding hostage the country's first Indo-Fijian Prime Minister, Mahendra Chaudhry, and various Members of Parliament. It was the beginning of nearly six months of violence and terror. The rebels held Chaudhry and other members of his ruling coalition for fifty six days. Even after their release, violent attacks against Indo-Fijians in rural and urban areas continued as the political and economic situation spiralled out of control. It was not until mid-November 2000 that the country returned to some semblance of normality.

During his stay at the Parliament Complex, Speight and his supporters not only overturned the government but overturned the Parliament buildings as well. An estimated 1,500 people flocked into the Parliament Complex in Veiuto, many of them having travelled to Suva from the interior of Viti Levu (Field et al. 2005). They dug large lovo pits (earthen ovens) on the Parliament grounds, hung their laundry on the Parliament roof to dry and used whatever space was available as toilets. When they evacuated the area, they left the Parliament buildings strewn with rubbish and used condoms. Journalist Michael Field described the Parliament shortly after Speight and his followers abandoned it:

> A misty rain was slowly lifting over burnt out cars, rubbish, broken chairs, stray dogs and a once beautiful complex of wooden buildings that had been trashed. ... Through the drama hundreds of people had turned offices into campsites, dug up the grounds to cook pigs and taro and everywhere they drank kava and then used the rooms, and anywhere else, to shit and piss on Fiji's democracy. The parliamentary library was turned into a laundry where clothes hung from books to dry. The water pooled everywhere and the place stank of rotting food. (Field et al. 2005: 228)

The Parliament buildings were not the only ones to suffer. On 19 May 2000, the same morning that Speight took over the Parliament, urban rioting rocked Suva's downtown business district. A pre-planned march against the government had taken place in the city that morning and when Speight's actions became public, the marchers turned violent and began to loot downtown shops and businesses.

I was conducting fieldwork in nearby Nausori Town when shopkeepers there hurriedly began to board up their stores and close down the main thoroughfare. My neighbours, who had fled from their offices in Suva earlier that morning, described hordes of people racing through the city, some intent on destruction, others scrambling to get out of their way. That afternoon we watched the TV footage together. Shop after shop had windows smashed and merchandise looted. Some businesses had been set alight, while others stood in the midst of broken glass and piles of trampled goods. In total, an estimated 167 business were damaged, with twenty set on fire, all in one morning (Field et al. 2005: 103). For many Indo-Fijians, the destruction of Suva's business district became the central image of the coup's devastation. They expressed their horror not through references to the taking of hostages or personal assaults, but by invoking the terror they felt at downtown Suva's destruction (Trnka 2002, 2008).

While the economic damage to the city was substantial, the symbolic damage was more significant. The destruction of so many shops and businesses was viewed by many as the first step in tearing down the city, and with it, Fiji's claims to modernity. These fears were recurrently evoked through images of *jungli*. Repeatedly, the Fijians who were involved in the violence were referred to as *junglis*. On other occasions, Indo-Fijians remarked that such violence stemmed from rural areas that were themselves characterised as jungli. As people spoke of the looting, they also expressed their fears of the possible disappearance of Fiji's urban infrastructure. Some suggested that this was the beginning of the city itself being overtaken by *jungli*.

Derived from the Sanskrit word 'jangal' (from which the English word 'jungle' originates) *jungli* connotes a wild and uncultivated state that has not been transformed through human endeavour. The term *jungli* is frequently used in Fiji in both Fiji Hindi and in English to describe unruly behaviour. An ill-mannered, misbehaving child might, for example, be referred to as *jungli*. For similar reasons, the term is also commonly used by some Indo-Fijians as a racial epithet for indigenous Fijians. The racist element of *jungli* discourses was particularly prevalent during the coup as talk of supposed Fijian 'primitivity' became part of daily conversations attempting to explain the political crisis (see also Trnka 2008).

While such descriptions were rife amongst many Indo-Fijians, indigenous Fijians took part in these discourses as well. In mid-June 2000, in the midst of the political turmoil, a Nausori-based indigenous Fijian friend warned me that further trouble was afoot. As the site of an upcoming rugby game between two teams from the interior provinces, Nausori Town was preparing for more violence. 'There might be shops broken into since a lot of people are coming down from Naitasiri', Timoci told me. I asked him why he thought that Fijians from Naitasiri were likely to be violent and he replied that they are violent because they are 'from the jungle'.[5]

While it is often used to describe unruly behaviour or people who are thought to be badly behaved, the term *jungli* is clearly also a spatial referent used to connote not only 'primitivity' but also to locate the origins

---

5. Another variant, used by both Indo-Fijians and indigenous Fijians, described those responsible for the violence as 'bush people', referring, in this context, to the inhabitants of interior areas of Viti Levu.

of that primitivity in a certain kind of physical space: the jungle or the bush. The term 'jungle' itself is furthermore similarly used to implicitly denote a lack, be it a lack of human cultivation, or in more current usage, a lack of development. As its etymology reveals, the original meaning of 'jungle' was 'in strictness only waste, uncultivated ground' (Yule and Burnell 1985: 470). Only later did 'jungle' come to be applied 'to forest, or other wild growth, rather than to the fact that it is not cultivated' (Yule and Burnell 1985: 470). As used by Indo-Fijians today, the term indicates a space that has not been 'cleared' or 'cleaned' (*sāf karna*) and thus transformed into an appropriate site for human habitation. First there was jungle, I was told, and then it was cleared away and the country was 'developed'.

Parts of Fiji remain, however, covered in jungle and fears abound over the Jungle as a space out of which wildness can still disseminate. During the 2000 coup, many were concerned that should this *jungli*-ness come out of the bush and encroach upon the polis, then civility itself might be overthrown. Embodied by those who enacted the political overthrow and the violence that coincided with it, the inherently polluting quality of *jungli* was viewed as a threat not only to the Chaudhry government, which was indeed thrown out of power by the coup, or to the safety of Indo-Fijians, who were the targets of much of the violence, but to the law, order, and progress thought to be epitomised by the City.

The attribution of violence and lawlessness to the Jungle was further encapsulated by the phrase 'law of the jungle' as used to comment on the 2000 coup. In a press release, the leading opposition party, the National Federation Party (NFP), condemned the lack of law and order following the coup, stating that:

> from May 19th members of the Indo-Fijian community have fallen victim to acts of terrorism and thuggery. These unarmed and defenceless citizens have been forced off their homes and farms. Houses have been ransacked, some burnt down, livestock has been slaughtered, and crops have been stolen by criminal elements. *This is the law of the jungle*.[6]

All of these examples - Indo-Fijians' fearful talk of 'jungles', Timoci's concern over the behaviour of people 'from the jungle', and the opposition party's condemnation of the 'law of the jungle' – evoke an opposition between the City and the Jungle. They furthermore demonstrate how the Jungle becomes the repository of wildness and danger which, if not mastered by more civilising forces, threatens to overwhelm the City and turn civility on its head. According to this logic, if the jungle is not

---

6. *Fiji Times*, 12 August 2000, p. 21. Emphasis added.

contained, sites of commerce and cosmopolitanism become rubbish heaps, just as libraries become laundries. The city's physical destruction – the merchandise and litter heaped on the streets, the broken windows and buildings set on fire – are thus seen as embodying the devolution of Fiji's most cultivated site into a wasteland.

Identities of transformation and labour

Many Indo-Fijians spoke of the damage to Fiji's capital as if it entailed not only the destruction of parts of the city, but a personal attack against themselves and their place in the nation of Fiji. In the midst of discussing the events of 2000 or watching news coverage of these events, they interjected assertions of their contributions to Fiji's development. They described in detail how Indo-Fijians had cleared the land, laying the foundations for Fiji's modernity, all of which, they declared, was being swept away by the looting. In order to understand the links many Indo-Fijians make between labour, national development and the city of Suva, it is essential to know something of the history that brought their ancestors to Fiji.

An estimated 318,000 Indo-Fijians live in Fiji today (Fiji Islands Bureau of Statistics 2006). For the most part, they are the descendants of the indentured servants (*girmitiyas*) who were brought over by the British to make the colony economically viable. Following Fiji's cession to Britain in 1874, the colony's first Governor General, Arthur Gordon, was wary of the effects of colonisation on the indigenous population. Gordon and his administration therefore initiated a series of policies to ensure the preservation of indigenous Fijian culture. These included codifying indigenous Fijian 'traditions', ensuring the inalienability of indigenous Fijian land by setting aside 83 percent of land for indigenous land owning units (*mataqali*), and requiring that indigenous Fijians retain their communal, subsistence lifestyle by prohibiting them from entering into wage labour (Kelly and Kaplan 1999: 237–57). Simultaneously, Indians were brought over from North and South India to provide a labour force for the colony. From 1879 to 1916, some 60,000 *girmitiyas* were brought over to work on Fiji's sugar plantations. The conditions they encountered were often brutal, including extensive illness, hunger and violence. Upon the completion of five years of service, they were free to settle in the colony, or, if they had sufficient funds, to return to India.[7] Many started up

7. Another five years of service would have earned them a free passage home. Very few, however, took this option. See Lal (1992).

sugar cultivation of their own or entered various small trades. By necessity, Indians were integrated into the wage labour economy, unlike indigenous Fijians, and over time they became a leading force of economic development in Fiji.

Today, many Indo-Fijians perceive labour (*kām*) and in particular, its transformative capacities, as a central feature of Indo-Fijian identity. The work of the indentured labourers or *girmitiyas* is often credited with transforming Fiji from a 'backward' place dominated by 'jungle' into a forward-looking, developed, or at least developing, nation. While the speeches of politicians and statesmen stress the co-operative nature of this endeavour,[8] in private conversation, assertions of Indo-Fijian industriousness are often made at the expense of other groups in Fiji. 'When Fijians were here, it was only jungle. Then Indians came and cleared it', one Indo-Fijian woman told me. 'Indians have built everything we have. But they want us to go back to being labourers, like during *girmit* [indenture]!' another woman exclaimed angrily while watching television news coverage of the coup. An Indo-Fijian man summed it up: 'Indians are the ones who developed this country. They did the hard work.' In such local discourses, Indo-Fijians frequently describe the role their ancestors played in Fiji by using the image of 'clearing away the jungle'. Such clearing away of the bush to prepare land for cultivation is, moreover, conceptually associated with the nation's overall economic and technological development. The epitome of their contributions is, for many, encapsulated by Fiji's capital city which stands for commerce, productivity and progress. This depiction of Fiji's development not only highlights Indo-Fijian contributions to Fiji but does so by leaving out the roles played by British colonialists and, more importantly, indigenous Fijians.[9]

Such claims of the historical importance of Indo-Fijian labour to Fiji are especially important during times of political turmoil when many Indo-Fijians feel pressed to show their allegiances and contributions to Fiji. Over the decades since the abolition of indenture, Indo-Fijians' position in the nation and indeed their right to remain in Fiji have come under repeated threat. In response, their origins as *girmitiyas* who were brought to Fiji to

8. See Kelly (1988b). In colonial times, the cooperative nature of these contributions was evoked by the image of the nation as a 'three legged stool' supported by Indo-Fijian labour, indigenous Fijian land, and British capital and administration. See Scarr (1983); Kaplan (1995: 107); Lal (1995: 37); Kelly and Kaplan (2001: 131, 174); Trnka (2005).

9. For more on the place of ethnic identity and perceptions of racial difference in these discourses see Trnka (2002, 2008).

develop the nation's economy have become the central platform of their bid to demonstrate their loyalties to Fiji.

The two political coups in 1987 as well as the 2000 coup were motivated by political and economic concerns rather than the need to assert indigenous rights. Yet grassroots indigenous Fijian support for the 1987 and 2000 coups was drummed up through the use of racist discourses that cast indigenous Fijians as the rightful owners of Fiji on the basis of their status as indigenous peoples and depicted Indo-Fijians as 'foreigners' (*vulagi*) and usurpers of Fiji's bounty (Trnka 2002; Kelly and Kaplan 2001; Rakuita 2002). In response, the positive connotations of clearing the land (*desh sāf kiya*) for cultivation, thus setting Fiji on its course of development, were invoked by many Indo-Fijians as part of defending themselves as bona fide citizens of Fiji (Trnka 2005, 2008). Citing the various roles they had played in Fiji's colonial past, with Indo-Fijians engaged in enterprise and commercial agriculture while indigenous Fijians were restricted to communal, subsistence living, many Indo-Fijians spoke of 'development' as something they and their forefathers had had a unique role in cultivating.

The language they used, moreover, resonated metaphorically with other practices of cleaning or purifying. About 77 percent of Indo-Fijians are Hindus for whom practices of ritual cleanliness (*sāf karna* or making oneself *sāf* or clean) are a crucial aspect of religious practice and identity. While they were largely stripped of their caste status during indenture, an intricate cultural and religious sensibility of the importance of purity remains. Not only do Indo-Fijian Hindus engage in various practices of purifying their bodies prior to prayer, but there are also strong cultural sanctions against anyone who might break these pollution prohibitions (Trnka n.d.). They are just as quick to instruct outsiders on how to observe pollution prohibitions should they wish to enter a temple or partake in a Hindu ritual, as they are to monitor other community members' enforcement of these rules.

Given the almost complete dissolution of caste, pollution is viewed as a temporary state (Jayawardena 1971) caused by such things as the consumption of meat, eggs or alcohol; not having washed recently; a recent birth or death in the family; and for women, menstruation. All of these states preclude a Hindu from taking part in religious rituals. Many of them can, however, be modified. Avoiding polluting foods, for example, or in special cases, using a combination of birth control pills to alter one's menstrual cycle are seen as transforming a person from being 'polluted' to being 'clean'. While there are limits to what one can do, complying with pollution prohibitions is often viewed by Indo-Fijians as an agentive act (cf. Gottlieb 2002; Pedersen 2002). Emphasis is placed not only on 'being' clean, but on the bodily control (cf. Reinhart 1990) implicit in 'transforming' one's body from a state of impurity into one of cleanliness.

There is, furthermore, great concern over the possibility of an impure person or object negating another's purity. To take one example, a menstruating and thus 'unclean' (*mailā*) woman cannot enter a temple or she will endanger the other devotees' ability to pray and commune with the deities.

While much more can be said about the various collective negotiations and enforcements of purity in which Indo-Fijian Hindus engage, my point here is that just as bodies can be transformed from dirty to clean, the land and the nation as a whole are spoken of as undergoing a positive transformation through Indo-Fijian labour. Moreover, cleanliness, in its many forms, is a state that must be cultivated and yet its cultivation is always in danger of being undone by those who are impure.

Cross-cultural conceptions of cleanliness and *jungli*

Since the publication of Mary Douglas' groundbreaking study *Purity and Danger* in 1966, anthropologists and other scholars cannot help but be aware of both the cultural specificities of 'dirt' and its sociological importance. In her classic text, Douglas powerfully demonstrated how the cultural specificities of what gets categorised as clean and orderly on the one hand, versus the unruly, anomalous or dirty on the other, varies considerably from culture to culture. She also, however, drew out commonalities in the workings of systems of purity and cleanliness across societies. One of her findings was that religious communities, including but by no means limited to Hindus, employ the opposition between pure and impure acts, objects, animals and persons to consolidate corporate identities. Ideas of what separates the clean from the unclean, Douglas concluded, are used to provide order in our lives, amongst other things by 'protect[ing] the political and cultural unity of a minority group' (Douglas 2005: 153). Other scholars have since expanded on this insight by asserting the relational, rather than innate, qualities of purity/impurity as well as demonstrating the historically and culturally-specific dynamics through which ethnic, and in particular colonial and post-colonial, identities are constituted as 'clean' or 'dirty' (see Aretxaga 1995; Jackson 2002; Malkki 1995; Pedersen 2002; Rouse and Hoskins 2004; Valeri 1990, 2000).

Similarly, the image of the City as haunted by the threat of an eagerly encroaching Wilderness is hardly unique to Indo-Fijians and some of the dynamics I have described here parallel tensions observable elsewhere. Specifically, fears of the jungle and of 'the law of the jungle' have wider cultural and historical purchase as the danger attributed to the Jungle is invoked in a variety of historical and geographic sites. I will briefly note only one here, taken from colonial India, but there are many others (e.g. Birtles 1997; Taussig 1987).

Given that the term 'jungle' derives from Sanskrit, India is an obvious place to look and indeed we find that this part of the world has a rich history of imagery of *jungli*. In colonial India concerns over the encroaching jungle were rife. Anthropologist Piya Chatterjee (2001) provides vivid descriptions of how nineteenth and early twentieth century British colonial planters viewed the jungle as a space of both danger and fertile possibility. In her examination of tea plantations in Northern Bengal, India, Chatterjee discovered a fear of and fascination with the jungle that, similar to Fiji, came to define not only spaces, but also people, bodies and assessments of civility. Interestingly, British colonial planters' assessments of labour in Northern Bengal were quite at odds with those in Fiji. In colonial Fiji, the British did their best to exclude indigenous peoples from plantation labour. In Northern Bengal, however, the British endeavoured to employ, and indeed paid the highest rates to, aborigines or so-called *jungli* labourers because they were seen as best suited to transform the jungle due to their own 'jungle-like' physical constitution. Thus, while similar categories of people and spaces and indeed the same language are employed, the comparison between India and Fiji also reveals the historical and geographic specificity of how colonial labour was both organised and imagined.[10]

10. While its roots may lie in the jungles of India, evocations of the danger of the jungle crop up in all manner of descriptions of societies on the brink of 'lawlessness'. A second example could be made with respect to New Orleans where jungle metaphors were rife during the tragic flooding that took place in the city in September 2005. Dozens of newspaper articles and blogger accounts of the flooding and subsequent looting of New Orleans described the city as succumbing to the 'law of the jungle' (see also Marable (2006); Congleton (2006); Fletcher (2005). Anti-African-American racism (which in some respects bears a striking resemblance to anti-indigenous Fijian racism in Fiji), histories of slave labour and the current economic realities of the United States all came together to translate a site of natural tragedy and appalling government neglect into the imagery of the Jungle encroaching on the City. Just as there is no shortage of images of the jungle's danger to the polis, the phrase 'law of the jungle' is used to describe a range of sites, many of them distinctly un-tropical. The phrase crops up in a variety of contexts to indicate self-interested brutality. According to the BBC, 'the law of the jungle' was at work in 2005 in a Kashmir quake zone, the *China Economic Review* found it in the Chinese legal system, and *The Guardian* used it to characterise Tony Blair's economic policies while he was Prime Minister (see A.A. Khan, ' "Law of the Jungle" in Quake Zone', BBC News, October 31, 2005, as available at *http://news.bbc.co.uk/1/hi/world/south_asia/ 4390744.stm*; S. Lubman, 'Law of the Jungle', China Economic Review, September 2004, 24–25, as available at *http://www.carnegieendowment.org/ pdf/2005–04–18/lubman_pub1.pdf# search='law%20of%20the%20jungle*; T. Juniper, 'Blair's Law of the Jungle is Not Sustainable', Guardian, October 5, 2005, as available at *http://www.guardian.co.uk/print/0,3858,5301139–105907,00.html*.)

Perceptions of an inherent tension between the City and the Jungle are not uniquely Indo-Fijian. But the specific cultural significance of 'the City' and 'the Jungle' depend on the cultural and political-economic context in which such imagery is used. Delving into an indepth, ethnographic examination of one such case (i.e. Indo-Fijian perceptions of Suva) illuminates how the interaction between colonial histories and current political and economic crises is played out in such conceptualisations. As I have shown, many Indo-Fijians view the City, as represented by Suva, as having been built primarily by the labour of a single cultural group. In this manner, they have come to see themselves as embodying the transformative powers of cultivating and converting the dirty and unruly into the clean. In times of crisis, the City, as a clean, orderly and civilised space transformed by human labour, is perceived to be under threat from the wild primitivity of the Jungle. Threats to the City are, moreover, viewed as the possible end of not only Indo-Fijian enterprise but of Fiji's chances for development, advancement and modernity. A combined analysis of colonial histories and policies of ethnically-specific labour, current cultural and religious perceptions of cleanliness and responses to contemporary political turmoil reveals what generates the power behind this fearful image of a City under threat.

A city forever 'clean'

By alluding to the inherent 'cleanliness' of the City, I do not, however, mean to suggest that Indo-Fijians or other residents of Suva are not aware of, or concerned about, threats to urban well-being that clearly originate within the city's boundaries. With increasing rural-to-urban migration, intensified by recent losses of rural land leases, Suva's population is swelling. Lack of basic infrastructure, including the provision of clean water and appropriate waste disposal, have led to an increasing incidence of diseases such as typhoid. Environmental disasters also clearly highlight the tensions and dangers of city life. For the most part, urban residents accommodate to these problems. They avoid dangerous areas, boil their tap water before drinking it (an uncommon practice in urban areas as recently as seven years ago) and otherwise adjust to the increasing dangers of city life.

Sometimes, however, the hazards require more stringent measures. In July 2005, Suva's main rubbish dump, located in Lami, was on fire for one week, spewing a cloud of toxic gas across the city and leading to the evacuation of local residents. For seven days the fire service attempted to extinguish the fire as shifting winds spread the dioxin-filled smoke across Suva. But the rubbish continued to burn until the Public Works Department finally covered up the dump with soil. According to local physicians, there were immediately discernible health effects from the fire, including increases in respiratory infections. No one knows for sure what the long-term health implications of this catastrophe might be, as the exact chemical components of the emissions are unknown, but medical authorities in Suva have suggested that residents who inhaled the gas might later experience liver damage, blindness, nausea, vomiting and abdominal pain, though these effects might take five to ten years to appear (Gurdayal 2005; Vunileba 2005). I was conducting research in Suva at the time of fire and did not encounter a single resident who was not concerned about the possible health impacts of the blaze. Local residents were advising one another on precautionary measures, such as staying inside and keeping their windows closed, and those who could were voluntarily evacuating the city.

In suggesting the intrinsic 'cleanliness' of the City as opposed to the Jungle, I do not thus intend to imply that urban residents are oblivious to the basic dirtiness and dangerousness of urban life. Rather, my point is that in Indo-Fijian perceptions of the City, the urban represents a 'clean' modernity that stands in opposition to the wild, dirty and unruly Jungle. Just as Alley has argued that Hindus' perceptions of the Ganges River as spiritually 'clean' and 'purifying' does not indicate that they lack of awareness of the pollutants within the Ganges (Alley 1998), I am suggesting that many Indo-Fijians simultaneously view the City as a symbol of modernity and cleanliness and invest Suva with these meanings whilst recognising the inherent problems of living in the capital.

Conclusion: Fiji, the way the world should be?

Like most parts of the Pacific, the image of Fiji that is used to entice foreign tourists is that of a country characterised by pristine waters and clean, white sandy beaches where visitors can escape the stresses of their (mostly urban) lives. Some of this sentiment is encapsulated in the popular slogan *Fiji, the way the world should be* which has been widely used by the Fiji Tourist Bureau to promote an image of Fiji as uniquely peaceful and 'unspoilt'. Relatively little advertising text is given to promoting the attractions of 'cosmopolitan Suva'. Yet for many of Fiji's own residents, it is the city of Suva, despite all its drawbacks, that offers them a glimpse of how they imagine 'the world should be'. As such, the City is seen as in need of protection from the dangers inherent in the 'unspoilt' nature that surrounds it.

At the same time, Suva's residents are well aware of the pollution, disease and other difficulties of living in the capital. Suva might be the epitome of 'modern-living' in Fiji, but for many of Fiji's inhabitants, it is the lives they imagine that they can have overseas that are the ultimate attraction. Since 1987, political instabilities and economic crises have led thousands of Fiji's inhabitants to migrate overseas. The overwhelming majority of them (recently about 80–85 percent) are Indo-Fijian. Most go to New Zealand, Australia, Canada and the U.S., countries that have well-established networks of Indo-Fijian expatriates. These nations are also viewed as being the most 'developed' and economically viable destinations for new immigrants. Thousands more, however, are unable to obtain overseas visas and are destined to remain in Fiji. For many of them, the city of Suva continues to hold out the hope that the 'development' they seek might yet be achievable in a Fijian city.

References

Alley, K.D. 1998. 'Old Cities, New Masters', *City and Society* 10 (1): 167–82.
Appadurai, A. 1998. 'Dead Certainty: Ethnic Violence in the Era of Global Uncertainty', *Public Culture* 10 (2): 225–47.
————2006. *Fear of Small Numbers: An Essay on the Geography of Anger.* Durham: Duke University Press.
Aretxaga, B. 1995. 'Dirty Protest: Symbolic Overdetermination and Gender in Northern Ireland Ethnic Violence', *Ethos* 23 (2): 123–48.
Bienstock, R., ed. 2003. *Let's Go New Zealand Including Fiji.* New York: St. Martins Press.
Birtles, T.G. 1997. 'First Contact: Colonial European Preconceptions of Tropical Queensland Rainforest and Its People', *Journal of Historical Geography* 23 (4): 393–417.
Brown, C.H. 1978. 'Coolie and Freeman: From Hierarchy to Equality in Fiji', unpublished Ph.D. thesis, University of Washington.
————1981. 'Demographic Constraints on Caste: A Fiji Indian Example', *American Ethnologist* 8 (2): 314–28.
Chatterjee, P. 2001. *A Time for Tea: Women, Labor, and Post/colonial Politics on an Indian Plantation.* Durham: Duke University Press.
Comaroff, J. and J. Comaroff. 1991. *Of Revelation and Revolution: Christianity, Colonialism, and Consciousness in South Africa.* Chicago: University of Chicago Press.
Congleton, R.D. 2006. 'The Story of Katrina', *Public Choice* 127 (1–2): 5–30.
Douglas, M. 2005 [1966]. *Purity and Danger.* London: Routledge.
Field, M., T. Baba and U. Nabobo-Baba. 2005. *Speight of Violence: Inside Fiji's 2000 Coup.* Auckland: Pandanus.
Fiji Islands Bureau of Statistics. 2006. *Key Statistics, March 2006.* Suva: Government of Fiji.
Fletcher, K. 2005. 'Myths in the Making', *British Journalism Review* 16 (4): 12–8.
Gill, K. 1988. 'Health Strategies of Indo-Fijian Women in the Context of Fiji', unpublished Ph.D. thesis, University of British Columbia.
Gottlieb, A. 2002. 'Afterword', *Ethnology* 41 (4): 381–90.
Gurdayal, M. 2005. 'Residents Cry Foul', *Fiji Daily Post*, 11 July 2005, p. 2.
Jackson, M. 2002. *Politics of Storytelling: Violence, Transgression and Intersubjectivity.* Copenhagen: Museum Tusculanum Press.

Jayawardena, C. 1971. 'The Disintegration of Caste in Fiji Indian Rural Society' in *Anthropology in Oceania: Essays Presented to Ian Hogbin*, L.R. Hiatt and C. Jayawardena (eds), pp. 89–119. Sydney: Angus and Robertson.

Kaplan, M. 1995. ' "Blood on the Grass and Dogs Will Speak": Ritual Politics and the *Nation in Independent Fiji' in Nation Making: Emergent Identities in Postcolonial Melanesia*, R.J. Foster (ed.), pp. 95–125. Ann Arbor: University of Michigan Press.

Kelly, J.D. 1988a. 'Bhakti and the Spirit of Capitalism in Fiji: The Ontology of the Fiji Indians', unpublished Ph.D. thesis, University of Chicago.

────── 1988b. 'Fiji Indians and Political Discourse in Fiji: From the Pacific Romance to the Coups', *Journal of Historical Sociology* 1 (4): 399–422.

────── 1998. 'Aspiring to Minority and Other Tactics Against Violence in Fiji' in *Making Majorities*, D.C. Gladney (ed.), pp. 173–207. Stanford: Stanford University Press.

Kelly, J.D. and M. Kaplan. 1999. 'Race and Rights in Fiji', *Research in Politics and Society* 6: 237–57.

────── 2001. *Represented Communities: Fiji and World Decolonization*. Chicago: University of Chicago Press.

Lal, B.V. 1992. *Broken Waves: A History of the Fiji Islands in the Twentieth Century*. Honolulu: University of Hawaii Press.

────── 1995. 'Managing Ethnicity in Colonial and Post-colonial Fiji' in *Lines Across the Sea: Colonial Inheritance in the Post-colonial Pacific*, B.V. Lal and H. Nelson (eds), pp. 37–48. Brisbane: Pacific History Association.

Madraiwiwi, J. 2007. 'Mythic Constitutionalism: Whiter Fiji's Course in June, 2007?' Paper Presented at the workshop *The Fiji Coup – Six Months On*. Canberra: The Australian National University, June 5, 2007. As available on the Fijilive website, www.fijilive.com.

Malkki, L. 1995. *Purity and Exile: Violence, Memory, and National Cosmology among Hutu Refugees in Tanzania*. Chicago: University of Chicago Press.

Marable, M. 2006. 'Katrina's Unnatural Disaster: A Tragedy of Black Suffering and White Denial', *Souls* 8 (1): 1–8.

Mbembe, A. 2003. 'Necropolitics', trans. L. Meintjes. *Public Culture* 15 (1): 11–40.

Pedersen, L. 2002. 'Ambiguous Bleeding: Purity and Sacrifice in Bali', *Ethnology* 41 (4): 303–15.

Rakuita, T. 2002. 'Taukei-Vulagi Philosophy and the Coup of May 19, 2000', *Pacific Studies* 25 (4): 93–108.

Reinhart, A. K. 1990. 'Impurity/ No Danger', *History of Religions* 30 (1): 1–24.

Rouse, C. and J. Hoskins. 2004. 'Purity, Soul Food, and Sunni Islam: Explorations at the Intersection of Consumption and Resistance', *Cultural Anthropology* 19 (2): 226–49.

Scarr, D. (ed.) 1983. *The Three-Legged Stool: Selected Writings of Ratu Sir Lala Sukuna*. London: Macmillan Education.

Taussig, M. 1987. *Shamanism, Colonialism and the Wild Man: A Study in Terror and Healing*. Chicago: University of Chicago Press.

Trnka, S. 2002. 'Foreigners at Home: Discourses of Difference, Fiji Indians and the Looting of May 19', *Pacific Studies* 25 (4): 69–92.

———2004. 'Upahar Gaon' in *Bittersweet: The Indo-Fijian Experience*, B.V. Lal (ed.), pp. 135–50. Canberra: Pandanus.

———2005. 'Land, Life and Labour: Indo-Fijian Claims to Citizenship in a Changing Fiji', *Oceania* 75 (4): 354–67.

———2008. *State of Suffering: Political Violence and Community Survival in Fiji*. Ithaca: Cornell University Press.

———n.d. 'A Negotiated Purity: The Passion and Politics of Pollution Debates among Diasporic Hindus in Fiji,' unpublished ms.

Valeri, V. 1990. 'Both Nature and Culture: Reflections on Menstrual and Parturitional Taboos in Huaulu (Seram),' in *Power and Difference: Gender in Island Southeast Asia*, J.M. Atkinson and S. Errington (eds), pp. 235–72. Stanford: Stanford University Press.

———2000. *Forest of Taboos*. Madison: University of Wisconsin Press.

Vunileba, A. 2005. 'Safety of Fumes from Fire Unconfirmed', *Fiji Times*, 11 July 2005, p. 3.

Yule, H. and A.C. Burnell. 1985 [1886]. Hobson-Jobson: *A Glossary of Colloquial Anglo Indian Words and Phrases*. London: Routledge and Kegan Paul.

CHAPTER 5

Gendered Fears of Pollution: Traversing Public Space in Neoliberal Cairo[1]

ANOUK DE KONING

Sexual harassment on Egyptian streets; women simply cannot walk in this country without being pestered by male voyeurs. ... Some of the language used on the streets to harass women is shockingly obscene and sometimes violent, with vulgar anatomical references becoming the pathetic norm. A friend of mine gags every time she recalls a male passer-by who bestowed her with a list of the various sexual acts he would like to practice on her. Another colleague has had to endure *the trauma of having a stranger on the street brush his hand against her hips* ... Male harassers place the blame on women for evoking their own dirty sexual fantasies ... [Yet] the problem is not in women's attire, as demonstrated by veiled women far from being exempted from harassment in the streets.

Shaima'a Bakeer, *Community Times*, June 2004 (my emphasis)

1. This contribution is a revised version of a chapter of my book on the changing socio-cultural landscape of middle-class Cairo under conditions of neoliberal policies and a search for global inclusion (see De Koning 2009a). It has had many incarnations, which have been read and commented on by several people, all of whom I would like to thank for their help in thinking through this argument. I would particularly like to thank Eileen Moyer, Mohamed Waked, Pam Zuurbier and Rivke Jaffe for their thoughtful comments and encouraging enthusiasm. I have earlier presented parts of the present argument at the conference 'Negotiating Urban Conflicts', Technical University Darmstadt in April 2005 (for the proceedings of the conference, see De Koning 2006b); a longer version has appeared in *Antipode* (De Koning 2009b). This article has profited much from a follow-up research trip in 2004 and my stay as a visiting scholar at the International Center for Advanced Studies at NYU during Spring 2006, both made possible by the generous financial support of the Netherlands Organization for Scientific Research (NWO).

This excerpt from an essay in the English language publication *Community Times* reflects a common comment on sexual harassment in the streets of Cairo. The author expresses her frustration with the way her passage through public space is hampered by unsavoury comments and unwanted physical contact. As I argue in this chapter, this scene can also be read as an expression of the tensions that accompany new class configurations in Egypt's new liberal age, and their manifestations in Cairo's cityscape. I am particularly interested in the complex ways in which her commentary knits together issues of gender, class and public space, with pollution and defilement. It is indicative of a central paradox in present day Cairo. Women's public presence is one of the most significant markers of the new upper-middle class culture that has developed in Cairo in the 1990s. This public presence is, however, fragile and evokes severe anxieties about the possible harm that can come to female upper-middle class bodies in the public spaces of the city. These anxieties are often expressed in terms of pollution.

Purity and defilement are central issues with respect to the way young upper-middle class women move through public space. The urban trajectories of young, female upper-middle class professionals are governed by fears of pollutants that lie waiting in the urban environments they traverse. An improper gaze can constitute injury to the upper-middle class female body; 'a brush of hand' can leave a traumatic mark. This defilement is both physical and metaphorical as both female bodies and reputations are held to be vulnerable to improper interference. These pollutants are crucially connected to the presence of non-upper-middle class others, those who are perceived to be of a lower 'social' or 'cultural level', and are therefore seen as unable to grasp the subtly negotiated respectable public presence of young upper-middle class women. As I argue in this chapter, the bodies of young upper-middle class women in public have become an important site where new class configurations of Egypt's new liberal era are elaborated and contested. Tropes of pollution and defilement are central to these spatially embedded contestations as they intersect with contemporary negotiations of gender and class.

This contribution is based on twenty months of ethnographic research among young professional Cairenes. The fieldwork was carried out from September 2001 to February 2003 and from May 2004 to July 2004. It included participant observation and interviews with differently positioned middle class professionals, mostly in their mid twenties to early thirties. Participation in a number of loosely knit social networks was key to the ethnographic research on which this article relies. Particularly important was my involvement in an on/offline group organising trips to the desert and social events in the city; membership consisted almost exclusively of young upper-middle class male and female professionals.

Being roughly the same age, and, like these upper-middle class professionals, able to easily combine Arabic and English repertoires, I was an easy going companion on outings. These contacts and social activities introduced me to upscale parts of the city and specific ways of inhabiting urban space. I learned about the logics and rules that guide young upper-middle class professionals as they move through the urban landscape. I also draw on some of my own spatial experiences to understand that mixture of metropolitan anonymity, ascribed social identity and urban social life that shapes interactions in Cairo's public spaces.

Class, gender and urban space

In Cairo I made the acquaintance of a number of high-powered, young upper-middle class women who routinely move around the city, from home to work to gym to coffee shop to cinema to concert before returning home to sleep, wake up early and once again cross half the city to reach work. They were in constant contact with their friends over their mobile phones, coordinating where and when to meet, relatively indifferent to the surprisingly vast distances covered in order to socialise. Frequent mobile phone contacts while moving across the city also connected them to their families, reassuring those at home of their safety and good conduct, and informing them of their whereabouts. These young professionals are perhaps the most visible exponents of what has been called Egypt's new liberal age (Denis 1997): young, classy women, relatively fluent in English, who are employed in the internationally oriented segment of Cairo's economy and claim knowledge of global trends and cosmopolitan fashions.

Many of these young upper-middle class women live highly mobile and public lifestyles, outside the purview of the family. Their presence in both professional and social public life has become normalised, even critical to upper-middle class lifestyles, which are marked by the mixed-gender character of contacts and places. The highly mobile and rather public lifestyles of female professionals are valued cultural capital in parts of the upper-middle class.[2] Their negotiations of space and the public performances can thus be seen as part of a particular class project.

2. What constitutes the ideal upper-middle class marriageable woman is often the subject of heated debates. Conspicuously cosmopolitan lifestyles provide one of the positive models for marriageable upper-middle class women. Class-specific forms of religiosity and modesty provide different, but equally attractive gendered models (see Mahmood 2005). These two models are not mutually exclusive. Many women I knew tried to create their own blend, amidst constant wondering about and anxious discussions of men's preferences.

Egypt's adoption of a more neoliberal economic course since the early 1990s has given rise to new lines of segmentation in education, the labour market and consumption that increasingly divide Cairo's professional middle class (see De Koning 2009a; Mitchell 1999, 2002). While large segments of the professional middle class are suffering from vast unemployment, declining real wages and the withdrawal of a whole range of government subsidies and services, there is a still tentative formation of a distinct professional upper-middle class that is employed in the more internationally oriented, up-market segment of the urban economy and inhabits Cairo's upmarket spaces. Upmarket circuits comprised of private schools, universities and hospitals, as well as upscale residential areas, and shopping and leisure venues like upmarket coffee shops have been crucial to the elaboration of these new divisions within Cairo's middle-class. These venues and spaces are set apart from less exclusive Cairene spaces by their high prices, cosmopolitan claims and the frequent use of English in names, menus and social interaction, as well as climate control, immaculate cleanliness and maintenance. They have carved out public spaces for new upper-middle class lifestyles and forms of sociability, and simultaneously inscribe the urban landscape with new social divisions. Most notable among these venues are the upscale coffee shops that have mushroomed in upper-middle class areas since the mid-1990s. These coffee shops have enabled a specifically young, upper-middle class urban presence (De Koning 2009; 2006a). The *Community Times*, from which I quoted earlier, is another exponent of this trend. It is one of the many publications that address themselves in English to this relatively exclusive, and lucrative, segment of society.

In this chapter I examine the way these female upper-middle class professionals in their late twenties and early thirties negotiate two types of public spaces.[3] First, I turn to the controlled spaces of the upmarket coffee shops that have become central spaces for a young, upper-middle class urban presence. In these socially closed spaces the management of a respectable public presence takes centre stage. Secondly, I discuss the open

---

3. I use public and private to denote the spaces of the home versus more open, societal urban spaces. I take the term public space to indicate a tendency towards accessibility, rather than a clearly defined and bounded domain. We can thus think of publicness as complex set of characteristics. Coffee shops, for example, are public when compared to the private spaces of the home. They are, however, privately owned, protected from view and have numerous explicit and implicit entrance requirements. In this sense, they differ considerably from open public spaces like streets or parks.

and less class-specific spaces of street transport, which are marked by constant efforts at shielding the pure, unsullied upper-middle class female body. I argue that the routines employed in inhabiting/traversing Cairo's public spaces can be seen as attempts at managing public visibility and at the same time protecting the vulnerable, easily defiled body.

In each of these contexts, fears surrounding possible pollutants are ubiquitous. Much anxious effort is directed at securing both respectable public visibility, and unscathed passage through the urban jungle, from one safe upmarket space to the next. While these pollutants, *pace* Douglas, certainly provide occasion for repeated confirmations of moral order, the sense that emerges from their urban trajectories is one of continual battle against pollution in an environment that refuses to heed upper-middle class demands. Rather than the creation of a stable moral order, these experiences of purity and danger have to be understood against the background of contestations of new inequalities and distinctions, and the urban developments that express and sustain these new socio-cultural configurations in Egypt's new liberal age.

Dilemmas of public visibility

Young upper-middle class women negotiate their being in public against the background of longstanding dilemmas of female public presence and visibility. Specific forms of women's public visibility have a chequered history in twentieth century Cairo. They have been a central arena for contestations over modernity and authenticity (see Ahmed 1992; Abu-Lughod 1998). Cosmopolitan or 'westernised' elite practices have long been taken to indicate modernity and sophistication. During much of the twentieth century, France provided Cairenes with central reference points for distinctive cosmopolitan practices and lifestyles. In the last two decades France has been overtaken by the United States (cf. Abaza 2001; Armbrust 1996, 1999; for a comparative case, see, e.g., Guano 2002). In Cairo such cosmopolitan referencing, however, not only intimated elite class membership and sophistication; it could also be taken as a sign of alienation and rootless Westernization, which was associated with moral looseness. According to Walter Armbrust (1999, cf. 1996), the mixed-gender character of elite leisure practices – the mingling of women and men in public spaces – has provided the focal point for contestation throughout the twentieth century. Being visible could thus be part of a claim to a cosmopolitan elite belonging that hinges on a certain public female presence, but it could also be taken to indicate moral and sexual looseness. These two interpretive possibilities continue to haunt interactions in public space, and elicit continual efforts at managing interpretations of public presence. The question, then, is how this public female presence and visibility is negotiated and how the oftentimes contradictory exigencies of public visibility and propriety are managed.

These women's negotiations of Cairo's public spaces can be seen as efforts to perform a classed and gendered self that is respectable and in place, thereby attempting to prescribe certain interpretations of their gendered performances. 'Social level' is a central criterion in judging whether a certain woman is able to respectably indulge in casual mixed-gender contact and play with features that otherwise suggest a lack of respectability. Wearing 'naked' [*°iryaan*] clothes, for example, need not indicate a lack of respectability as long as the wearer's good origins are beyond doubt. These clothes are then framed as part of respectable class-specific norms and lifestyles, as much as the stylish clothing of upper-middle class *muhagabbaat* [veiled women]. These assumptions imply that women – and men – from a high social level know how to conduct mixed-gender interactions properly, since it constitutes part of their respectable class normalcy.

Though spending time in public leisure spaces is an important aspect of the daily routines of upper-middle class women, such outings are largely restricted to unambiguously classy places with a large degree of social closure. The trajectories of these women are invariably based on class maps: places that are safe for women are classy places. Cairo's upscale coffee shops, directly or indirectly modelled on US examples such as Starbucks, have played a crucial role in this respect. Such coffee shops provide upper-middle class professionals, and particularly young professional women, with new opportunities for socialising, finding partners and other forms of networking and self-presentation (De Koning 2006a, 2009a). They allow for casual mixed-gender sociabilities in conspicuously cosmopolitan settings. As Amal, a professional in her early thirties from a well-to-do family, put it: 'Coffee shops were able to gather girls from their houses and the club. Before, we did not have places where we could spend time after work.'

These upscale coffee shops have created a protected niche for non-familial mixed-gender sociabilities in contested public geographies of leisure. They have been able to wrest such mixed-gender sociabilities away from associations with immorality and loose sexual behaviour that cling to less exclusive mixed-gender spaces outside of the redemptive familial sphere. This rather exclusive context helps to frame a woman's appearance and comportment as upper-middle class and thereby guarantees a certain interpretation of her presence in that space. Coffee shops legitimise a woman's presence by marking it as part of an upper-middle class professional lifestyle, thus framing it as normal and respectable. Coffee shops and their relatively affluent mixed-gender publics can therefore be seen as the latest manifestation of distinctive cosmopolitan practices, which, as I argued above, have a long and contentious history as markers of elite status.

These upper-middle class performances of gendered respectability are dependent on the safe space of the coffee shop. Social closure is a crucial feature of any coffee shop that wants to appeal to an upper-middle class audience (De Koning 2009a, 2006a). Even though internal and external borders are heavily guarded, there is a continuous anxiety about the possible presence of unsuitable others in these spaces. The fear of attracting those of a lower social level indicates the importance of guarding the class markers of a place. Unsupervised meetings of unmarried men and women can only claim respectability when such a class standing is beyond question. The fear of the presence of others is also stirred by the conviction that these others might not abide by the implicit rules of gendered sociability. Overwhelmed by the availability of young women, men might flirt or harass. Conversely, some women might come with the aim of picking up wealthy male customers. These fears echo assumptions about less exclusive leisure spaces with a mixed-gender public, which are thought to be market places for easy relationships. Mixed-gender sociabilities were assumed to be normal and respectable only for a certain class of people. Accordingly, venues were judged on the 'level' of their public and the extent to which their mixed-gender interactions were assumed to be respectable.

Tamer, a middle class professional in his late twenties, sketched out a scale of venues along lines of respectability. The 'style of people' frequenting a certain venue was crucial to his judgment. He remembered a one-time visit to a 'cheap' open-air coffee shop in Maadi, an outlying upper-middle class district of Cairo.

> The style of people was not that great, I did not feel comfortable. When I go out, I do not want to encounter some rancid girl, *some bii´a* ['vulgar' person] that disgusts me.[4] The atmosphere was definitely not classy. This is even a bigger problem for girls. I can't take my fiancée to some of the places I visit with my male friends. The places I visit with her have to have people of a 'clean' level, where everyone minds their own business and nobody looks at you in a non-respectable way or laughs really loud.

4. In upper-middle circles *bii´a*, literally 'environment', had overtaken older terms like *sha^{c}bi* and *baladi* as an expression of socio-cultural dislike and distance. Unlike these older terms, *bii´a* does not refer to the lower classes or their presumed habits, but rather to a 'failed' middle class. Vulgar would be the best way to translate the term.

The coffee shops located on Gamaaᶜit id-Duwal Street, a major shopping street and thoroughfare in Mohandisseen, present a clear example of the places he would never visit with his fiancée, he said, explaining how a specific space could sully a female reputation. 'In these coffee shops most of the girls are prostitutes. I can't go there with my fiancée. Others will think that she is not my fiancée, but my girlfriend. She will be seen as one of those girls.'

Karim, a professional in his early thirties had once entertained the idea of starting his own coffee shop and had clearly given the logics of the coffee shop a lot of thought. He explained,

I would need a female crowd, because this will attract a male crowd. You have to keep a place comfortable for women. It has to be closed, clean and part of the staff needs to be female. You need to keep a certain standard of people coming in. If a woman finds a man who harasses her, or a woman who looks like a prostitute, she will not come again because people might say that she could be one of them.

The ill-fated story of the Fashion Café, another coffee shop on Gamaacit id-Duwal Street, bolstered his analysis. The owner of the Fashion Café had wanted to create a café with large windows that opened up to the street, 'like cafés on the Parisian boulevards'. This idea proved fatal in the Cairene context. Karim said that the crowd that began to frequent the café consisted largely of men who came to meet girls. 'People came who could create problems, who came to flirt/harass [yiᶜaaksu]. Female patrons stopped coming, and another type of women started to come.' According to Karim, the closed design of most upscale coffee shops is crucial, since it hides patrons from the view of passers-by in the street:

The 'ahwa [male-dominated sidewalk café] does not have a door. Coffee shops, in contrast, are closed. Not every passer-by will see you when you sit there; you do not get influenced by other people. My girlfriend would not like to sit in a place where she would be seen and would have to hear comments. She would refuse to sit in the street. She prefers a safely closed place.

Polluting gazes

Protecting women from view is an old theme in Cairo's leisure architecture. Many older restaurants have a second floor where families or mixed-gender groups can sit hidden from view. As Karim's comments indicate, the maintenance of visual boundaries remains an important feature of places that are considered appropriate for a mixed-gender public. While such visual protection is most obviously focused on blocking views from the street, it also extends to the gaze of patrons of a doubtful social level or social origins. The impact of such a gaze is illustrated by a comment Amal once made. This professional from an affluent family once emphatically stated that she would not 'go in the water' (swim in a bathing suit) if she did not feel sure of the social level of the others present. 'They might be *bii'a and eat you with their looks*' (my emphasis). Nihal, an upper-middle class professional in her early thirties, similarly emphasised the issue of being looked at and the 'social level' of those who look. She summarised the logics of the coffee shop as a safe space as follows:

> A place has to have a certain standard, it shouldn't be cheap. This guarantees your safety. It guarantees that our kind of people go. This is crucial with respect to the image of women in a certain place. If people look at me in a certain place, it is enough to make me wonder what they say about me. It makes me insecure.

The look or gaze is central to comments and stories about coffee shops. It is a specific gaze that is viewed as problematic and even harmful: the invasive look of undeserving men directed at respectable and classy women. The essential question was who could be seen by whom. The recurrent references to 'a certain standard of people' and 'our kind of people', as well as the frequent negative mention of less classy others indicate the importance of 'social level' with respect to mixed-gender spaces. 'Social level', a concept of social differentiation that combines notions of class and culture, determined the interpretation of specific looks. A look might be part of an appropriate and desired visibility, or might be harmful and defiling, depending on 'social level.'

Just as the look of a *bii'a* ['vulgar'] person can be harmful, those of classy others are invited, even desired. Yet, being seen was hardly ever discussed, except for in comments about the shallowness, vanity, opportunism and lack of respectability of those 'others' who made it their priority to be seen in the latest, hippest place or who wanted to be seen in order to find a partner. The desire to be seen was apparently too contentious, and could evoke accusations of shallowness and, in the case of women, charges of disrespectability. Public visibility thus figures as a central, yet highly ambiguous trope.

In the comments cited earlier the gaze emerges as an active agent of pollution and defilement that physically impacts the female body. It is also able to impute a bad reputation, and suggest a lack of respectability, which also taints the pure upper-middle class body. Nihal's story is telling in this respect. Nihal told me of her one-time venture out to a disco that was not clearly marked as upper-middle class. She felt embarrassed as soon as she entered. She estimated many of the women present to be 'easy' with regards to sexual morals and suspected that some might be prostitutes.

Despite her self-identification as a proper upper-middle class woman, she felt she was included in this group of loose women as a result of her mere presence, and felt tainted by the experience.

Other women told me similar stories, imbued with similar feelings. Some stressed the social repercussions of being seen in a certain place, whereas others emphasised their sense of embarrassment or even defilement by being identified as less than respectable. This sense of pollution and shame can be elicited by anything from personal misgivings to subtle signs of others present, from benevolent teasing and flirting to concrete interventions. While a woman may feel the presence of such interpretations because of the concrete actions of others around her, such interpretations may however also be attributed to an abstract, imagined public. What struck me is the extent to which such interpretations become inscribed in the body and come to determine a woman's sense of self.

These stories about women's presence in public leisure venues are, moreover, haunted by the spectre of prostitution. They reflect a constant concern about the 'level' of the female patrons and the nature of the relationships between men and women in public leisure venues. Elizabeth Wilson's sketch of the dilemma of the 'public woman' in the nineteenth century city illuminates a central ambiguity that surrounds these women's public presence. As Wilson argues, 'the prostitute was a "public woman", but the problem in the nineteenth-century urban life was whether every woman in the new, disordered world of the city, the public sphere of pavements, cafes and theatres, was not a public woman and thus a prostitute. The very presence of unattended - unowned - women constituted a threat both to male power and a temptation to male "frailty"' (Wilson 2001: 74). A similar ambiguity, based on the fraught relation between morality and visibility, continues to provide the central backdrop to women's negotiations of public space in numerous settings, among others in contemporary Cairo. It pervades the ambiguous views of young upper-middle class women who move – apparently unowned – through public space. The core of this ambiguity consists of the contrasting possible interpretations of a young woman's presence in public. Does her presence indicate a disreputable sexual openness, or is it part of a more respectable lifestyle and everyday routine (cf. Ossman 1994: 160)? Public visibility can indicate (immoral) availability.

As long as its class framing is beyond question and disreputable others are kept out, the space of the coffee shop prescribes the interpretation of these women's public lifestyles and sexy appearances as normal and respectable.[5] In the streets, where up-market norms are not hegemonic and a clear class framing is absent, such (self-) representations may well be overturned. The

5. The gendering of public (and private) spaces and the spatial inflection of gendered conceptions of propriety present old, yet recurring themes in urban landscapes (see, e.g., Bondi and Domosh 1998; see for Cairo also Abaza 2001b).

same fashionable *cut* [sleeveless top] becomes in the best case something out of place, but may also be seen as disreputable and taken to indicate easy morals, an open invitation to comments and even harassment. A young professional who was also a frequent visitor of the coffee shop scene told me of his annoyance with some of his friends. They insisted on harassing women they perceived to be less than respectable. A girl smoking or wearing tight clothes in the streets would qualify as such in their eyes. He would chide them for their behaviour by asking, 'Doesn't your sister dress just like her?' Such inversions indicate the extent to which impromptu identifications are framed, and to a large extent determined, by specific spatial contexts.

It is difficult to capture and mediate the intensity and corporeally experienced character of interactions in Cairo's public spaces, or the intense self-awareness of many women when they move through public space. Gillian Rose argues that women are constituted as explicitly embodied, located subjects. Many men, in contrast, enjoy a masculine illusion of freedom from the body and its inevitable locatedness. These differential forms of subjectification give rise to specific experiences of space, Rose argues:

> Women of all kinds are expected to look right, and to look right for a gaze which is masculine ... The threatening masculine look materially inscribes its power onto women's bodies by constituting feminine subjects through an intense self-awareness about being seen and about taking up space ... Women's sense of embodiment can make space feel like a thousand piercing eyes ... it is a space which constitutes women as embodied objects to be looked at. (Rose 1993: 145–146)

Rose's analysis resonates with the experiences and stories of the women I knew in Cairo. While I take up the themes of the male gaze and female embodiment that Rose articulates, I explore the specific dynamics of 'the gaze' in the Cairene context and ask what these particulars can tell us about the constitution of female upper-middle class bodies and gendered identities.[6] As I argued above, the undeserving, hungry gaze appears as an active pollutant of physically and symbolically pure and respectable female bodies.

---

6. Feminist discussions of the objectification of women have largely focused on the abstract workings of a (heterosexual) masculine gaze (for a discussion of feminist debates about the male gaze, see Rose 1993, esp. Chapter 5). Though I explore the particular ways in which women are constituted through a constantly observant male gaze, I do not want to suggest the existence of a universal male gaze that figures women (see for a thorough critique Wilson 2001: 83).

Traversing the urban jungle

In contrast to the closed coffee shops, Cairo's streets are largely characterised by male entitlement (cf. Ghannam 2002, Chapter 4).[7] Women, particularly young women unaccompanied by men, have a liminal and ambiguous status. They are supposed to be on their way somewhere, have a clear destination and not linger for too long. Hanging around in the streets, especially on their own, is taken as an open invitation for men to make contact. The male prerogative to judge, comment or accost these women was only partially staved off by the high class status of my female acquaintances. This prerogative is most readily expressed in frequent *muᶜaksaat* [flirts/harassment], which, as the comment at the beginning of this chapter made clear, present an important nuisance and deterrent in women's urban trajectories. Indicative of their liminal and ambiguous status in public space, and the related discomforts, are the efforts of most of my female acquaintances to carefully plan their schedules and meetings to avoid time gaps during which they would have to spend time waiting alone in a public space. Waiting alone in open public spaces is often taken as an invitation for unknown men to make contact, and thus exposes women to not only physical pollutions, but also importantly, the symbolic defilement of being seen as open for sexualised contact.

Many women told me that before leaving the house, they go over the different places they would visit and the kind of self-presentation required in them. Women's strategies in crossing the city depend on social maps of Cairo that indicate what to expect in certain places, and mark these places with a sense of ease and tension, safety and danger. Their choice of itineraries invariably displayed extensive knowledge of diverse urban spaces, as well as the specific logic that informed their movement through these spaces.

These women negotiate their public presence in and through highly diverse spaces that are characterised by different grids of framing and understanding social identities and interactions (cf. Secor 2002). A young

---

7. Streets in upmarket areas like Zamalek and Maadi differ significantly from their lower-class counterparts, as do shopping streets from big thoroughfares and more residential streets. Despite such significant differences, a dominant male presence and women's liminality are shared features of Cairo's street life. Streets moreover share a certain indeterminacy with respect to class. Some residential areas constitute marked exceptions to these gendered definitions of the street, while women peddlers who occupy sidewalks in central streets defy notions of women's liminality.

woman's presence is subjected to constant observation and judgments. Such judgments are based on looks, class markers and signs of modesty such as the *higaab* or loose fitting clothing. Different styles of women's dress have become central to and iconic of different styles of femininity. As Secor (2002) argues with respect to regimes of veiling in Istanbul, specific attires allow for certain interpretations and interventions in public space and are therefore crucial with respect to the micro-politics of interaction in public spaces. Such markers are evaluated with respect to possible definitions of a woman's presence in a specific place at a specific time.

As we have seen in the case of the coffee shop, 'public space' can take on a prescriptive quality, demanding certain class and gender-specific performances. Public space can, however, also denote an 'outside', a less scripted social space where rules are unsure, interactions are not scripted, the others one might encounter unknown. It can even invoke images of an urban jungle (cf. Mitchell 1995; Kaviraj 1997). Kaviraj (1997) argues that these are two contrasting ways of perceiving open spaces. In the context of the public park in Calcutta, these two conceptions of space – the former tied to the British colonial presence, the latter to more local understandings of open spaces, spaces outside the house – create a hybrid understanding of what he calls 'pablik', a space that retains some of the wild and unrestricted qualities of the 'outside', while it is also perceived to be everyone's rightful possession, since it belongs to the state, and therefore to everyone. In the case of Cairo, both prescriptive and wild conceptions of public space pervade experiences of being in public. At times 'being in public' was first and foremost about representation, about the management of public social identities. At other times, it was rather the concept of the anonymous mass, the open spaces, or the sense of an unpredictable urban jungle harbouring manifold threats and pollutants that determined the experience of public space. It is the latter conception that dominates the experience of less scripted, open social spaces such as the streets. The sense of a dangerous urban jungle focuses primarily on the (sexualised) threats it presents to the female body. Anxieties about the propriety of being in public are displaced by, or perhaps translated into, fears of pollution and defilement of the highly fragile and vulnerable upper-middle class female body.

The avoidance and barring of unwanted gazes and unwarranted contact are crucial upper-middle class strategies in public space, including in the context of transportation. Two common means of transport have come to symbolise the two extremes of experiences in public space: the bus has come to stand for forced proximity and possible harassment, while the car represents control, protection and absolute freedom of movement. Everyday comments about public transport resonate with assumptions about the vulnerability and preciousness of the female upper-middle class body. A woman should not get tired, should be at ease and free of the unwanted touches of other bodies. Whereas a man might brave these nuisances, a woman should never be forced to undergo the horrors of crowdedness in an open yet closed space like the public bus, where one is condemned to the proximity of others and their unclean bodies, and worst of all, physical harassment. The cheapest 'red' public bus, charging 0.25 LE[8] regardless of distance travelled, has become a symbol of the 'poor Egypt' as imagined by those who are not part of it. A friend told me that her colleagues tended to comment on *mu'aksa* by saying, 'as if we are in a red bus'. The public bus was used as a metaphor for extreme instances of uncivilised harassment, thought to typically occur on this cheap type of transport. While buses form part of the daily routines of most Cairenes, men and women, most upper-middle class women told me that they had never and would never enter a public bus. The two acceptable means of public transport were the new service lines of luxury air-conditioned buses (2 LE) and the subway, where the first two compartments are reserved for women only.

Stories of harassment in public transport abound. When the subject of public transport came up, so did stories of the dangers of the minibus or microbus, which invariably featured men waiting to harass women moving on their own. These stories express a deep-seated vulnerability felt by young women moving on their own through Cairo's cityscape. This anxiety about their vulnerability is also apparent in countless, more mundane routines that constitute ways of moving through urban space. It speaks to the conceived wildness of the urban jungle, implying that when a woman leaves the safe confines of her home, workplace or other secure, intimate spaces, all sorts of things might happen in an urban landscape replete with pollutants and threats.

Cairo is generally said to be safe. Nevertheless, fears of sexual violence, especially rape, were commonplace. The fear of sexual violence gave rise to profuse advice and warnings whenever a woman readied herself to leave a 'safe' space and travel to her next destination. Concerns about women's movement focused on their unscathed passage through public space. As noted above, their presence in public was not seen as problematic *per se*. Rather, anxieties centred on the numerous dangers of harassment and defilement that were seen to accompany such being in public, the numerous cracks in the social and physical layers that would otherwise protect these upper-middle class bodies and reputations. Whereas rape represented the ultimate desecration, even a look could harm and defile the pure, unsullied and properly sexualised female body.

8. In 2002 the Egyptian Pound (LE) was worth between €0.20 and €0.25. A ticket on the 'red bus' came to €0.05; by comparison, a short taxi ride would cost around €1.

The necessity of taking public transport or moving by foot through the streets exposes upper-middle class women to infringements on their established routines and preferred lifestyles. Hoda, one of my respondents, commented that she had had to change her style of dress when she moved house after marrying. Now that she had to take a taxi from home to a subway station located in a popular neighbourhood, she had stopped wearing tight clothes and obvious make-up, to avoid being too visible and thus warranting comments. 'You cannot wear professional clothes, such as a skirt, unless you have a car', she said. She complained that, as a result, she was not able to present herself as a professional career woman. For many middle-class women who can afford it, and even those who cannot, the car has become an indispensable item. The car allows a woman to dress as she likes and protects her from unwanted encounters. It allows her to be *bi-rahitha*, at ease. The second best thing is the taxi, a favourite but expensive option for many non-car owners.

In contrast to the stories of danger and defilement that surround public transport, the car thus becomes the symbol for, and guarantor of, a perfect world of professional life, self-representation and respectable socialising. In addition to physical protection, it provides a mobile framing of the self that confirms a certain class standing, akin to the fixed spatial framing of the upmarket coffee shop. As a man in his early thirties remarked, 'A woman who takes a taxi still has a relation to the street. She will eventually return to the street and can therefore be flirted with. A woman with her own car can dress in whatever way she likes. Nobody will harass her.' The public lifestyles of young upper-middle class women depend on the financial means to sit in certain places and to use certain modes of transport – in short, to move exclusively in upmarket Cairo. The car crowns attempts to create a controlled environment. It transports women unscathed and free of unwanted interventions, from one safe space to the next.

Nihal sketched her paramount image of the young upper-class woman: driving a Cherokee with closed tinted windows, air-conditioning on, moving between different places dominated by her own norms of respectability and sociability. The ability of many upper-middle class women to engage in their preferred lifestyle and specific modes of sociability and self-presentation depends on such class closure and control over their environment. Moving around with these female professionals, the map of Cairo seemed to shrink to include only those areas where their distinctive lifestyles are the norm: the upmarket districts of Mohandisseen, Zamalek, Maadi and Heliopolis. Safe passage between these upmarket districts relies strongly on the ring road, fly-over bridges and inner-city highway that now connect these different areas. They allow one to move from one part of upmarket Cairo to the next, without having to descend into the disorder, crowdedness and poverty that characterise Cairo's poorer spaces (cf. Tomic et al. 2006). For some, spaces outside this class-specific economy seemed to be only a vague and distant reality. These other spaces were marked as dirty, full of bacteria and health hazards, uncouth people and harassment. Some of these spaces outside upmarket Cairo, such as the popular or informal housing sectors (ʿashwaa'iyyaat, see Bayat and Denis 2000), were places never to be visited, unless by accident, when one gets lost and is stranded in a popular area like Dar es-Salaam, full of unknown but lurking dangers.

Performing fragile identities

[The daughters of the high aristocracy] dreamt solely of a regular sojourn abroad, lived surrounded by electronic gadgets and refused to go out into the streets, afraid that the contact with all those poor drifting about the sidewalks would defile them. They would only go out by car, and then exclusively to closed establishments: restaurants, cinemas or beaches where they could be sure they wouldn't encounter any plebs.
They were right. Wherever they went, the atmosphere grew tense. Their beauty was almost impermissible. Even if the girls laughed very modestly, it looked like a provocation. When they pushed up their hair, the gesture would become erotically charged. The pointed breasts under their shirts inflicted more chaos than a machine gun. Their transparent cheeks seemed made to be kissed.

Rachid Mimouni (1991:88; my translation)

This passage is taken from *Une peine à vivre*, a novel about the life of a dictator in an unnamed country by the Algerian writer Rachid Mimouni. It describes the lives of women in a far more privileged position than the women whose trajectories have informed this chapter. Yet, it sketches a similar ironic situation in which elite fears and anxieties surrounding less exclusive places and their inhabitants combine with the segmented everyday realities of a divided city. Elite norms increasingly clash with those of other city dwellers, thereby confirming the impossibility of 'going out in the streets'. As Mimouni writes, they were right not to leave their exclusive surroundings. Even the simplest gesture could be 'misread', creating confusion, inciting harassment and the defilement of otherwise pure and respectable embodiments of upper-middle class femininity.

In the conspicuously cosmopolitan, yet respectable spaces of the coffee shop, morality, particularly female respectability, remains a central focus of anxieties and contestations. This focus on female respectability brings to mind the earlier centrality of the 'women's question' in longstanding discursive battles over modernity versus authenticity, colonial domination versus national liberation, and Western secularism versus an Islamic modernity (see, e.g., Ahmed 1992; Armbrust 1999; Abu-Lughod 1998). When moving out of these safe, upmarket spaces, the focus shifts from negotiations of professional femininity to a concern with unscathed passage through an urban space replete with pollutants and threats.

While their class status gives them a certain leverage vis-à-vis male entitlements in the streets, most upper-middle class women I knew preferred to resort to more reliable strategies of class closure to secure their unscathed passage through Cairo's public spaces. Their trajectories were invariably based on class maps. This points to what seems a crucial contradiction at the core of these high-mobility and rather public routines: the condition for their existence is social closure, the avoidance of any disturbance and the ability to skirt unwanted contacts. Only in the spaces of upmarket Cairo could they be *bi-rahithum* [at ease] and dress and socialise as they saw fit, without being harassed or seen as disreputable. Other spaces held the dangers of a bad reputation that could easily rub off on an otherwise respectable upper-middle class woman, and the threat of defilement posed by undeserving gazes and unwarranted touch. The possibility of disrespectability and defilement hampered the unscathed passage through public space that functioned as a precondition for the public lifestyles of many upper-middle class women.

The dangers that being in public represented for the upper-middle class female body were simultaneously symbolic and physical. A respectable woman was taken to have a pure, unsullied body. Yet, just as upper-middle class women's reputations were easily damaged or ruined, upper-middle class bodies were easily harmed and defiled. The sense of privilege that emanates from this female presence as a manifestation of a certain class project, was matched by a strong sense of fragility and threat. In the context of her discussion of citizenship and everyday practices in Istanbul, Secor argues that 'Spatial stories, whether they trace tactics of anonymity or strategies of identity, should ... be seen as political narratives operating through the streets of the city' (2004: 363). I argue that the negotiations of the city discussed in this chapter similarly evidence a form of political contestation. In this light we might understand upper-middle class female bodies as a central battleground for new class configurations and contestations, literally embodying both the power and the fragility of Cairo's professional upper-middle class in Egypt's new liberal age.

Conclusion

Upmarket Cairo is characterised by myriad forms of class closure. The previously outlying districts of Mohandisseen, Maadi and Heliopolis and their desert expanses along the three main highways out of Cairo increasingly constitute the city for many upper-middle class Cairenes.

New forms of segmentation and segregation are imprinted on physical and imaginary maps of the city, while the desert becomes a new frontier where Cairo's affluence and cosmopolitan ambitions can be realised in most lavish manner (De Koning 2009a; Mitchell 1999; Denis 1997).

In the context of her discussion of exclusive urban developments in São Paulo, Teresa Caldeira argues that the tendency to spatialise social distance is connected to 'the inability [of more privileged inhabitants] to impose their own code of behaviour – including rules of deference – onto the city' (2000: 319). In many cities, increased crime rates seem to form the focus of social fears that accompany growing social inequalities, and provide a main motive for all kinds of closure in the urban landscape (see e.g. Low 2001; Caldeira 2000). In Cairo, property crime is perceived to be relatively limited and does not seem to form a major focus of such social fears. Class-based cultural differences, often centred on sexuality and gender, seem to provide an important rationale underlying distance and closure. These assumed cultural – and moral – differences, or rather, the supposed lack of cultural development among the lower classes, are seen as the source of the countless urban pollutants that threaten the pure, unsullied, privileged female body. These are the focus of anxieties and give rise to a tendency towards social avoidance and class-homogeneous spaces.

Lifestyles of young upper-middle class women are strongly predicated on class closure. In turn, arguments about gendered behaviour and the need for the protection of 'classy' women in turn come to legitimise class segregation and highly exclusive forms of urban development. Many of the women featured in this chapter were concerned about defilement, harassment and even worse things that might happen in public spaces that were not explicitly marked as upper-middle class and appropriate or safe for women. These fears concern non-upper-middle class public spaces and tend to have strong implicit or explicit classist undertones. Female upper-middle class bodies are perceived as highly vulnerable to material and symbolic defilement. The sources of pollution are the male masses that occupy those 'other' spaces outside of upmarket Cairo.

As in earlier times, class-specific, gendered practices provide a central battleground for contestations of inequality. The public presence of these young, well-to-do women represents one of the most tangible representations of changing class formations in the urban landscape. Their public visibility provides occasion for contestations of these new inequities. For more privileged Cairenes, in turn, fears of defilement by the masses in Cairo's streets and buses serve to legitimise a further avoidance of these socially open spaces.

References

Abaza, M. 2001. 'Shopping Malls, Consumer Culture and the Reshaping of Public Space in Egypt', *Theory, Culture & Society* 18 (5): 97–122.

Abu-Lughod, L. 2005. *Dramas of Nationhood: The Politics of Television in Egypt.* Chicago: Chicago University Press.

Abu-Lughod, L. (ed.) 1998. *Remaking Women: Feminism and Modernity in the Middle East.* Cairo: AUC Press.

Ahmed, L. 1992. *Women and Gender in Islam.* New Haven: Yale University Press.

Armbrust, W. 1996. *Mass Culture and Modernism in Egypt.* Cambridge: Cambridge University Press.

——— 1999. 'Bourgeois Leisure and Egyptian Media Fantasies' in *New Media in the Muslim World: The Emerging Public Sphere*, D. F. Eickelman and J. W. Anderson (eds), pp. 106–32. Bloomington: Indiana University Press.

Bayat, A. and E. Denis. 2000. 'Who is Afraid of *Ashwaiyyat*', *Environment & Urbanization* 12 (2): 185–99.

Caldeira, T. P.R. 2000. *City of Walls: Crime, Segregation, and Citizenship in São Paulo.* Berkeley and Los Angeles: University of California Press.

Denis, E. 1997. 'Urban Planning and Growth in Cairo', *Middle East Report* Winter: 7–12.

Ghannam, F. 2002. *Remaking the Modern in a Global Cairo: Space, Relocation, and the Politics of Identity.* Berkeley: University of California Press.

Guano, E. 2002. 'Spectacles of Modernity: Transnational Imagination and Local Hegemonies in Neoliberal Buenos Aires', *Cultural Anthropology* 17 (2): 181–209.

Kaviraj, S. 1997. 'Filth and the Public Sphere: Concepts and Practices about Space in Calcutta', *Public Culture* 10 (1): 83–113.

De Koning, A. 2006a. 'Café Latte and Caesar Salad: Cosmopolitan Belonging in Cairo's Coffee Shops' in *Cairo Cosmopolitan: Politics, Culture, and Urban Space in the New Middle East*, P. Amar and D. Singerman (eds), pp. 221–34. Cairo: AUC Press.

——— 2006b. 'Negotiating the City: Everyday Forms of Segregation in Middle Class Cairo' in *Negotiating Urban Conflicts: Interaction, Space and Control*, H. Berking (et al.) (eds), pp. 99–112. Bielefeld: transcript.

——— 2009a. *Global Dreams: Class, Gender and Public Space in Cosmopolitan Cairo.* Cairo and New York: American University in Cairo Press.

——— 2009b. 'Gender, Public Space and Social Segregation in Cairo: Of Taxi Drivers, Prostitutes and Professional Women', *Antipode* 41 (3): 533–56.

Low, S. M. 2001. 'The Edge and the Center: Gated Communities and the Discourse of Urban Fear', *American Anthropologist* 103 (1): 45–58.

Mahmood, S. 2005. Politics of Piety: *The Islamic Revival and the Feminist Subject.* Princeton: Princeton University Press.

Mimouni, R. 1992. *Straf voor het leven*. Translation of Une peine à vivre [1991]. Amsterdam: Maarten Muntinga.

Mitchell, D. 1995. 'The End of Public Space? People's Park, Definitions of the Public and Democracy', *Annals of the Association of American Geographers* 85 (1): 108–33.

Mitchell, T. 1999. 'Dreamland: The Neoliberalism of Your Desires', *Middle East Report* Spring: 28–33.

———2002. *Rule of Experts: Egypt, Techno-Politics, Modernity*. Berkeley: University of California Press.

Ossman, S. 1994. *Picturing Casablanca: Portraits of Power in a Modern City*. Berkeley: University of California Press.

Rose, G. 1993. *Feminism and Geography: The Limits of Geographical Knowledge*. Cambridge: Polity Press.

Secor, A. J. 2002. 'The Veil and Urban Space in Istanbul: Women's Dress, Mobility and Islamic Knowledge', *Gender, Place and Culture* 9 (1): 5–22.

———2004. '"There Is an Istanbul That Belongs to Me": Citizenship, Space and Identity in the City', *Annals of the Association of American Geographers* 94 (2): 352–68.

Tomic, P., R. Trumper and R. H. Dattwyler. 2006. 'Manufacturing Modernity: Cleaning, Dirt and Neoliberalism in Chile', *Antipode* 38 (3): 508–29.

Wilson, E. 2001. *The Contradictions of Culture: Cities: Culture: Women*. London: Sage.

Chapter 6

The Choice between Clean and Dirty: Discourses of Aesthetics, Morality and Progress in Post-Revolutionary Asmara, Eritrea

Magnus Treiber

Tsryet mer'aya wuHlul hzbi iyu.
('Cleanliness is the token of a smart society')
ERI-TV, 25 November 2001, 8.45 p.m.

Travel reports in the mid 1990s covering Asmara, capital of then newly independent Eritrea, Africa's youngest state, vied with one another in praising the city's extraordinary architectural beauty and obviously unexpected urban character.[1] Journalists, sensing a new era about to dawn for the small, war torn country bordering on the Red Sea, described a 'petite Rome' (Lathullière 1995) with a 'touch of cultivated urbanity' and 'Italian flair' (Mack 1993). Until today, most reports do not fail to mention the numerous Italian street cafés alongside Asmara's principal boulevard, Liberty Avenue (*godena harnet* in Tigrinya, the dominant local language) or the properly attired old men who attend them, catching the visitor's eye because of their habit of wearing suit, waistcoat and hat in any kind of

---

1. A previous version of this article was presented at the 8th biennial EASA conference, Vienna 8–12 September 2004, in the panel 'Environmental and Ecological Issues in Cities: An Anthropological Approach', convened by Rivke Jaffe and Eveline Dürr. I am indebted to their critical comments on my article and their efforts to realise this book.

weather (de Vries 2004). Correspondingly, Asmara's grandfathers are nicknamed *tekabano*, a word borrowed from Italian meaning 'coat hanger'. The word *asmarino* in turn, does not simply refer to an Asmara dweller. Rather, it is the local nickname for a male urbanite said to be typical for the city: clever and witty, arrogant and macho, eloquent and work-shy at the same time, rarely solvent, but always generous. As a saying goes, an *asmarino* would always prefer to spend his last money on a new shirt – instead of on food.

Urban life, identities and aesthetics in today's Asmara still demonstrate references to the colonial past and contemporary urban change. Contested concepts of purity and danger are evident in the city's topography as well as its turbulent history. This chapter analyses the ways in which symbolic pollution has figured in the discourses and actions of both those in power and less influential city dwellers. Cultural distinctions of 'clean' and 'dirty' are played out in and on the city's built environment. Aesthetic and moral distinctions between different urban places and material interventions in the physical environment link to historically evolved discourses of modernity and progress. Following an outline of Eritrea's colonial history and its struggles for independence in the late twentieth century, the chapter focuses on Asmara's *warsay* generation of post-independence youth and the ways in which they draw on conceptions of symbolic pollution – dirt and danger – in differentiating between bars and hangouts. Such distinctions can be understood as responses to Eritrea's poverty and violence, and point to broader negotiations of gender and class within urban space.

This chapter is mainly based on ethnographic fieldwork, conducted over several periods of varying length from 2001 to 2005 in Asmara. Data has been gathered mainly through participant observation. Contract research on behalf of Eritrea's Cultural Assets Rehabilitation Project (CARP) from September to November 2001 also included semi-structured interviews with architects and urban planners as well as a sample of Asmara's residents. In August and September 2007 additional ethnographic fieldwork among urban refugees was done in Shimelba refugee camp in Tigray province and in Addis Ababa, Ethiopia (Treiber 2003; Treiber 2005; Treiber and Tesfaye 2008).

Claiming modernity: a historical outline

In 1889, Abyssinia's local military leader, Ras Alula, and his warriors left their camp, established few years earlier in the small but economically prosperous village of Asmara, in order to fight the Mahdists. Italian forces, already present in the coastal plains, took this opportunity to get rid of their persistent Abyssinian rival by climbing the Eritrean mountains and occupying Alula's base (Erlich 1996). Situated on the edge of the Eritrean highlands at an altitude of 2,300 metres, a few kilometres behind the Eastern escarpment and its breathtaking view of the Red Sea, Asmara was of infrastructural importance for military and commercial purposes and was soon made the new administrative capital of the young Italian colony.

Early urban planning dates back to the 1890s, but was not realised to any large extent until the 1930s, the height of Mussolini's Fascism, when Italy invested in transforming Eritrea economically and socially, in order to prepare its invasion into Ethiopia in 1935. Renowned Italian urban planners and architects arrived to design a complete modernist city from scratch, in the architectural styles of Italian Modernism and, more specifically, Rationalism, though one can also still find the monumental style of Mussolini's fascist ideology, built from the late 1930s through to the Italian defeat against Allied troops in 1941 (Gebremedhin 2003; Denison et al. 2003a; 2003b).[2] Colonial architecture symbolised civilised superiority and inscribed technological modernity and social segregation into the city's topography, as well as into the colonial territory as a whole, perceived as a blank experimental ground for socio-technological change (cf. Rabinow 2003; Scott 1998). Four urban areas were outlined and grouped around a central boulevard, then carrying the *Duce's* name: first, the *zona nazionale*, a European zone, characterised by large spaces, representative villas and green gardens; secondly, the *zona indigeni*, a native zone at the other edge of the town, crowded by simple mud houses alongside winding narrow streets, lacking basic sanitation facilities (cf. Sahle 2000); thirdly, a mixed zone enabling mutual business contacts, including the market areas; and finally, an industrial zone in the outskirts (Denison et al. 2003a; Abraham 2003). Treated as inferiors and considered dirty and dull, Eritreans were nevertheless needed as workers, soldiers and servants in the fascist colony, so that they had access, albeit limited, to symbols of modernity such as machinery and weapons, household technology, lifestyles and modern mass culture in the form of Asmara's huge and massively promoted cinemas (Locatelli 2003).[3] With the British victory over the Italian forces in 1941 came the possibility of democratic institutions and techniques, such as schools, parties, unions and

2. For a more detailed summary of World War II in Eritrea and the defeat of the Italian colonial troops in Keren, see Ofcansky and Treiber 2007.
3. While the cinemas alongside the main boulevard were not accessible to Eritreans during the period of racial segregation, they were opened up after the British victory. During the Italian years there was at least one – smaller and less representative – cinema for the 'natives' (Denison et al. 2003b: 160–7).

newspapers. These provided the evolving urban middle class in particular with opportunities to access, appropriate and enjoy commodities and assets that symbolised modernity, despite economic decline after World War II.

In the 1950s, Ethiopia began to enforce its imperialist claims to the former Italian colony and then British-administered UN mandate, supported by the USA who had maintained a military monitoring facility in Asmara since 1942. The Ethiopian Emperor Haile Selassie, his Ethiopian legation and Eritrean supporters, made up of orthodox clergy, the Unionist party and degraded poor, found themselves facing educated, self-confident and organised urban working and middle classes. These groups were beginning to form one of the pillars of growing Eritrean nationalism in the 1940s and 1950s.[4] The Ethiopian monarchy that took over from British administration was perceived as undemocratic, undeveloped and anti-modern in every sense (symbolised by the fact that the royal Ethiopian soldiers crossing the Ethiopian-Eritrean border in 1952 did not wear shoes). It instantly enforced its rule through repression and unpopular laws, dismantling the official and in principal UN-guaranteed Ethiopian-Eritrean federation. A general strike in 1958 was followed by the full annexation of Eritrea in 1962 (Killion 1997). The first resistance movements were founded, but Asmara remained under tight Ethiopian military control, although it was almost liberated during the chaotic and unpredictable years following the Ethiopian revolution in 1974, the demise of Haile Selassie in Addis Ababa and the rise of a ruling military committee (the *derg*) under Ethiopia's new autocratic leader, Mengistu Haile Mariam, alleging its own notion of development and modernisation (Donham 1999). The Soviet Union's economic and military support enabled Revolutionary Ethiopia to retain the Eritrean towns and cities and win back much of Eritrea's countryside. As the *derg's* revolutionary modernism in Eritrea was, however, limited to rhetoric and repressive means, life in Asmara, occupied by thousands of Ethiopian soldiers, deteriorated. Poverty and dirt, violence, repression and raids, internal military coups, urban guerrilla activities and punitive actions against civilians shaped daily life in the formerly prosperous city. Asmara came under increasing siege again after 1988, which finally forced the *derg* to fly in all supplies until its defeat.

4. The other pillar of Eritrean nationalism in the decades after World War II was rural Islam, in opposition to and afraid of Christian Orthodox domination. In consequence several religious tensions and even clashes between Muslims and Orthodox Christians occurred (Killion 1998: 73, 390–1).

During the reign of the Ethiopian Emperor Haile Selassie, and even more so during the era of Mengistu Haile Mariam's *derg*, Asmara's architectural shape hardly changed, while the degeneration of the built environment increased, to such an extent that, on entering the city in 1991, the victorious troops of the Eritrean People's Liberation Front found a city that was severely run-down and in a state of disrepair, despite being saved from the ravages of war. The subsequent head of Eritrea's official Cultural Assets Rehabilitation Project (CARP), a former EPLF-fighter, recalls the haunting smell of the city's ramshackle sewage system, a harsh antidote to his nostalgic anticipation of return to the place of his youth (Tzeggai 2001).

Creating nation and subjects: The Eritrean People's Liberation Front

The rapidly growing Eritrean People's Liberation Front, the nationalist guerrilla movement founded in the early 1970s by critical deserters of its predecessor, the Eritrean Liberation Front, soon managed to dominate the struggle for national liberation, attracting thousands of young men and women. This included young Eritreans from urban middle class families, who were studying at Asmara or Addis Ababa universities, with a Maoist-inspired ideology of national liberation, education and development. Its concept of self-reliance, adapted from the Chinese Red Army's 'Long March' and from Julius Nyerere's Tanzanian development policy, can be read as a cathartic concept of national development through revolutionary purification of foreign domination and manipulation. To this collective end, morally strong, authoritarian and consequently anti-individual guidance was needed, provided by the EPLF's inner circle (Pool 2001).
Songs and poems, written by educated liberation fighters 'in the field' (in the mountains of the rural Sahel region of Northern Eritrea), romanticised Asmara. Transferring childhood memories into a clean, safe and joyful utopian place to be reached and realised in an unforeseeable future, these texts expressed melancholy as well as the motivation to finally end guerrilleros' daily hardships and return to the civilised city. In 'September in Asmara', Ararat Iyob (1999: 42) writes:

> They [the Ethiopian soldiers] look with wonder / at the abandoned houses and apartments / asking themselves why they [the liberation fighters] left / this beautiful place / to lie on hot sand / thorns biting their feet.

After the EPLF's military victory and the entry of its – disarmed – troops into the Eritrean capital, political initiatives were taken to repair and reinstall the city's infrastructure, but also to clean the city of the previous government's agents, and to eliminate rampant petty crime, vice and moral disorder (cf. Wacquant 2003). In its 'high-modernist' mission the new revolutionary government never differentiated between physical and moral or cultural pollution (Scott 1998; cf. Lindner 2004: 19–26). Restorative interventions in Asmara's physical, built environment were paired seamlessly with interventions aimed at social and moral restoration. An authoritarian campaign of national values, promoting a collective culture of discipline and moral purity, was issued. This was an attempt to wipe out all forms of disobedience and ambivalence (cf. Harrison 1999; Bauman 1991), which were considered a threat to the nation's newly won purity, resources and development (cf. Patel and McMichael 2004).

In the mid 1990s, the national capital Asmara had become a city of half a million inhabitants. Street cleaners and construction workers were secured through so-called food-for-work programmes. Children were rewarded for collecting discarded plastic bags (a short-lived opportunity, though in 2005, ten years later, plastic bags, which had again become a major form of urban pollution, were forbidden overnight). A programme of alternative, ecologically sustainable tourism was even drafted (Hartmann 1998). Towards tourists, taxi drivers, who were usually demobilised freedom fighters, praised Asmara as a safe place: 'no beggars, no thieves'. In fact government forces, from time to time, transferred beggars and prostitutes who lived in the former native quarters to the countryside or into the military training camp at Sawa, founded in 1994. Eritrean youth, who had grown up in Addis Ababa and moved to Asmara for work and educational opportunities, were warned explicitly by local police not to bring in 'bad habits' – such as loitering – from the Ethiopian capital, which was perceived as a dirty, ugly, anonymous and criminal Moloch: 'This is not Addis Ababa, we work here.'[5]

Among Western sympathisers and governments, post-independence Eritrea's normative, clear-cut and modernist policy of 'zero tolerance' (Wacquant 2003: 198) was admired as effective and emancipatory. In the common euphoria preceding the border war with neighbouring Ethiopia, there was little attention for the fact that the success of the government's moral and physical hygiene and corporate body politic relied to a significant extent on the effective and exclusionary creation of fear, a well-known guerrilla tactic (Harvey 2003). People who resisted, like a small number of Jehova's witnesses – who did not take part in the country's referendum for independence in 1993 and refused the newly introduced national service in 1994 – were considered traitors who polluted the selfless and nationalist revolutionary mind with their subversive and 'foreign' religious ideology (Donham 1999: 143). Consequently, such

5. Biniam, field informant, 10/2001.

people were treated as waste, dumped in military prisons in Sawa and elsewhere (Amnesty International 2004).

Eritrea's *warsay* generation

Today's Eritrea is ruled by a group of high officials of the former Eritrean People's Liberation Front around President Isayas Afeworki, who have successfully impeded democratisation and criticism from both inside and outside the EPLF. They have imprisoned dissidents, oppositional activists and journalists after the 2001 border war with Ethiopia and established a system of strict ideological control. Ten percent of the population is at present conscripted into the army, where they suffer lawlessness, harassment, rape, torture and extrajudicial executions, but also general boredom in remote army camps in the countryside. Amnesty International estimates that thousands are in jail because of desertion and political opposition (2004). Young adults between 18 and 40, both male and female, are required to complete the compulsory national service. This officially consists of six months of military training and one year of community service in development projects or governmental institutions. In reality the national service, in Tigrinya *agelgulot*, seems to be open-ended. Anyone assigned to Asmara or accepted as a student of one of the country's 'technical colleges'[6] is already privileged and safe from military service – at least in the short-term. Those who fulfil their national service in the capital's bureaucracy are mostly academics who have finished their studies or even worked as experts for regular salaries before being conscripted into the army. In the biopolitical terminology of the Eritrean government (Foucault 1976), national service conscripts are called *warsay*, the Tigrinya word for 'my inheritor', describing the role of the post-independence generation in defending what the EPLF once fought for. Currently they are paid 500 Nakfa[7] monthly, which officially equates to approximately $30, but unofficially is closer to $20. In early 2005, demobilisation cards were issued to men aged 35 years and women aged 27 years and their salary was raised to pre-war standards, normally around 1000 Nakfa. However, these young men and women were not released from their assignment, nor did the pre-

6. As it did not fulfil its duty to train a national cadre – to produce only a technical and administrative elite, but not an intellectual and critical one – the University of Asmara has been shut down incrementally in the last years. New students are now assigned to so-called technical or business colleges under military administration.
7. The Eritrean currency Nakfa is named after the town Naqfa (or Nakfa) in Northern Eritrea, which as EPLF's successfully defended rear base played an important strategic and symbolic role in the Eritrean liberation struggle and historiography, cf. Abdela and Treiber (2007).

war salary account for post-war inflation and price increases due to drought and food shortages. Students and draft dodgers – despite harsh punishments, many of the latter pour back into Asmara from the army camps – are usually impecunious and try to get support from relatives and to earn some pocket-money in more or less irregular jobs. Although Asmara has some industry, which traditionally produces textiles, shoes and alcoholic beverages, most urbanites hold badly-paid jobs in the service sector, own a small business or workshop, or work in the capital's national administration. Trade is concentrated in the hands of companies owned more or less openly by the state's single party. Interestingly, the UN organisations present in the capital – including the now dissolved United Nations' Mission to Ethiopia and Eritrea (UNMEE, 2000–2008), commissioned to watch the two countries' common border – supply many, at least temporary, jobs, even to those who otherwise would have to prove that they have completed their national service. Consequently, these organizations are a popular employer for *warsay*, students and draft dodgers, and generally ignore the government's strict ban on employing national service conscripts.

Due to these conditions, risky and illegal migration of thousands of *warsay* to Ethiopia and Sudan – and from there to Europe and North America – has become popular in the last few years. Those still living – legally or illegally – in Asmara are trying to save up the US$ 2500 or more, often with support of local relatives if present, required to pay the trafficker.

The Eritrean leadership has lost all of its moral credit. General poverty, open corruption among the leadership and military elite, and brutal implementation of disciplinary biopolitics that turn the individual into a mere subject to the imaginary national collective, show that post-revolutionary ideas of a clean life and common developmental progress are now no more than shallow propaganda. Refraining from political statements of any kind (which might be documented by Asmara's numerous secret government informants), young urbanites, locked in a state of prolonged adolescence, develop their own aesthetic ideas of a clean life, leading to quite different, even rivalling urban lifestyle milieux (Treiber 2005; cf. Behrens 2007: 20–3; Park 1925).[8] These – in their

8. Fieldwork in Asmara was conducted between May 2001 and May 2005, during several stays of different lengths, in order to study the *warsay* generation's life and survival strategies in daily life (Treiber 2005). In order to analyse urban spaces and locations, as they are chosen, arranged and appropriated by *warsay* who are assigned to the capital, Pierre Bourdieu's ideas of field, capital and habitus proved useful and inspiring (1993). A separate research project concerning urban perspectives on Asmara's colonial built environment, undertaken in cooperation with the governmental 'Cultural Assets Rehabilitation Project' (CARP) between August 2001 and May 2002, provided additional insight into urban dwellers' aesthetic preferences and their pragmatic ideas of modernity (Treiber 2003). Fieldwork with Eritrean migrants in the USA and in an Ethiopian refugee camp was conducted in April and August 2007 (the latter together with Lea Tesfaye).

perspective 'a-political' – notions of cleanliness should be seen in the historical context of Italian colonisation, British administration, Ethiopian occupation, the liberation war and independence. Such notions hint at the historical emergence and implicit continuity of urban middle class values and ideas despite political changes and ruptures. Today, creative agency is restricted to available spare time. Work as a *warsay* is considered forced labour and since *warsay* are not paid sufficiently, many men and women in their forties still live with their parents, siblings and further relatives, sometimes even in a single room. While living and working conditions pose essential restrictions, bars and cafés provide some individual choices – at least after office hours.

Clean life in a clean city?

In Tigrinya, *tseruy* or *tsefuf* means 'tidy' or 'neat'. *Tsa'eda* ('white'), reminiscent of colonial rule and education, stands for moral cleanliness, for hope and virtue and for 'European'. However, it can also be used in the phrase *ertra tsa'eda*, literally 'white Eritrea', referring to post-independence development,[9] as expressed in the words *haddish* for 'new' or *zemenawi* for 'modern'.[10] While doing research work for CARP in the autumn of 2001, interviewees usually used the English word 'clean' to sum up these aspects. 'Clean' represents the streets of Asmara's city centre that are cleaned daily, the renovation works undertaken there, the new and representative buildings in the centre and in the newly constructed outskirts and the dressed-up urban dwellers, strolling up and down *godena harnet*, the main boulevard, in the evening. It represents safety in comparison to other African capitals, peace after devastating wars and development towards European standards as successfully achieved by Singapore.[11] In other words, 'clean' to these urban dwellers generally

9. See, e.g., the private Eritrean diaspora website www.garaadom.de.
10. On the discourse of colonial modernity in Eritrea see Teklehaimanot (1996) for the field of education and Locatelli (2003) and Denison et al. (2003a, 2003b) for the field of architecture and urban planning. On (post)colonial concepts of urban modernity and hygiene cf. Kaviraj (1997).
11. In the Eritrean development discourse in the prospering years between the wars, the so-called Asian Tigers, especially Singapore, became a popular shining example of successful development for small states without abundant natural resources. Referring to these countries and their specific histories implied placing collective commitment above individual rights and democratic decision-making, without further explanation.

means 'civilised' – imagining an integrative urban lifestyle.[12] Logically, its antonym would not only be *zeytsefuf* ('not clean'), but *Hmaqh* ('bad') referring to dirt, disrepair, poverty, desperation, crime and war (cf. McDonogh 2003; Girtler 1995; Douglas 1966; 1981).[13]

Since the early 1990s, renovation work in Asmara has increased considerably, at least during the boom period before the devastating 1998–2000 border war with Ethiopia and the subsequent impasse which

Figure 6.1. Downtown Asmara, former *zona nazionale* or *campo cintato*.

12. In the context of post-colonial India, Kaviraj alludes to the 'European model of public sphere', taken over by a 'middle-class educated elite' (1997: 92), and to its 'unmistakable strand of control, of order and discipline' (1997: 99). That the idea of Asmara as a clean city is shared even by North Ethiopian Tigrayans, who firmly oppose the Eritrean regime which they consider arrogant and offensive, is demonstrated by the following statement. To stress how exceptionally neatly his wife runs the common household, Habtom, a 40–year-old man from the Tigrayan capital Mekele, explains that '… she has been in Asmara before [as a housemaid and work migrant]'. Fieldwork in Tigray, 08/2007.
13. See also this report from an oppositional news agency: 'General Oqbe Abraha was uniformly believed to be a clean fighter, but when the G-1 was building its case against him, it invented a corruption charge – then declared him guilty through its "special court" '. *Gedab News*, 8 October 2006.

Figure 6.2. Street café alongside 'godena harnet', Liberty Avenue.

hit the gastronomic business sector especially hard. Renovated cafés, bars and nightclubs have become eye-catchers in an environment where disrepair is still predominant. These establishments represent modernity, post-war development and civilised urban life, or, to paraphrase local terminology, 'cleanliness'. It is easy to demonstrate how attractive renovated cafés along *godena harnet* are to Asmara's citizens – just try to obtain a seat in one of them in the late afternoon, after office hours.

From a preservation perspective, construction and renovation works rarely respect the historical style and aesthetics of Asmara's built environment. The present-day owners and tenants of hotels, cafés or bars – most real estate is actually owned by the government – have a pragmatic interest in a clean and attractive exterior and interior, in functioning sewage facilities and a reliable water supply. The ongoing construction and renovation works increasingly create a polyphony of styles, absorbing aesthetic concepts from Europe, North America, the Middle and Far East, as well as Africa, using available building material from Arab, Asian or African countries (Treiber 2003), thus polluting the pure Rationalist architecture in the eyes of local and international preservationists (Denison et al. 2003a: 8–9). The Mask Place is such a renovated bar and will be discussed in more detail.

'The Mask Place'

The Mask Place is a well-known bar in the city centre, located west of the cathedral, not far from *godena harnet* and the President's office, in a single-storied building occupying a street corner plot. Large windows provide views of the interior, where a massive wooden bar – representing the stereotype of a Kenyan beach bar – dominates the entrance area. Wooden masks – uncommon in this part of Africa – and a large West African painting provide an exotic atmosphere. As urban Eritreans are currently discovering music and fashion from Central and West Africa, the interior of the Mask Place can be considered stylish and en vogue, probably even contributing to the launch of the West African fashion trend, as it emerged a few years ago. Since then, several other chic bars have been established, including Green Pub in the Intercontinental Hotel, Sunshine-Hotel-Bar, Caravelle-Club, the cocktail bar Zara or Roof Garden and Golden Fork restaurants. The Mask Place itself always appears to be well attended. When I asked Mussa, 25 years old at the time, why he liked coming there, he answered, 'It is clean there.' Here, 'clean' stands for the renovated architecture, the quality of food and service and the social exclusivity guaranteed by high prices and a guard at the entrance door, who chases away the undesirable: children selling chewing-gum, beggars and drunkards.

Young adults, who are the Mask Place's regular guests, identify with the bar's physical and social cleanliness, and enjoy being identified with it. To see and to be seen is a common motto here. Especially after sundown, the front windows make the softly illuminated interior a social showroom, and it goes without saying that being here requires clean and classy clothes as well as good behaviour. Violence and drunkenness are not tolerated. Guests will limit themselves to one or two drinks only and women will most likely abstain from cigarettes and alcohol, in order not to be taken for and treated as prostitutes. Cleanliness here also implies moral integrity, supporting Mary Douglas' view that strict bodily control is a sign of clear-cut ideals of social order and purity (cf. Douglas 1981: 106–12; Bourdieu 2005: 76). But it is notable that young adults gather in the entrance area around the bar, where only few bar stools offer seating, as they cannot afford to sit down in the restaurant section, where one must order dinner. This part of the Mask Place seems to be reserved for the city's successful businesspeople and foreign development experts. Young adults in the Mask Place have made a virtue of necessity. By occupying the bar section, they come close to and even try to be part of an exclusive milieu, despite the financial impotence they suffer as students and academics (cf. Rigi 2003; Whyte 1993; Gandoulou 1989; Goffman 1969).

Under these conditions, the acceptance of renovated bars after office hours and on weekends provides time and space to realise specific notions of life-quality despite a lack of financial power, dependency on relatives and senior officials, and constant political and military repression. Outfit, manners, academic education and social exclusivity are markers of their concept of a clean and civilised society, opposing combat gear, military order, mistreatment and incapacitation (cf. Douglas 1966: 12–3). Young adults who regularly frequent the Mask Place or other stylish and expensive bars in Asmara constitute a milieu of people, who have enjoyed education but lack access to regular salaries. In the terminology of Pierre Bourdieu (1993: 118–19), they are not yet able or permitted to convert their symbolic capital into economic capital, which leads them into an extended adolescence. Nevertheless, these young adults have a shared idea of a lifestyle that they could afford under other circumstances, and they simulate this in their spare time, occupying specific spaces and places (cf. Fuest 1996; Gandoulou 1989).

'Bar Diana'

Until his recent migration to Khartoum, Biniam was a regular guest in Bar Diana, where he came for tea or coffee in the afternoon or for a couple of beers and a chat with friends in the evening. Like the young adults in the Mask Place's bar section, he and most of the other guests were students at Asmara University or a technical college or *warsay* in the capital's bureaucracy. Even most of the draft dodgers present have an academic education – but the contrast between both places could not be more evident. Bar Diana is just a ten-minute walk from the Mask Place at *godena*

Figure 6.3. Popular local bar in Asmara.

harnet, located in the heart of the city, opposite from St. Mary's cathedral. Yet, despite its prominent location it is easy to miss its entrance. A narrow shop window containing piled-up Heineken accessories and a dark-toned glass door prevent passers-by from sneaking a peek inside. If one moves to the dim, smoky back of the bar room, one is completely safe from being seen from outside. Bar Diana has not been renovated and consequently does not allow its guests to be identified with physical, social and moral cleanliness. On the contrary, as Hagos and Mussa, both regular guests at the Mask Place, demonstrated. Hagos warned me not to ruin my reputation – 'this is not a place, where a man with manners should be seen' – and Mussa obstinately refused to join me there. Others even call it a dangerous place (cf. Douglas 1966: 13–4).

Biniam realises this: 'those people would consider me dirty.' He believes this assumption would be based on both his disorderly family situation and his different notion of life-quality. He is a father of two small children by different mothers, and as such morally stigmatised. Besides this, he refuses to be judged on the basis of his clothes, and questions the standard ideal of life-quality as hypocritical.[14] There are only a few drunks in Bar Diana, both

---

14. On the meaning of clothes in social integration and segregation, see Tranberg Hansen (2004) for an overview, and Gandoulou (1989) for Brazzaville's specific urban culture.

young and old, who do not care about their clothes and prefer to spend their limited budget on alcohol. All others pay careful attention to their appearance and regularly exchange and borrow stylish garments from each other, though the Bar Diana's young adults are not ready to invest more in clothes than they consider reasonable. They want to be able to drop into the bar without changing their clothes beforehand. They choose to reserve some money with which to get drunk and enjoy loud music – or, as in Biniam's case, they need to contribute to the support of children or relatives. Few women frequent Bar Diana where beer is cheaper than in the Mask Place and getting drunk is not frowned upon. Bar fights do not occur often, though regulars at the Mask Place like to exaggerate them. A small group of women, who were deported from Ethiopia during the border war, are among Bar Diana's regular guests. Having grown up in the larger and more liberal city of Addis Ababa, they want to enjoy the same urban liberties as men. As they already feel ostracised and isolated, they do not care about their reputation and are used to drinking and smoking. These habits are normally seen as a sign and privilege of prostitutes, but while a few might occasionally work as a prostitute, these women are in Bar Diana to enjoy themselves like the other guests. They too want to be accepted and respected in the milieu of the 'dirty', without the need to feign more potency than they actually possess.[15]

Moral ascriptions of cleanliness

Following Mary Douglas, the Mask Place shows how control of the body is enforced, as a space where strict social control and clear-cut concepts of purity and impurity are in full evidence. This bar can be described as a highly formal place, in contrast to Bar Diana, which is a less structured place of informality, intimacy, mixed roles, social integration and collective inebriation. Such characteristics oppose and conflict with the Mask guests' ideals of order and purity (cf. Douglas 1981: 106–9; Kaviraj 1997: 99). Bar Diana's guests do not accept the segregative vision their counterparts express through manners, clothes and behaviour, where, in the context of a lack of material capital, aesthetics are employed to enforce a social hierarchy of high and low lifestyles (cf. Bourdieu 2005). Yet, the behaviour

15. On female spheres of decision and possible action alongside and across moral boundaries of purity and gender, see Nageeb (2004) in the context of Muslim fundamentalism in Khartoum, Girtler (2004) on prostitution in Vienna. McDonogh (2003: 265), writing on 'moral mapping' in Barcelona's nightlife quarters, states that: ' "Spatialising" immorality allows others to differentiate themselves as virtuous by location and behaviour as space and virtue reinforce each other while intimately dividing social worlds. Good Barcelona men relax in good bars in good neighborhoods, possibly with good women (who might also stay at home).'.

of both groups can be explained as alternative responses to what is perceived as inhuman repression and arbitrariness. While guests in Bar Diana abolish order through integration, guests in the Mask Place prefer to replace a 'bad' order by a more 'civilised' one.

The differentiation of Asmara's young urban adults into two opposing milieus echoes *Street Corner Society*, William Foote Whyte's classic study from the 1940s. Whyte (1993) differentiated young urban men in an Italian-American Boston neighbourhood into 'corner boys' and 'college boys'. Still, there is considerable difference in the way those youths chose their milieu and lifestyle. In Whyte's 'Cornerville', it is the lack of education, and the associated chances of a normal professional career, that steer young men toward a certain milieu. In Asmara, most young adults who reside in the city, whether legally or illegally, have enjoyed an academic education. Almost all of the less educated young Eritreans have been assigned to rural army camps and so they are permanently absent from Asmara (cf. Whyte 1993; Gandoulou 1989). Uneducated have-nots and drunkards will tend to join people in Bar Diana, Bar Eden or Bar Segen, while wealthier citizens will be more inclined to frequent the Mask Place, Bar Zara, Green Pub or other chic places. All the same, many in both milieus of young adults share similar situations in life, as they are impecunious though well-educated, and suffer common conditions of political and military repression and conservative gender morality.

The example of Abraham demonstrates the dynamics of the choice between clean and dirty. He switched locales, changing from Bar Diana to Mask Place, and in doing so lost the sympathy of his former Bar Diana companions, who then treated him curtly and with contempt. Abraham obviously expected to get greater social respect and, in the long run, improved access to social resources such as well-paid jobs and women from wealthier families with good reputations. But as young urban adults, the *warsay* and draft dodgers are currently unable to realise the 'appropriate' life they imagine. Abraham has joined a social game, which at the moment has nothing more to offer than different social ideals of what constitutes a clean life. This is in contrast with Rigi's (2003) description of dispossessed urban youth in post-Soviet Kazakhstan, where flourishing crime and prostitution are in fact seen as an alternative route to tangible material and social advancement. It also contrasts with Gandoulou's (1989) account of unemployed but trendily dressed school and university graduates in Brazzaville, where sophisticated clothes, manners and spatial choices not only symbolise but reify a higher social status.

Examining young urban adults in present-day Asmara shows how collective lifestyle and social milieu are individual choices, even in a situation of general repression and total future insecurity, which may result in being arrested for unknown time by the next military police patrol or even shot because of a missing ID card.[16]

It also illustrates how reciprocal moral ascriptions – 'dirty and dangerous' or 'hypocritical' – are contested among young adults who share similar circumstances but differ in their ideas of what constitutes quality of life. Such ideological differences are manifested in decisions regarding the built environment and translated into a semantic opposition of 'clean' and 'dirty'. This can be seen as an attempt to establish social, quasi-natural differences between milieus where ideological or, following Bourdieu, symbolic differences prevail (cf. Bourdieu 1993; Kaviraj 1997: 112–13). Far removed from the environmental issue of preserving and maintaining Asmara's colonial city centre, acceptance and rejection of physical renovation and physical cleanliness are used to define and legitimise a concept of social status and a claim on individual progress, without the economic means one believes one could acquire, should one only be allowed to.

Figure 6.4. Remembering and rebuilding Asmara in Shimelba refugee camp, Tigray/Ethiopia – *Mask Pastry.*

16. See Massimo A. Alberizzi, 'Eritrea: Fotografie di morte', *Corriere della Serra*, Sept. 13, 2005, www.corriere.it/Primo_Piano/Esteri/2005/09_Settembre/11/ speciale_eritrea.shtml, also 'Eritrea: Photographs of Death', *asmarino.com*, Sept. 12, 2005, http://news9.asmarino.com/content/view/551/86/

Postscript: Rebuilding Asmara in the refugee camp

Looking out over Shimelba refugee camp, situated in a dry valley in Northern Ethiopia, it is easy to identify a 'boulevard' intersecting the accumulation of simple mud houses, reminiscent of *godena harnet*. Loud music is played all day, inviting the Eritrean refugees who are concentrated here into numerous little bars and cafés, established with financial support from relatives abroad. The makeshift cafés have been carefully designed from mud, which can be moulded quite easily before becoming solid. The characteristic bar counter and even the cash desk, similar to those in Asmara, have been constructed from mud. For years, thousands of successful Eritrean refugees wait to be scheduled for resettlement in Europe or North America, suffering from paternalism, boredom and destitution (Treiber and Tesfaye 2008). While wandering through the camp, familiar names pop up: Diana Entertainment and Hollywood (now makeshift cinemas), The Golden Fork (a restaurant), Caravelle-Club, Green Pub and – twice, even – the Mask Pastry. The ground may be dusty, but the different ideas of a clean life, hoped to be realised one day in the First World, have been transported from Asmara and rebuilt as well as possible. 'We miss Asmara so much', say Haben and Adeam, two 19–year-old girls and Jehovah's Witnesses.

References

Abdela, S. and M. Treiber. 2007. 'Naqfa' in *Encyclopedia Aethiopica*, S. Uhlig (ed.), vol. 3. Wiesbaden: Harrassowitz Verlag.

Abraham, M. 2003. 'Early History of Asmara' in *Asmara: A Guide to the Built Environment*, E. Denison, G.-Y. Ren, M. Abraham and N. Gebremedhin (eds), pp. 26–39. Asmara: CARP.

Amnesty International. 2004. *Eritrea, 'You Have No Right to Ask': Government Resists Scrutiny on Human Rights*. AFR 64/003/2004, May 2004.

Appadurai, A. 2000. 'The Grounds of the Nation-State' *in Nationalism and Internationalism in the Post-Cold War Era*, K. Goldmann, U. Hannerz, Ch. Westin (eds), pp. 129–42. London, New York: Routledge.

Behrens, R. 2007. 'Kritische Theorie der Stadt', *Widerspruch: Münchner Zeitschrift für Philosophie* 46: 13–38.

Bourdieu, P. 1993. *Sozialer Sinn: Kritik der theoretischen Vernunft*. Frankfurt am Main: Suhrkamp.

——— 2005. 'Taste of Luxury, Taste of Necessity' in *The Taste Culture Reader: Experiencing Food and Drink*, C. Korsmeyer (ed.), pp. 72–8. Oxford and New York: Berg.

Denison, E., G.-Y. Ren and N. Gebremedhin. 2003a. *Asmara: Africa's Secret Modernist City*. London and New York: Merell.

————2003b. (eds) *Asmara: A Guide to the Built Environment*. Asmara: CARP.

de Vries, F. 2004. 'The Italian Colony Time Forgot', *Sunday Independent*, 1 August 2004.

Donham, D.L. 1999. *Marxist Modern: An Ethnographic History of the Ethiopian Revolution*. Berkeley, Los Angeles, Oxford: University of California Press.

Douglas, M. 1966. *Purity and Danger: An Analysis of Concept of Pollution and Taboo*. London: Routledge.

————1981. *Ritual, Tabu und Körpersymbolik: Sozialanthropologische Studien in Industriegesellschaft und Stammeskultur*. Frankfurt am Main: Suhrkamp.

Erlich, H. 1996. *Ras Alula and the Scramble for Africa: A Political Biography, Ethiopia and Eritrea, 1875–1897*. Lawrenceville and Asmara: Red Sea Press.

Foucault, M. 1976. *Überwachen und Strafen: Die Geburt des Gefängnisses*. Frankfurt/M.: Suhrkamp.

Fuest, V. 1996. *'A Job, a Shop, and a Loving Business': Lebensweisen gebildeter Frauen in Liberia*. Münster: LIT-Verlag.

Gandoulou, J.-D. 1989. *Dandies à Bacongo: Le culte de l'élégance dans la société congolaise contemporaine*. Paris: L'Harmattan.

Gebremedhin, N. 2003. 'Architecture of Asmära' in *Encyclopedia Aethiopica*, S. Uhlig (ed.), vol. 1, p. 379. Wiesbaden: Harrassowitz Verlag.

Gedab News, 8 October 2006. 'Update on the "G–15", the "G–1" & the People'. Accessed on www.awate.com.

Girtler, R. 1995. *Randkulturen: Theorie der Unanständigkeit*. Wien: Böhlau.

————2004. *Der Strich: Erotik der Straße*, 5th edn. Wien: LIT-Verlag.

Goffmann, E. 1969. *Wir alle spielen Theater: Die Selbstdarstellung im Alltag*. München: Piper.

Harrison, S. 1999. 'Cultural Boundaries', *Anthropology Today* 15 (5): 10–3.

Hartmann, R. 1998. *Eritrea. Neubeginn mit Tourismus. Ein integratives Planungs- und Entwicklungskonzept*. Arbeiten aus dem Institut für Afrika-Kunde 99. Hamburg: Deutsches Übersee-Institut.

Harvey, D. 2003. 'The City as Body Politic' in *Wounded Cities: Destruction and Reconstruction in a Globalized World*, J. Schneider and I. Susser (eds), pp. 25–44. Oxford, New York: Berg.

Hepner, T. M. R. 2008. 'Transnational Governance and the Centralization of State Power in Eritrea and Exile', *Ethnic and Racial Studies* 31 (3): 476–502.

Iyob, A. 1999. *Blankets of Sand: Poems of War and Exile*. Lawrenceville NJ, Asmara: Red Sea Press.

Kaviraj, S. 1997. 'Filth and the Public Sphere: Concepts and Practices about Space in Calcutta', *Public Culture* 10 (1): 83–113.

Killion, T. 1997. 'Eritrean Workers' Organization and Early Nationalist Mobilization, 1948–1958', *Eritrean Studies Review* 2 (1): 1–58.

————1998. *Historical Dictionary of Eritrea*. African Historical Dictionaries, vol. 75. Lanham and London: Scarecrow Press.

Lathullière, M. 1995. 'Erithrée: Dans un pays exsangue, Asmara s'éveille', *Jeune Afrique Économie* 205 (16 October): 26–7.

Lindner, R. 2004. *Walks on the Wild Side: Eine Geschichte der Stadtforschung*. Frankfurt/M.: Campus.

Locatelli, F. 2003. 'Colonial History of Asmära' in *Encyclopedia Aethiopica*, S. Uhlig (ed.), vol. 1, pp. 374–5. Wiesbaden: Harrassowitz Verlag.

Mack, G. 1993. 'Eritrea: Der Krieg, Der Hunger, Der Aufbruch', GEO 4: 127–50.

McDonogh, G.W. 2003. 'Myth, Space, and Virtue: Bars, Gender, and Change in Barcelona's Barrio Chino' in *The Anthropology of Space and Place: Locating Culture*, S. Low and D. Lawrence-Zúñiga (eds), pp. 264–83. Oxford and Malden: Blackwell.

Nageeb, S.A. 2004. *New Spaces and Old Frontiers: Women, Social Space, and Islamization in Sudan*. Lanham: Lexington.

Ofcansky, T. and M. Treiber. 2007. 'Kärän, Battle of' in *Encyclopedia Aethiopica*, S. Uhlig (ed.), vol. 3. Wiesbaden: Harrassowitz Verlag.

Patel, R. and Ph. McMichael. 2004. 'Third Worldism and the Lineages of Global Fascism: The Regrouping of the Global South in the Neoliberal Era', *Third World Quarterly*, 25 (1): 231–54.

Park, R. 1984 [1925]. 'The City: Suggestions for the Investigation of Human Behavior in the Urban Environment' in *The City*, R. Park, E. Burgess and R. McKenzie (eds), pp. 1–46. Chicago, London: University of Chicago Press.

Pool, D. 2001. *From Guerillas to Government: The Eritrean People's Liberation Front*, Oxford, Athens: James Currey.

Rabinow, P. 2003 [1982]. '*Ordonnance*, Discipline, Regulation: Some Reflections on Urbanism' in *The Anthropology of Space and Place: Locating Culture*, S. Low and D. Lawrence-Zúñiga (eds), pp. 353–62. Malden MA, Oxford: Blackwell.

Rigi, J. 2003. 'The Conditions of Post-Soviet Dispossessed Youth and Work in Almaty, Kazakhstan', *Critique of Anthropology* 23 (1): 35–49.

Sahle, A. 2000. 'The People of the Narrow Streets', *Eritrea Profile*, 2 September 2000.

Scott, J. 1998. *Seeing Like a State: How Certain Schemes to Improve the Human Condition Have Failed*. New Haven, London: Yale University Press.

Teklehaimanot, B. 1996. 'Education in Eritrea During the European Colonial Period', *Eritrean Studies Review*, 1 (1): 1–22.

Tranberg Hansen, K. 2004. 'The World in Dress: Anthropological Perspectives on Clothing, Fashion, and Culture', *Annual Review of Anthropology* 33: 369–92.

Treiber, M. 2003. 'Urban Perceptions of Asmara' in *Asmara: A Guide to the Built Environment*, E. Denison, G.-Y. Ren, M. Abraham and N. Gebremedhin (eds), pp. 68–73. Asmara: CARP.

————2005. *Der Traum vom guten Leben, Die eritreische warsay-Generation im Asmara der zweiten* Nachkriegszeit, Spektrum 92, Berliner Reihe zu Gesellschaft, Wirtschaft und Politik in Entwicklungsländern, Münster: LIT-Verlag.

————2007. 'Dreaming of a Good Life: Young Urban Refugees from Eritrea Between Refusal of Politics and Political Asylum' in *Cultures of Migration: African Perspectives*, H.P. Hahn and G. Klute (eds), pp. 239–60. Berlin: LIT Verlag.

Treiber, M. and L. Tesfaye. 2008. 'Step by Step: Migration from Eritrea' in *Hot Spot Horn of Africa Revisited: Approaches to Make Sense of Conflict*, E.-M. Bruchhaus and M. Sommer (eds), pp. 280–95. Berlin: LIT Verlag.

Tzeggai, G. 2001.'Urbanising Asmara'. Paper presented at the Eritrean Studies Association's conference 'Independent Eritrea: Lessons and Prospects', Asmara, July 22–26.

Wacquant, L. 2003. 'Toward a Dictatorship Over the Poor? Notes on the Penalization of Poverty in Brazil', *Punishment & Society* 5 (2): 197–205.

Whyte, W.F. 1993 [1943]. *Street Corner Society: The Social Structure of an Italian Slum*, 4th edn. Chicago and London: University of Chicago Press.

CHAPTER 7

Using Pollution to Frame Collective Action: Urban Grassroots Mobilisations in Budapest

SZABINA KERÉNYI

Introduction

The perception of pollution has general, cross-cultural features – most commonly pollution is understood negatively, as the opposite of cleanness and order, and is perceived as something undesirable. In cities, pollution is usually visible and measurable in very concrete ways, as it is evident in the quality of air, or its physical presence can simply be observed. Urban pollution is also a concept that is often shared publicly, as it tends to affect public space and thus applies to everyone. Pollution has become an integral part of urban problems, and one that is generally dealt with at the policy level. Following transitions to democracy in post-Communist countries, citizens' involvement in decision-making processes has remained very low. In Communist times, contentious politics were simply absent (or if not, were generally connected to oppositional activities), with very few exceptions of environmental activism from the mid-1980s on. The repertoires of civil action have been very narrow up to the present day, while citizens' initiatives, therefore, tend to seek non-institutional channels. This contribution focuses on such non-institutional discourses on urban pollution, and explores conceptualisations of urban pollution by the environmental and associated movements, in a large post-transitional Central European city, based on fieldwork conducted in Budapest, the capital of Hungary. The paper is based on research that took place between 2005 and 2007 in Central European post-communist cities, focusing on grassroots urban mobilizations. The fieldwork consisted of interviews with activists, and is also based on primary materials (produced by the activists, such as leaflets, websites, public statements, petitions), as well as 'external' texts regarding those actions.

In post-communist Europe, environmental activism is entering a new era following the emergence of the first institutional groups after democratisation nearly two decades ago. While, especially in geopolitical regions without a strong tradition of social movements, they are usually expected to maintain an agenda focussing on 'classical' environmental issues, today's global environmental movement has moved beyond those expectations. In Hungary, the some major divisions inside the environmental movement can be drawn along urban-rural lines, which in this particular, over-centralised case tends to mean an antagonistic relation between Budapest and the rest of the country. For many years, the contrasts between city and 'province' have also dominated environmental discourses, but urban issues were rarely articulated explicitly. In the early years of the new millennium, however, a new meaning of greenness has developed from the loose networks of professional environmental protectors, and a vision of the built environment – the city – has begun to be outlined.

The role of urban pollution for social movements will be approached through the theoretical frame of urban injustices, and discussed by applying the literature on framing in social movements, which considers how frames can provide a basis for discourses, with the capacity to convert them into social action. After reviewing the theoretical concepts of framing, this contribution briefly introduces the development of urban issues and the urban environmental movement. Following this, concrete expressions of mobilisations against pollution will be outlined through three different approaches to the redefinition of space: the Critical Mass movement, which claims different uses of existing urban public space; the squatters' search for underground and alternative spaces; and an initiative to preserve the existing built cultural heritage in the city. This chapter's main focus is on the potential of urban pollution as a frame for social movement mobilisation and collective action. Pollution, as will be argued, is defined on both a material and an abstract level – both mark borders between 'ritual' cleanness and uncleanness, or between sustainable and harmful practices, in city life. Both levels are connected in experiences of urban space and urban objects, where the movement initiates the use of alternative spaces or alternative uses of 'common' spaces, and offers a normative concept for a sustainable and 'clean' city.

Conceptualising pollution for urban social movements: A culturalist perspective

The term urban social movements, indicating movements concerned about urban issues and social problems related to the city, was propagated most strongly by Manuel Castells and is rooted in classical urban sociology, with a particular emphasis on class relations (Castells 1977). Castells' initial work did not regard movements as a potential challenge to existing social relations (Pickvance 2003); this is, however, a crucial point in the self-definition of the grassroots movement in Budapest. Another important distinction is that the category of class seems entirely irrelevant – neither class nor neighbourhood, nor other ascriptive factors play a particular role for these movements. Instead, these groups are best seen as an identity-based network of informal groups and actors, which are culturally constructed as locally conscious activist groups concerned about a range of problems in the city. The local consciousness is, however, not so much territorially bounded as culturally constructed, and is an important identity issue. As Pickvance (2003) points out, there has been a gap between the study of urban movements and theories on social movements – this chapter is concerned with urban social movements defined in a generic sense by the same author: movements engaged in non-institutional politics, aiming at radical changes in the social system (Pickvance 2003).

As Fine (1995: 127) notes at the start of his paper on discourse in social movements, 'culture is a concept that, like mushrooms on a dewy summer morning, is now discovered everywhere'. Although the discovery of culture is hardly a new phenomenon and can at best be called rediscovery, it is true that, in social movement studies, the culturalist approach is relatively new. While achieving a consensus on a definition of culture is impossible, it is necessary to give an outline in order to understand how culture is conceptualised within the research conducted on social movement studies, and to provide a possible theoretical background for urban green movements.

The introduction of a cultural perspective in social movements research is linked to theories of framing, starting with Goffman's (1974) oft-cited *Frame Analysis*, adopted about a decade later by Snow et al. (1986). Opposed to the initial understanding of culture as a background for structural changes, Ann Swidler's (1986) 'tool kit' metaphor introduced a general analytical perspective of culture as an instrument, a way of perceiving the world rather than a set of norms that direct actors. Even more importantly, her work put the discussion on culture in the spotlight. The innovation of Swidler's model of approaching culture lies in her replacing the dominant Geertzian understanding of culture - as defining values and goals of actions - with a perception of culture as a set of publicly available symbols through which people experience and express meanings. Culture, then, does not define the ends and goals of action, but rather provides general knowledge frames for perceiving and interpreting the world: a 'tool kit' for actors, which is used in constructing strategies of action. For Swidler, culture is not simply how things are perceived, but how symbolic practices are used, combined and changed. This concept improves on previous, more static approaches that are insufficient to understand processes of challenge, contestation and change (Williams 2004). Swidler (1986: 277) has shifted the focus of analysis to the process of the construction of strategies, in which 'culture has an independent causal role because it shapes the capacities from which such strategies of action are constructed'.

The processes of identity construction and strategy building can be reviewed through the concept of framing, through which the actors name the grievances and identify 'enemies', as well as communicate the message, which is not purely symbolic but also points to the strategy chosen to realise the goals (Tarrow 1998). Framing for social movements 'refers to an interpretative schemata that simplifies and condenses the "world out there" by selectively punctuating and encoding objects, situations, events, experiences, and sequences of actions within one's present or past environment' (Snow and Benford 1992: 137).

Doug McAdam (1996: 340), according to whom 'the principal weapon available to the movement is its strategic use of framing processes', stresses that most academic work on framing concentrates on the system (the institutionalised structures as the environment in which the movement arises), rather than on the concerns of the activists. Nevertheless, he himself divides movement framing into categories from the viewpoint of the system: its stability and threats to it, and institutional responses to the threats. The basic problem with this scheme is that it reduces movement activities to mere responses to the institutional system. Social movements, however, and at least as importantly, contribute to the establishment of cultural contents, goals and values of the movement community, which resonates in their social-cultural embeddedness. In the urban context, pollution serves as the 'master frame' in which the actors name a collective action frame and define a concrete grievance. Framing is significant in the mobilisation process of collective action, and serves as a 'label', a naming or a reference to the movement's goals and character, defined in reference to the actual social-political environment.

Framing pollution in the urban action arena

Cleanness and pollution, as recognised since Mary Douglas's essential work appeared, are not absolute categories but cultural constructions. Complex cultural systems carry various related meanings within the given framework. 'As we examine pollution beliefs we find that the kinds of contacts which are thought dangerous also carry a symbolic load. This is a

more interesting level at which pollution ideas relate to social life. I believe
that some pollutions are used as analogies for expressing a general view of
the social order' (Douglas 1969: 3). Pollution as such is not merely a matter
of hygiene – it goes far beyond, encompassing a complex of moral
perceptions that are constructed around all the threats and taboos that
pollution represents within a system. In an urban green movement
discourse, pollution is more than the undesired garbage on the street or the
unhealthy air – it lies in various layers of understanding, representing a
whole system of pollutions that endangers life on Earth and constrains the
chances for future generations.

The dichotomy of cleanliness and pollution is always in the foreground
and exists on a metaphorical level in urban environments, forming a
crucial part of discourse. Pollution in cities is an everyday topic – the
quality of air, water and the public spaces in general are issues that are
discussed continuously and on which everyone generally has an opinion.
Such issues are often used as indicators of the level of 'development' of
societies. For example, it is widely held that western countries are more
'civilised' because their streets are clean and garbage is collected
systematically and properly. Consequently, dirt serves to define a political
division between Eastern and Western European countries, and similarly,
between 'uncivilised' and 'civilised' places.

Pollution, in green discourse, contains various messages, but the basic
division lies along the dichotomy between cleanliness and pollution,
which opens spaces for negotiating values and norms for the movement
society. On the policy level, for instance, discourses on pollution are less
dominantly represented. As environmental protection ranks extremely
low as a priority issue of institutional politics (as in most post-communist
countries, cf. Szabó 1994), it is not a focus of interest for authorities. In
addition, since the regime change, the political scene in Hungary has been
strongly polarised, and environmental issues have an exceedingly low
potential to enter the arena of 'hard' political issues (Kerényi and Szabó
2006). Protection of the environment is narrowed down to specific spheres,
such as international treaties (which similarly get low publicity), and come
under probably the least influential ministry, the Ministry of Environment.
Partly as a consequence of the polarised political atmosphere,
environmental protection has not managed to enter public awareness,
although some polls have shown that on an individual level, people are
interested in protecting the environment but do not hold it to be an
explicitly political – and thus, important – issue.

At the grassroots level, however, pollution serves as a uniting factor in
the otherwise extremely diverse green movement. For the urban green
movement, the cultural content of pollution is expressed through the
rejection of an entire set of values, which they identify with urban
pollution. Beyond its physical attributes, pollution marks the frontline of

identities in the urban green subcultures, constructed along an antagonism symbolised by the opposition of pollution versus cleanness. Pollution here is rejected along with the consumerist urban lifestyle represented by the masses, while cleanness symbolises the alternative worldview, lifestyle and general attitudes, the actors in the green subcultures share. This opposition corresponds symbolically to the opposite poles of 'holiness and impurity' described by Mary Douglas (1969: 7–29). The first column, below, gives examples of categories rejected by the movement actors (as impure instances), followed by a second column of their 'sacred' counterparts.

pollution	cleanness
consumerism	sustainability
competition	solidarity
material goods	idcological values
preference for standard	diversity
short-term profit-making	preservation of natural and cultural resources

Figure 7.1. Environmentalist concepts of pollution and cleanness.

In this manner, pollution has become a central concept to which the movement links diverse, crucial and basic meanings. It therefore has the capacities to become a 'label' or a 'master frame' for the movement subcultures, who can express viewpoints on the alternative society through it. Pollution becomes a general frame, marking the line between 'purity and danger', that is, it serves as a boundary between desirable and unacceptable behaviours, thus posing guidelines for moral codes of norms, while on the physical level it divides clean spaces from polluted ones. In this case, the symbolic level of cleanness and pollution is dominant, as the urban environment of Budapest, a dynamic metropolis with two million inhabitants, is generally and literally dirty everywhere.

Pollution as a conceptual frame is, however, not sufficient to produce social action in itself. As a frame, it must resonate in the domestic culture, and address a major injustice in the name of a group. The issues the movement addresses could easily fit into a political economy discourse that emphasises the importance of economic processes and criticises the outcomes of a capitalist system, speaks of a 'right to the city' and defends the rights of deprived communities (Fainstein 1997). While the movement does incorporate some of these views, contrary to the Marxist approach, its major grievances are not linked to distributive problems, nor do they stress the accumulation of capital. In other words, despite incorporating important points from the Marxist agenda, the aim of the movement is not economy-oriented.

Instead, urban movements act as 'critical communities' (Rochon 1998) that raise the issue of pollution and attach new societal values to it, refer to the 'green worldview' in the city. In this fashion, pollution becomes more than a disturbing urban phenomenon that involves health risks and aesthetic damage. It is employed to articulate a political agenda through pointing at a common responsibility for the urban environment in individual lifestyles. Rochon's process of value connection corresponds with the stages of frame alignment described by Snow et al. (1986), where the last two phases – frame extension and frame transformation – can be observed in the collective actions that emerge under the frame.

The conceptual frames of outlining culture and identity provide the basic resources for collective action. The urban environmental movement not only managed to locate itself and certain focal problems in the urban environment, but also turned the city into a basic source for self-definition, a ground for drawing on collective action frames. While in the first decade of its existence, the Hungarian green movement regarded the city as a place to escape from, in recent years the city transformed from a background or location into an interactive space that produces and challenges new meanings within the movement. This essential shift was brought about by a view of urban space as more than a source of grievances, in the form of classical urban issues such as pollution, the dominance of capital, and phenomena like homelessness, poverty and violence (Merrifield and Swyngedouw 1997). Rather, they also identified solutions located in the city. In other words, their collective action frames included both the diagnostic and the prognostic frames for urban conflict (Snow and Benford 1988). In addition, as will be demonstrated below, urban spaces themselves have become incorporated into their actions and play an important role in the action strategies.

As noted by Merrifield and Swyngedouw (1997: 14), urban streets and public spaces have traditionally been terrains of conflict and struggle. It must be stated that there is an analogous relation between political and the spatial strategies: the nature of contentions and the physical spaces of their articulation. As movements explicitly aim to avoid official and institutional structures and political channels, the spatial characteristics of the conflict display, for instance, a deviation from 'mainstream' urban spaces, in the case of the squatters. An alternative use of space is justified by the call for changes in practices regarding public space, in the case of cyclist mobilisations and actions for reclaiming the streets. In a third case, a demand is made, by the conservationist movement, for non-material (aesthetic, cultural, community, etc.) values to have priority over capital investment in urban planning. All three cases point at different ways of problematising urban conflicts by environmental movement actors, who constitute a minority of the urban population. Nevertheless, the collective action frames are not articulated in the name of a marginal cultural minority but as grievances of ordinary citizens, and thus resonate as urban injustice frames.

Using pollution as a frame for social action

During communist times, contentious politics were either non-existent or took form only as anti-authoritarian underground illegal activism, such as the *samizdat* movement. The few organizations that were tolerated by the regime consisted of a few environmental groups (exceptional even among those was the MME, the Hungarian Association for the Study of Birds, established in 1974), which became active from the mid-1980s on. The environmental movement can thus be considered to have had a special role in the Hungarian civil arena. The origin of the Hungarian environmental movement is widely accepted to lie in the Danube movement of the late 1980s, in which citizens mobilised against the project of building a dam on the northern part of that river, on the border between Hungary and Slovakia. The campaign was very influential and mobilised tens of thousands of people, mostly because it was closely linked to the (illegal) opposition against the Communist regime. After the fall of the regime and the democratic transition, the movement was not sustained, as the issue was transformed into a foreign affairs issue (Szabó 1994). The Danube movement, however, was important as a departure point for the Hungarian environmental movement. Although the majority of today's groups and actors did not participate in the campaign, they still consider it a starting point for the larger movement. In addition, for long afterwards, green groups nationwide did not succeed in finding a similarly large and important issue to mobilise the masses and realise social-political changes. As a result, the Danube movement marks the point where a common history begins to be constructed. The 1990s were characterised by slow network building in the institutional frames. Professional environmental NGOs were created across the country, and, despite permanent struggles over limited resources, the environmental sector has been relatively successful compared to other spheres of the civil society arena. Yet, for over a decade there were no significant and unified action campaigns, and in particular, no urban issues were addressed.

The breakthrough came in 2004 with a successful campaign (started in 1997 but peaking seven years later) against government plans to build a NATO military radar in a nature reserve on the Zengő hill in the Mecsek mountains. The protest was noteworthy for various reasons. First of all, it inspired a nationwide discourse, involving local residents, political actors, intellectuals, environmental groups, organised NGOs, informal networks and international social movement organisations, while the issue received remarkable media coverage. Secondly, the campaign was successful: in November 2005, after long months of battles, the government finally decided to drop the Zengő project and opted for an alternative location for the military enterprise. This success and the number of people participating led to the action being regarded as a second milestone in the history of the Hungarian environmental movement, after the Danube mobilisations (Kerényi and Szabó 2006). Furthermore, the issue unified actors from the countryside and from the capital, and urban problems were eventually incorporated into the discourse. Initially, the city appeared as the antithesis of a clean and sacralised nature that rises above the chaotic world of the everyday, one that should remain untouched. The city, in this perspective, was referred to as a pragmatic, realistic, but mostly negative attribute: 'the city can only temporarily satisfy our needs, but cannot provide us with the serenity a forest offers' (Vay 2005: 51).

Although the Zengő protests did not involve urban discourses directly, the successful mobilisations inspired environmental and grassroots activism in general, and enriched action repertoires with new techniques, such as articulated civil disobedience, which proved to be a crucial tool throughout the battle over the hill, or the 'boomerang pattern' (Keck and Sikkink 1998) of involving European institutions in the conflict. At least as important was the experience of a successful and powerful mobilisation of a network in itself, where local residents, local activists, conscience constituencies and Brussels-based organisations similarly had their well-defined roles. As the movement actors' scene in Hungary is relatively small, it was not surprising that some of the leading groups in the campaign were Budapest-based organisations. Direct consequences of the successful campaign were not only observable in the actions following the campaign for Zengő, but the activists themselves often talked about it and referred to the victory on the hill as a crucial point in the history of environmental contentions. But a new emphasis on local issues is certainly undeniable – since the successful Zengő campaign, where one of the major issues was the stress on locality and decision-making on a local level, the importance of the direct environment has apparently been brought to the foreground. Local mobilisations, fights for a street section, a square or a local market place have become increasingly professionalised, and received more public attention. Concrete visions and demands for localities were outlined as the Zengő campaign advanced; the shift of focus towards the local as an entity emerged on movement agendas. The following section will review three different patterns of urban grassroots mobilisation, each of which expresses a different type of claim to urban spaces, and their understanding of space is reflected in their action strategies. Even though they might appear quite diverse at first glance, they are all embodiments of local contentions in the city. Besides that, they all emerged around the period or shortly after the Zeng campaign; there is a strong mutual overlap in actors and networks, and, not the least important, they all articulate a certain alternative grassroots vision of the city, where pollution, the basic enemy of the city, is perceived in complex, symbolic ways by identity-based grassroots groups, in all three dimensions described by Castells: urban demands regarding living conditions and collective consumption, local cultural identity and local politics and citizens' participation (Castells 1983).

Alternative use of spaces

One way of experiencing urban spaces and expressing a demand for change has been the movement for reclaiming the streets. The movement's basic argument is that the city belongs to its dwellers, who have the right to live and move in it freely. Cars represent an obvious threat to this claim. Without simplifying the conflict to an opposition between the human and the machine, the activists argue that cars occupy unreasonable proportions of public space, pollute the air, and endanger those who transport themselves in a sustainable way: pedestrians, cyclists, skaters, mothers with prams. In recent years, several street demonstrations have taken place. Activists occupied a busy crossroad in the city centre (a flash mob action of the Radical Pedestrians in April 2006), organised a fiesta in a normally heavily polluted tunnel, covered a huge area with grass, played football and invited musicians (the Young Greens' birthday party in July 2006). The most popular demonstrations are those by Critical Mass (CM), an international cyclist movement initiated in San Francisco in 1992. Cyclists' protests have been organised under this name worldwide since then, with the symbolic message that once cyclists join together, they can take over the roads from the cars. While there were numerous cyclist demonstrations before in Budapest, they were organised by just one group and were rather small, with rarely over a hundred participants, and hardly remarkable. In comparison, thousands of people participated in the first CM demonstration, with an estimated number of over 20,000 activists participating on the car-free days that are usually organised twice a year, in April and in September.

The core of the CM, that is, the organisers, are biking courier and green organisations, whose primary goal is to popularise biking as a means of urban transport. On an analytical level, two layers can be distinguished, of what Kubal (1998: 543), following Goffman, identifies as 'front region' and 'back region' strategies: 'This front region/back region distinction purposefully highlights the contrast between carefully constructed, mass-mediated public frames and the comparably ephemeral frames produced among activists in back region environments.' The CM activists display an observable distinction between public-oriented versus internal discourses. The CM incorporates a dual strategy, where the front region is highly inclusive and addresses the broad masses, while the back region is negotiated among the urban cyclist subcultures and mobilises them beyond the level of biking in the city. In the front region, the strategy and the claims are simple. The goal is to attract increasing numbers of people and convince them that cycling is a pleasant alternative to car driving that is cheap, healthy and environmentally friendly. An additional objective is persuading the authorities to construct more bicycle routes in the city. The back region, however, is much more complex and includes a vision for an alternative city, offering more than a cheap and healthy form of transport: an alternative set of norms and values, an alternative urban lifestyle. Cycling symbolises a conscious attitude to urban life, a demonstration that is in support of sustainable values and, in particular, against the egoistic comfort of the dominant culture.

It is hard to define the cyclists as a community since practically anyone can become a cyclist. The community certainly does not include all of the thousands of people who participate in the CM, but rather those for whom cycling has an identity-forming component. The urban cyclist subculture, in part because it is so heavily influenced by green ideologies, distinguishes itself not only by its means of transport but also by its consumption habits, clothing and the way of spending leisure time, all of which are rejections of the values of the dominant, consumer society. As one activist formulated it, the 'hardliners' of this subculture are:

> those who reckon that the cars should fuck off, the city should be returned to those who live there – pedestrians, mothers with their babies, handicapped, dogs and cats, everyone. It is those who believe that cars, especially in the city, destroy people's life, and who think that there is an alternative, and they can take an active part in it. It has a community spirit, which is connected to the couriers, to a particular spirit, to this Budapest milieu.

Members of the cyclist subculture draw a double 'we and them' line. On one level they distinguish between 'hobby-cyclists' and those for whom biking realises a worldview. The more dominant boundary, however, is between the citizens who live a 'passive' and 'harmful' life, and the conscious cyclists, who do not simply 'use' the city but actively live in it and take on the mission of changing perceptions in favour of a sustainable urban lifestyle. While there is strong solidarity with other cyclists, there is also an 'external solidarity' (Hunt and Benford 2004) towards other groups seen as victims of the 'repressive car culture', such as old people, the disabled, and mothers with prams.

The front region strategy is very non-confrontational and deliberately inclusive; the first communiqué that was circulated, inviting people to join, articulated the desire to change biking attitudes in the city and to encourage better policies that would increase biking. This strategy has no targets or opponents; on the contrary, the first communiqué approached car-drivers with a friendly attitude: 'Many of us do have cars. The event, of course, is not aimed against car-drivers, since according to statistical data most of them are also bike-owners at the same time. Rather, our goal is to promote a sensible way of using cars'.[1] Nevertheless, it is a widely known fact that there is ongoing conflict in the streets between drivers and cyclists, mostly due to the fact that Budapest's bike routes are shared partly with pedestrian walkways and partly with car parking zones.

To the core cyclists, cars do not simply constitute a practical obstacle or an enemy on the road - the car is the symbol of mainstream, materialistic culture. In the background region it is highly unacceptable to drive a car, and while in popular culture the car has become a symbol of wealth and freedom, the activists see cars as a harmful product of the commercialised world. First of all, the car is harmful to the environment (beginning with the production process), so driving a car implies a comfort-oriented, selfish attitude. In addition, cars are seen as a commercial product and driving as an individualist and socially alienating act. Finally, cars are seen as enemies of a sustainable city since they take up too much urban space and are aesthetically disturbing. Many cyclist narratives consist of rumours of having seen their fellows driving a car, and the ridiculous excuses with which the culprits, once exposed, came up. For the 'hardcore', then, cycling is not simply a choice of transport or an eco-friendly alternative to driving a car. It is a symbol of belonging to a conscious community, it is rational, clean, and respectful of others and it is a healthy choice for the individual. But beyond that, it is a social act, and as the slogan says: 'you'll never bike alone'. Cycling as a social act that brings people together, as a political claim for a sustainable, city-friendly means of existence represents a demonstrative act against material embodiments of pollution connected to cars and a value-set that car

---

1. CM flyer – originally in Hungarian./

culture symbolises. The cyclist movement articulates a demand for revaluation of already existing surfaces in the city, and alternative, cleaner ways of using urban spaces. The next section reviews a reverse mobilisation: demands for activating neutral or marginal, underground spaces, alternative uses of certain spaces in the city.

Use of alternative spaces

Another crucial identity-based group within urban mobilisations consists of the squatters, who achieved remarkably dynamic mobilizations in the Budapest between 2004 and 2006. Within the grassroots urban discourse, the squatters represent claims for alternative, underground, out-of-focus spaces with the intention of turning them into lively cultural arenas. The mechanisms involved consist of activating spaces in the city through politicising formerly neutral areas, and creating alternative discourses on rights to use of space. Yet, despite a handful of attempts to occupy empty buildings and turn them into alternative cultural centres, there were no permanently existing squats in Hungary. This makes the squatters a peculiar phenomenon: the fact that the movement actually existed and had an influence on urban underground discourses, despite the lack of a physical space to locate itself, proves that the movement is present predominantly in symbolic spaces. No matter how marginal, there is an indisputable squatter culture that is produced and negotiated continuously, in minds and in discourses. Even though there was no actual squatting practice, the activists were still very concerned about certain norms and draw clear in-group/out-group boundaries.

The first building that appeared on the squatters' agenda was occupied in November 2004 by an informal group called Centrum. The building had previously been a Communist department store, the Úttörő ('Pioneer'), but it not been in use for three years. In the space of a few days, the activists cleaned up the place, did partial renovations (painting walls and connecting the water), and made it suitable for a 'community space'. They organised alternative exhibitions and film projections for about two weeks, before the authorities forced them to leave. Following this, there were a couple of further attempts to establish a squat in Budapest, but neither lasted longer than a few days. There is, however, a basement apartment known as AK57 that functions up to the present day as a squat: it is under control of (but not owned by) a group of young activists, who use it for clubs, meetings, discussions and art workshops. Additionally, every now and then people will live there temporarily. Apart from the club meetings, the activists spend time together in the context of other squat-related or green projects, or meet during different urban underground events. The squatters, then, are not a random group of actors, but a permanent and self-conscious community.

The insiders' rules are stricter than in any other green-related urban community, and are based dominantly on collective identities. In this case, there are no clearly distinguishable front-versus-back region strategies (or if there is a difference, it lies in the style and intensity of the messages). On the contrary, the strategies are developed in terms of strong group consciousness, the very construction of which is in itself a mobilising force. Two tenets dominate the squatters' ideology: the first is opposition to the dominant culture's norms and mechanisms, and the second the strategic avoidance of existing power institutions, referred to collectively as 'the system'. While, in a way, the second point follows from the first, they demonstrate completely different attitudes. The first tenet represents a dialogical relationship, as the movement's ideological values are constructed through reflections on societal values. The second aspect, in contrast, constitutes a complete rejection: the movement consciously ignores influences from institutions of state power, and avoids them in its strategies. Bureaucratic mechanisms are seen as part of the system that exists not to help people but to complicate processes and consequently constrain citizens' initiatives, making them passive recipients. Taking part in an illegal action is in first place a public provocation of authorities, and a demonstrative message to the broader public:

> The establishment of Centrum is in itself a demonstration against the urban policy and the practices in using urban spaces. Centrum demonstrates with its mere existence the demand for redefinition of public spaces and culture, and supports a more articulate care for the city.[2]

Opposed to mainstream society, the squatters often describe themselves as a 'progressive', proactive, dynamic community. Their aim is to construct a community that offers not only an ideological alternative to mainstream societal values and norms, but alternative behaviour as well. This means that in the 'squat' – that is, any temporary squat or AK57 – the activists take all decisions by consensus, deliberately constructing a flat, horizontal group without leaders. While members found it hard to describe the essence of belonging to the squatter community, both internal and the external solidarity are key concepts. The latter is drawn on the basis of social exclusions in the capitalist world, so other powerless, marginal groups in the city, such as homeless young people, alternative artists and social activists, are seen as allies.

2. Author's interviews.

Activist groups of underground artists and street activists could also be considered part of this group, not only due to their various links to the squatter groups but also because of the similarities in their claims to public spaces and understanding of the importance of cultural values versus the overwhelming motives of commerce and global economy in public spaces. Art can thus become a tool of politicisation: alternative or underground art, the least problematic description of which would be the opposite of 'mainstream' art, is often installed or even produced at the squatter centres. Tags, stickers and stencils are spreading all over the city, not necessarily with a specific artistic effect or political message. However, the very act of putting tags into places that were either neutral or used for commerce, in itself demonstrates a political protest against the overwhelming dominance of commercial and business surfaces on otherwise public places. Thus, on the one hand, these manifestations bring the debates on the 'public' into the urban discourse, and, on the other, represent perceptions of cleanliness in the city as 'commerce-free' areas. The last section will examine yet another example and a different approach to articulating pollution versus purity in the city – the mobilisation for conservation of the urban environment.

Conservation of spaces

Apart from seeking underground spaces or promoting their alternative use in the city, Budapest has witnessed urban mobilisations that aim at conservation of different mosaics in the urban environment, be they marketplaces (such as a more recent campaign for keeping the marketplace at Hunyadi square in the sixth district), trees in Nagymez street in the city centre, or old buildings, which tend to fall victim to the local government's contemporary urban planning. The conservationists' struggle is a different kind of effort to create a sustainable city that guarantees spaces for its citizens, and can be symbolised as a clash between profit-oriented functionalism and value-oriented aestheticism, or as the activists formulate it: Stalinist baroque versus cultural values. The urban conservationists do not comprise a permanently active movement or one that organises regular mobilisations. They are reactive, and their primary activity consists of negotiations with authorities (the municipality, the prosecutor's office, urban planners, urban representatives and so on). Protest, and illegal protest in particular, takes place only when negotiations fail.

The urban conservationists are grouped around an organisation called *ÓVÁS!*, established in June 2004 to protest against the tendency in urban planning to prioritise business enterprises and neglect 'non-commercial' values such as aesthetics or authenticity. Under particular threat is the old Jewish district in the city centre, where most houses are over a century old.

Many such buildings had begun to be replaced by so-called 'Stalinist baroque' glass buildings, predominantly office centres at odds with their architectural surroundings. Since the establishment of *ÓVÁS!*, urban conservationism has become an integral part of the urban environmental movement, gaining not only individual supporters but also the backing of a number of organisations, including environmentalist groups, the Art Relic Office and the Jewish religious community. The issue of protecting historical artefacts was also incorporated in the underground movement's agenda, with striking co-operation between the different urban movements. Urban conservationists participate in squatting actions, and joint (underground) art projects and exhibitions are organised. The issue of preserving buildings is also promoted by the cyclists, while the urban conservationists call for a sustainable city that is created to please the citizens, demanding less traffic and an increase of shared spaces (whether parks, playgrounds or alternative cultural centres).

Identity building among protesters (and protectors) is strongly symbolic. The conservationists are not delimited geographically or institutionally; there is no direct correlation with place of residence. Collective identities are outlined using the frame of injustice imposed on the targets, mainly the municipality, and the authorities. As an activist on Indymedia explained it: '[the city] survived two World Wars, Rákosi, Kádár, but the municipality will settle what the World Wars and dictators were unable to cope with.'[3] In the movement's discourse, the municipality is often called 'corrupt' or 'the law-breakers', while the in-group's demands of are very simple: they just want a city that is pleasant to live in. Activist narratives frequently refer to police brutality. The element of civil disobedience, used widely during the Zengő campaign, was clearly present at the conservationists' protests, where activists felt that to break laws in the name of a higher issue was morally acceptable, or even, the right thing to do. Pictures of the (partly) demolished buildings circulate online, on websites, lists and in forwarded emails. The use of aggression is common in narrations describing the 'other side', including extensive descriptions of the act of wrecking buildings.

A major dimension of the border drawn between 'us' and 'them' is the clash of values. While the municipality cares only about short-term profits, the activists fight for morally higher values, such as sustainability and respect for the rights of future generations. As one activist stated: 'These streets should be handed over to their inhabitants, the pedestrians and cyclists. It would change the atmosphere of the area, since the citizens would finally start to own the urban territories.'[4] Abstract values also

3. http://www.budapest.hu/engine.aspx/engine.aspx?page=zsidonegyed
4. http://epiteszforum.hu/?q=node/1065

emerge in the argumentation, including the aesthetic virtues and historical heritage of the endangered buildings that the municipality is accused of ignoring. Paradoxically, the same house at 40 Kiraly Street, that inspired one of the biggest mobilisations, is not generally considered beautiful, as one architect admits,[5] adding that its real value is intangible as the building is connected to a notable architect and was located on historical Budapest's main road. For the conservationist movement, thus, pollution is embodied in the neoliberal policy of local governments, while purity reflects a complex understanding embracing cultural values in the city.

Conclusions

This chapter has reviewed the meanings of pollution as perceived by urban social movements as mobilising frames in the Central European capital city of Budapest. Hungary, as a post-Communist country, does not have a long tradition of civil initiatives, and urban issues, in particular, have only recently begun to be addressed by social movements. Given this context, urban mobilisations typically avoid institutional channels, and function in the border area between legality and illegality. This contribution examined the issue of pollution using the culturalist approach of framing in social movements studies. It presented pollution as a master frame that is conceptualised as an urban injustice in material and symbolic forms, which overlap in causing damage to the city at various levels – from air quality to various unwanted intrusions into urban public spaces. Pollution features on both physical and symbolic levels, outlining a complex set of targets to the movement actors, from urban policy to public awareness and cultural values.

Urban social movements are defined as a loose, non-institutional network of actors, comprising culturally constructed locally conscious groups. Locality is not territorially bounded, but is rooted in urban identities, which, in various forms, mobilise against pollution. The case studies have reviewed three different patterns of mobilisation, which correspond to different spatial experiences and the appropriate understandings of pollution, and accordingly, adapt different strategies of action. The cyclist movement calls for an alternative use of spaces in the city, demanding more space for this city-friendly means of transport, while the use of cars is understood beyond its pragmatic instances. The squatters and underground artists activate alternative spaces through politicising formerly neutral spaces, and mobilise against the neoliberal urban

---

5. Quotation from the first public statement of Centrum.

planning practice of overwhelming urban spaces with commercial motives, and thus polluting the urban landscape and public spaces. The 'conservationist' pattern predominantly claims a reservation of cultural heritage as well as the scarce natural resources in the city.

The spatial demands of the movements reflect perceptions of pollution versus purity/ cleanliness, which do, however, overlap, and as the groups belong to the same urban grassroots family, so do the mobilisation patterns represent different emphases of the same grassroots agenda.

References

Castells, M. 1977. *The Urban Question*. Cambridge: MIT Press.
———1983. *The City and the Grassroots*. Los Angeles: University of California Press.
Douglas, M. 1969 [1966]. *Purity and Danger: An Analysis of the Concepts of Pollution and Taboo*. London: Routledge.
Fainstein, S. 1997. 'Justice, Politics, and the Creation of Urban Space' in *The Urbanization of Injustice*, A. Merrifield and E. Swyngedouw (eds), pp. 18–44. New York: New York University Press.
Fine, G.A. 1995. 'Public Narration and Group Culture: Discerning Discourse in Social Movements' in *Social Movements and Culture*, H. Johnston and B. Klandermans (eds), pp. 127–43. London: UCL Press.
Goffman, E. 1974. *Frame Analysis: An Essay on the Organization of Experience*. New York: Harper and Row.
Hunt, S.A. and R.D. Benford. 2004. 'Collective Identity, Solidarity and Commitment' in *The Blackwell Companion to Social Movements*, D.A. Snow, S.A. Soule and H. Kriesi (eds), pp. 433–55. Oxford: Blackwell.
Keck, M. E. and Sikkink, K. 1998. *Activists Beyond Borders: Advocacy Networks in International Politics*. Ithaca: Cornell University Press.
Kerényi, S. and Szabó, M. 2006. 'Trans-National Influences on Patterns of Mobilisation within Environmental Movements in Hungary', *Environmental Politics* 15 (5): 803–20.
Kubal, T.J. 1998. 'Collective Action Frames', *The Sociological Quarterly* 39 (4): 539–54.
McAdam, D. 1996. 'The Framing Function in Movement Tactics' in *Opportunities, Mobilizing Structures and Framing*, D. McAdam, J.D. McCarthy and M.N. Zald (eds), pp. 338–57. Cambridge: Cambridge University Press.
Merrifield, A. and E. Swyngedouw. 1997. 'Social Justice and the Urban Experience: An Introduction' in *The Urbanization of Injustice*, A. Merrifield and E. Swyngedouw (eds), pp. 1–17. New York: New York University Press.
Rochon, T.R. 1998. *Culture Moves: Ideas, Activism, and Changing Values*. Princeton: Princeton University Press.

Snow, D.A. and R. Benford. 1988. 'Ideology, Frame Resonance, and Participant Mobilization', *International Social Movement Research* 1: 197–217.

————— 1992. 'Master Frames and Cycles of Protest' in *Frontiers in Social Movement Theory*, A. Morris and C. McClurg Mueller (eds), pp. 133–55. New Haven: Yale University Press.

Snow, D.A., E.B. Rochford, Jr., S.K. Worden and R.D. Benford. 1986. 'Frame Alignment Processes, Micromobilization, and Movement Participation', *American Sociological Review* 51 (4): 464–91.

Swidler, A. 1986. 'Culture in Action: Symbols and Strategies', *American Sociological Review* 51 (2): 273–86.

Szabó, M. 1994. 'Greens, Cabbies, and Anti-Communists: Collective Action During Regime Transition in Hungary' in *New Social Movements*, E. Larana, H. Johnston and J.R. Gusfield (eds), pp. 287–303. Philadelphia: Temple University Press.

Tarrow, S. 1998. *Power in Movement: Social Movements and Contentious Politics.* Cambridge: Cambridge University Press.

Vay, M. (ed.) 2005. *Zengő: Ökológia, Politika és Társadalmi Mozgalom a Zengő-konfliktusban. Budapest*: Védegylet.

Williams, R.H. 2004. 'The Cultural Contexts of Collective Action: Constraints, Opportunities, and the Symbolic Life of Social Movements' in *The Blackwell Companion to Social Movements*, D.A. Snow, S.A. Soule and H. Kriesi (eds), pp. 91–115. Oxford: Blackwell.

CHAPTER 8

Cleanness, Order and Security: The Re-emergence of Restrictive Definitions of Urbanity in Europe

JOHANNA ROLSHOVEN[1]

The time to talk about cleanness, order and security has returned: during the past decade, discourse on the urban realm, with respect to its health and unhealthiness, has found new expressions in recent policies of managing public urban space. While there is clearly a quest for clarity and certainty behind the triad of cleanness, order and security, this contribution takes a closer look at the surface phenomenon, which is becoming generalised in Swiss and European towns. Specifically, the so-called *Wegweisungsbestimmungen* in German-speaking countries are examined in order to illustrate the discourse of 'health' and the city, and how these two have been related historically and in the contemporary.

These *Wegweisungsbestimmungen*, bylaws that allow custodians of the law to send people away from specifically defined public spaces, indicate where the process of defining and redefining urban space is headed. They provide the police with the power to restrict certain people from remaining in urban areas, without the need to provide evidence of an offence. These laws relate to the use of urban public space in general and are aimed at tackling the much invoked 'crisis' of the city. This 'crisis' is seen as the outcome of processes of social transformation that are accelerated and condensed in cities. Through these processes, the city has become the primary site for the production of cultural meaning.

1. I am grateful to Rivke Jaffe for her editing of the English in this text.

Harshening police legislation is intended to maintain if not improve 'order and security'. This practice of 'cleaning' by displacing unwanted people is paralleled by another, thematically and aesthetically linked form of control over space: increasing attention to waste management.

Such developments call for a renewed discussion of the dangers associated with urban spaces and places and related security needs. A better understanding is needed of perceptions and emic strategies regarding the use of urban public space, and of the city as a place of unexpected encounters. Using a historical perspective, this contribution analyses the contemporary discourse on the city for *topoi* and characterisations of cleanness, sanitation, health and morals that determine perceptions and practices of urban space and places. In the critique that has accompanied the urban evolution towards modernity, health and the city have always been fundamental mutual references, mirroring society and space. A more microscopic look at everyday urban life will reveal, on the one hand, varying discourses and representations, and on the other hand differing individual practices and perceptual habits. Such an examination reveals how an official discourse of unacceptable living conditions contrasts with the 'natural' ways in which the cities' inhabitants experience and deal with the concrete inconveniences and disorder of everyday life. By examining Swiss, and more broadly European, policies that aim to increase control over public urban space, this chapter analyses the ideologies and power relations that underlie such policies. In practice, order, safety and cleanliness are achieved through the removal of unwanted persons, rather than garbage alone, disregarding the positive effects of chance encounters and a certain randomness in public space on urban liveability. Following a historical overview of discourse on social contagion and urban health, contemporary connections between urban space and morality are explored through the case of *Wegweisungsbestimmungen*, which are in turn situated in a broader European context, characterised by the reemergence of more restricted definitions of urban freedom.

Contagious elements and the epidemiology of social classes

A brief historical overview reveals the basis of contemporary understandings of terms such as cleanness and health. There is an observable shift from a view of air, water and soil as 'natural' pathogenic media, to the differential ascription of 'moral' pathogenicity and the spatial differentiation between social classes in the development of the modern city. There have been two major paradigm shifts in the development of modern urban health policy. The first was a shift in which water, rather than air, came to be seen as the carrier of disease and death; in the second, disease transmission came to be seen as a social question, rather than one of fate.

Until the mid-nineteenth century, issues of hygiene were not a point of discussion, and the connection between individual lifestyle and risk of disease was not recognised. The belief that dirt carries disease only became established around that time, as a consequence of scientific attempts to understand causes of epidemics in the rapidly growing cities. As a result of increased economic interaction with the Middle East, the second cholera pandemic reached European metropolises in 1832. Mortality rates were staggering and in some cases, population losses were so dramatic that the urban population decreased by half. Cholera was a source of great fear and accelerated scientific attempts to comprehend the connections between disease and infection, specifically intensifying medical-scientific research on the mechanisms of transmission and the possibilities of prevention. In the eighteenth century, air was still considered to be the transmitting agent, with, interestingly, no real distinction between population classes. This changed in the nineteenth century, as water became viewed as the conduit for pandemics. New planning ideologies tried to reunite both the geographical and the social 'toilette', as French historian Alain Corbin (1982: 21) notes.

As the science of medical hygiene developed, so did urban sanitation policies, a set of measures aimed to improve urban hygiene. The term 'sanitation' began to emerge not only in medical reports, but in the writings of social reformers, architects, business people and journalists as well. The deodorisation of public space, a measure derived from the miasma theory around 1800, led to sanitation policies that might appear quite modern, including the recommendation to demolish fortresses and widen streets, so that air could flow freely into the city.

In Paris, around 1800, recommendations were made, in the interest of deodorisation, to build large squares and wide streets, tear down the old city fortifications and clean the city regularly. Citizens became obligated to sweep in front of their door, while garbage collection and public toilets emerged as new institutions. The remodelling of Paris by Hausmann can be seen as a first instance of gentrification, as it drove the poor out of the city centre and, since they were an unattractive sight, forbade them to spend time in the newly created boulevards. Twenty years earlier, plans had been discussed in which beggars and convicts would have to work as road sweepers, following the example of Switzerland. Corbin (1982: 126) quotes a 1780 report by Antoine L. Lavoisier, who wrote admiringly that Bern was the cleanest city he had ever seen. Every morning, 'convicts chained to the shafts [pull] large four-wheel carts through the streets ... female convicts are tied with longer and lighter chains to the carts ... partly to sweep the streets, partly to load the refuse'.[2]

---

2. Corbin cites this proposal by Abbé Bertholon from Montpellier.

Early notions of urban health

As a modern idea of health evolved, so did the idea of individualised, 'industrialised' Man (Dauskardt and Gerndt 1993). This concept of Man emerged in close relation to notions of cleanness and security, linked to the origins and the reshaping of the modern city. Authorities focussed on the triad of dirt, disease and immorality, as they began to imagine a clean population. The history of the Modern city shows how the discourse of Modern plagues has always located these problems in towns. In the nineteenth century, the catalogue of nuisances encompassed bad air, diseases, epidemics, the masses, poverty, dirt and death. In the twentieth century main concerns came to include migration, traffic and pollution. In both historical periods, 'the urban question' was essentially identified with the issues of property and security. These two terms are paradigmatic and lead in a fairly straightforward way to the ambiguous term of 'sanitation' (*Sanierung*), which, in the context of conflicts over the use of urban space, has a semantic relation with *Wegweisung*.

The term sanitation and its variants have been used in historical and contemporary contexts with regard to urban buildings and infrastructures as well as people. The ambiguity that the term has retained is apparent in the contexts of its use.[3] Its use began to occur in Europe towards the end of the eighteenth century, with the emergence of urban health policy. In the nineteenth century, social reform, mass rural-urban migration and ensuing urban conditions aroused scientific interest and led to the development of new academic disciplines, shaping a common basis for health and urban planning policies. The enormous influx of people from the countryside following industrialisation forced municipal authorities to take measures to prevent the worsening of unhealthy conditions in their overpopulated low-income neighbourhoods. The population of Berlin, for example, went from 200,000 inhabitants in 1820 to twice that in the course of twenty years (Korff 1985: 345).[4] In Paris, the population increased from one to two million between 1841 and 1870 (Girouard 1987: 297).[5] The policies following migration to the cities shaped urban development throughout Europe from the second half of the

3. Interestingly in German *Sanierung* and *Assanierung* are synonymous. However, the latter word is rarely seen, and more often in the formerly Austro-Hungarian Eastern Central European context. See Keberlova (2002).
4. In the 1830s, Berlin's population increased annually by 6,000 to 7,000 inhabitants, but by the 1840s this tripled to 18,000 to 20,000 per year (Korff 1985: 345).
5. New York went from 200,000 inhabitants in 1830 to 7 million in 1930, while Chicago went from fifty inhabitants in 1830 to 3,376,000 in 1930 (Girouard 1987: 303).

nineteenth century on. Prague, Vienna, Cologne, Paris, Caen – to list just a few well-known examples – were subject to massive restructuring, intended to systematically clear the congested medieval city centres, replacing them with new, profitable and hygienic buildings. In Switzerland, this process occurred on a smaller scale due to the lack of large cities.

In Prague, the focus of the sanitation (*Assanierung*) was Josefstadt, an old Jewish neighbourhood. In the process, and in accordance with the anti-Semitic climate of the late nineteenth century, the poor population was evicted. In this manner, the sanitation came to include a 'rectification' of the population, to be followed by other gruesome measures, including those under Fascism in the 1930s and 1940s. More recently, *Assanierung* or ethnic cleansing featured in the International Court of Justice's cases on genocide in former Yugoslavia. Such examples demonstrate the lethal nature of the double meaning of 'cleansing'.

Topography and morals

The sources available on nineteenth century urban development show how, increasingly, a connection was made in the consciousness of the general urban bourgeoisie between topography and morals. In these early urban studies, investigative and controlling activities were intertwined.[6] Similar to other statistics related to ideas of a national economy during the Enlightenment (Rolshoven 1991: 41ff), this new type of social research saw itself as providing a rational disclosure of reality in order to optimise socio-political interventions. In its terminology and its aim, the survey – a basic urban research tool from the outset – demonstrates how methods of recording and control merged (Lindner 2004: 11).

Fundamental to the connection between urban space and morality was the dependence and the lack of rights ascribed to the non-propertied classes: a process of ascription necessary to legitimise the process of civilisation. We can only consider ourselves civilised if we construct an image of what is uncivilised. The development of urban settlements supported this process as industrialisation led to a more marked urban pattern of socio-spatial segregation than ever before. Dividing the proletariat from the bourgeoisie in urban space produced a 'geography of inequality', which increasingly minimised encounters between the social classes in public space (Sambale and Veith 1998: 38). This was not the case

---

6. Lindner (2004: 13) points to this connection as part of the 'panoptic regime' described by Foucault.

everywhere, and some cities in the northern Mediterranean were exceptions. The industrial town of Barcelona, for instance, is held as an example of integration due the concept of to its urban planning, promoted by the Catalonian urban planner Ildefons Cerdá in the nineteenth century (Hofer 2005).

By the end of the nineteenth century, urban water supply and sewage disposal installations were remodelled. Tap water and water closets became heralds of modern living, and as the bourgeois and the working classes became segregated, differences in lifestyle and health increased. Dirt (as the absence of water) and disease began to be linked to character and lifestyle, as physical work, poverty and dirt were seen as causally related. As Edwin Chadwick, a leading British proponent of the concept of sanitation, wrote in 1842: 'The hotbeds of fever and the places of physical disrepair are at the same time the sites of moral corruption, of untidiness and of crime' (quoted in Lindner 2004: 20).

Medical and moral discourse merged, as surveys of canal workers' health were followed by surveys of prostitutes' health, and swamps of fever and swamps of sin were seen to coincide (Lindner 2004: 25). Earlier urban studies aimed to document social disorder and to remedy the deleterious consequences of the overcrowded neighbourhoods and housing in which the poor population lived. It was noted, even before the March Revolution of 1848, that a crowd of people could also represent revolt, and that ideas and practices hostile to the existing society could be as contagious as physical disease (Lindner 2004: 27). With increasing frequency, scholars pointed to the 'danger of social vapours', or social infection (Corbin 1982: 69). The bourgeois became increasingly worried by the social, more than the natural causes of disease, as risk of infection became understood in literal as well as figurative terms.

Semantics and restricting public space

The bourgeois mentality which functions as the heritage of the concept of sanitation led to moralistic as well as practical, infrastructural measures. Realising the 'clean city' is, then, more than the pragmatic attention given to garbage. It is also an aesthetic imperative that considers which city inhabitants are legitimate within the projected image of the city. In this, expressions of spatial control, which also form the basis for sanitation, become manifest. In recent years, discussions on the use of urban space indicate the emergence of newly articulated discriminatory discourse. While this is not new either in Europe or the Americas, the economic developments of late modernity frame such discourse in a new manner. In German-speaking countries, a central term in this is the neologism *Wegweisung* ('sending away'). This ambiguous term, with many potential applications, has become part of the semantics of the urban space that frames our linguistic and physical movements (see also Rolshoven 2008).

The *Wegweisungsbestimmungen*, the regulations for sending people away, are legitimised by notions of security, order and cleanness. These regulations are partly new, and partly reactivated bylaws, which had been declared obsolete in the era of progressive modernist urban policy. The possibility of sending people away involves curtailing civic liberties, including the freedom of assembly and freedom of action. In Germany, for instance, a vagrancy law (*Landstreicherparagraph*) that defined non-residence as an offence, was created under Nazism but invalidated in the early 1970s. Yet the proposed – but recently rejected – constitution of the European Union calls for the reintroduction of this kind of laws.

In recent times, the idea of *Wegweisung* was especially observable in Switzerland, where these regulations were decreed in several cities as part of municipal police laws.[7] In Bern, for instance, they were applied in particular to the main train station and its surroundings. But in general the term has proliferated in the German-language countries. In Switzerland, Germany and Austria, a *Wegweisung* is a provisional court order prohibiting a potentially violent husband or father to come near his wife or children. In Switzerland, the term *Wegweisung* is also an act of the immigration police (*fremdenpolizeiliche Massnahme*), concerning the rejection of applications for asylum and usually accompanied by expulsion from the country. In Switzerland, *Wegweisung* also refers to expulsion from school (*Schulverweis*), an issue of increasing concern. In Germany, in contrast, the official term for being expelled from school is in some cases Rückholung, implying that those who skip classes must be brought back to school, if necessary by the police. In Austria, *Wegweisung* is also applied to the removal of trespassers in prohibited military areas (*Militärbefugnisgesetz*).

While the term, notion and practice appear rather Swiss, they are in fact quite international. In certain parts of Austria, unwelcome loiterers are persecuted by a contested *Landessicherheitsgesetz* passed in January 2005, whereas in Germany this group falls partly under the road-safety laws.

7. Bern, the Swiss capital was one of the first cities to decree such laws in 1988. In 2004 and 2005, 967 *Wegweisungen* were issued with 2,435 charges (Grünes Bündnis Bern 2006). The total revision of the police regulations in St. Gallen was accepted on 5 June 2005 with a surprisingly clear vote with 66 per cent voting in favour, despite the intense debate. Under the new regulations, the suspicion by itself of a threat to security and public order is sufficient for up to fourteen days of imprisonment. The town's police commander argued that St. Gallen was to become the region's safest and cleanest town. See *Die Wochenzeitung* 24, 16 June 2005, p. 6.

In certain areas, the police are already known for the semi-illegal practise of apprehending vagrants, transporting them to the edge of the metropolitan area and abandoning them there. Such actions are known in police insider terms as 'junkie jogging' or the 'Frankfurt city-cleaning policy'. There is a broader European trend to create new legal bases for such practices, but this is accompanied by a movement to strongly oppose this trend, through political and other means. For instance, a German law passed in 2002, the Prohibition of Entering and Loitering (*Betretungs- und Aufenthaltsverbot*), aimed in particular at the 'punk scene' in the Karlsruhe Kronenplatz, had to be repealed eighteen months later following an Administrative Court decision.[8]

In France, the law is changing towards more restrictive regulations. A decade ago, the Mayor of Strasbourg Catherine Trautmann, together with Pierre Bourdieu, Salman Rushdie and Toni Morrison, publicly called for a reinstatement of the traditional role of cities as spheres of civic freedom. Yet, more recently, a new treaty was signed in Strasbourg, ensuring coordination between local and national police, and giving the municipal police more liberties, particularly to prosecute unwanted groups – the marginal public (*le public marginal*) of beggars, drunks and loiterers – and remove them from public space. Again, this is an illustration of the aim of establishing cleanness and security.

In 2003, the British Parliament approved the Labour government's Anti-Social Behaviour Action Plan, the wording of which immediately revealed its political function. Polls show, for instance, that every third citizen in the UK considers loitering young people a major problem.[9] The discourse on anti-social behaviour enables the legal prosecution of behaviour that is not necessarily criminal but that is considered a nuisance (Blair 2000; Hooper and White 2000). Anti-social behaviour, according to British law includes:

> nuisance neighbours, rowdy and nuisance behaviour, yobbish behaviour and intimidating groups taking over public spaces, vandalism, graffiti and flyer-posting, people dealing and buying drugs on the street, people dumping rubbish and abandoning cars, begging and anti-social drinking, the misuse of fireworks.[10]

---

8. See *Amtliche Bekanntmachung der Stadt Karlsruhe*, July 2002, §§ 1, 3, 5, 6, 7, 49, 60 Abs. 1 u. 66, Abs. 2 des Polizeigesetzes von Baden-Württemberg (reproduced in http://www.heypunk.de/Artikel/punkverbot/, accessed 1 September 2006). For legal commentary on the Germany situation, see Hutter (1998); Simon (2001); Krebs (1991).

9. BBC Action Network, http://www.bbc.co.uk/dna/actionnetwork/A2283824. Accessed on 16 August 2006.

10. Home Office, http://www.homeoffice.gov.uk/anti-social-behaviour/what-is-asb/. Accessed on 16 August 2006.

Such definitions of anti-social behaviour share the connotations of the term *asozial* which was coined during the Third Reich (Sedlaczek et al 2004: 87ff). At the time, it indicated homeless, migrating and in part unemployed people, and implicitly allowed for them to be controlled, from registration to internment to annihilation. The term slowly began to lose this meaning in the post-war period, but after the 1970s, the word *asozial* started to become part of everyday language again and was increasingly used to denote young people, from hippies to punks. Adolescents, whether as individuals or groups, are most likely to be condemned for 'anti-social' behaviour in urban public space. A recent anthropological study in Graz described 'marginal' people as varied groups of mainly socially disadvantaged adolescents and young adults, including many from broken homes, as well as drop-outs and unemployed youth (Reiners et al. 2006: 22). These are joined by sympathisers from 'normal' circumstances – young people who approach them out of curiosity or teenaged rebellion – as well as drug users and those who have abandoned their original social context and for whom this kind of peer group functions as a survival mechanism (Reiners et al. 2006: 75–98). The symbolic dimension becomes evident when such small groups are compared to the total urban population. The core of these loose social groups numbers no more than some thirty people in Graz's city centre, compared to a total population of over 250,000. In Bern, the marginal group counts about sixty members, in relation to more than 125,000 inhabitants plus over 100,000 daily commuters.[11] Whether such groups are labelled as tramps, louts or punks makes little difference; these definitions follow local slang, regional taxonomic traditions or national jargon. Official language sometimes demonstrates the bureaucratic pains taken to neutralise discriminating terms, for instance the French acronym 'SDF' for *sans domicile fixe* (without permanent residence). Such efforts do not, of course, manage to negate the stigma attached to those considered undesirable in urban space.

Cultural change and urban transformation

To summarise briefly: the stigma attached to marginal urban groups and their framing as socially disruptive elements appears to be a phenomenon that has resurfaced in various European urban contexts. Depending on political ideology, municipal governments address marginal groups in different ways. The case studies described here demonstrate that cause and effect may become confused in the process. The British Anti-Social Behaviour Campaign, the French Fight Against Incivilities (Vidal-Naquet

---

11. Sources: www.graz.at; www.statistik.bern.ch; and www.pendlerstatistik.-admin.ch/. Accessed 25 and 27 August 2006.

and Tiévant 2005) and the Zurich Campaign for Safety, Intervention and Prevention, are all used to combat the phenomena of disorder. But are they really well-meaning initiatives meant to help urban residents deal with the burden of the increasingly heterogeneous urban population? Are they, so to speak, anti-uncertainty campaigns? Or are they repressive measures leading back to a pre-modern legal system in which the propertied classes determine the legal status of the individual, signifying a creeping infringement on the basic rights of the poor?

I am neither willing nor able to answer this question here but can analyse the ambiguity of any possible answer. The much-discussed 'urban crisis' is related to processes of global transformation that are accompanied by fundamental uncertainties. The effects of the global economy are clearest in urban centres, where one encounters divided labour markets, the skewed socio-spatial distribution of wealth and poverty, expanding informal economies, and competition for urban space including inner-city gentrification. In short, urban spaces have become socially polarised, accompanied by the 'marginalisation of all those groups that do not figure in the representation of the economic centre as a global growth-machine with a secure future' (Berking 2002: 14). This image, which hides from view the losers within this growth, represents the legacy of the modernisation drive and demonstrates the inability of integration in post-Fordist cities.

The clean and safe city as a remedy

As outlined previously, the concerns of urban citizens and authorities shifted over time from fears of physical pollution to fears of social contagion, and contagion began to be understood in both in a physical-natural and a figurative-symbolic sense. This historical mentality is still recognisable in contemporary notions of sanitation, which still include moral measures that go beyond technical or aesthetic forms of urban planning. An examination of present-day ideas of a 'clean city' reveals how the pragmatic attention given to garbage implies a certain control over urban space prefigured by the concept of sanitation. A discourse analysis of the self-representations of European cities reveals the following parameters of the 'clean and safe city' of today.

First, there has been an observable increase in anti-littering campaigns, ranging from local slogans such as 'We keep Lower Austria clean!' to online fora such as Cleanuptheworld.org that take responsibility for keeping the entire world clean. Beyond practical matters of recycling, there have been conspicuous investments in the number, function and design of urban refuse containers. The formation of garbage patrols, monitoring the correct use of garbage containers or compost facilities, demonstrates the level of behavioural control sought. Another development is the discussions on the feasibility of forcing delinquents, the unemployed, or asylum seekers to clean public spaces. A prominent example in the media was British singer Boy George's sentence, following drug possession, to do volunteer work for the New York garbage collection services (CNN 2006). Under the label of urban security, waste patrols and police and para-police patrols increasingly focus on dispersing aesthetically disturbing groups of people, assisted by video surveillance systems in public space. Since the early 1990s, and increasingly after 11 September 2001, Britain has become the West's most equipped nation with respect to video surveillance, installing 4.2 million CCTV cameras or 'one for every fourteen people' (Murakami Wood 2006: 8, after McCahill and Norris 2003). These help document and prosecute violations of litter laws and the prohibited loitering of specific groups in public space. Furthermore, current discourses from architecture and urban planning display a fondness for 'straightening' and 'clearing up', creating large open spaces and long open axes of boulevards and using 'the new simplicity' of openness and transparency as guiding principles.

To illustrate the tendencies above with an example, the controversies surrounding the redesigning of Graz's main square show how such attempts at 'clearing up' are accompanied by processes of gentrification and invisible mechanisms of exclusion, aimed at those who are different or considered bothersome social elements. The architects commissioned to redesign the square wanted to 'open' and 'clear', providing a new pavement and removing benches. The new square is popular with everyone, including a small group of young people, labelled punks, who love to hang out there on a daily basis. The Styrian parliament, under pressure from the Mayor of Graz – who had called the main square his 'living room' – felt moved to adopt a new provincial security law, which charges 'offensive behaviour' and 'annoyance' in the public sphere with fines up to €2,000 or fourteen days of imprisonment. This enables the police to remove people with force if necessary, while the names of violators are registered by the office of social affairs (Reiners et al. 2006: 22ff, 43ff). As in the Swiss towns of Bern, Zurich, Winterthur and St. Gallen, it is argued that such measures are necessary to ensure pedestrians' sense of security and a positive shopping atmosphere and to prevent shop owners from suffering losses.

This last example shows how public space has increasingly become subordinated to private interests. The design measures implemented and the ensuing controversies attest to this in this and other examples, including the redesign of Bern's main station square or the decorating of Zurich's main shopping street with life-size lions, cows or teddy-bears. This international urban trend threatens to displace older models of urban planning, in which the city was envisaged as a community and a living space for heterogeneous groups. The presence of people from the margins of society contributes to social polarisation just by the idea that they might constitute a threat. Unlike their pre-modern precursors, the late-modern urban tramps have an active command of their image and they claim their own place in society. Their public 'appearance' on the stage that urban space provides follows ritualised sequences and staged patterns, while the fact of an ever-present audience is taken into consideration. 'The people have to see that we exist', a Bern 'punk' told a journalist.[12]

We are perched on the threshold of a new spatial order that must also be newly negotiated. Society's increasing complexity brings about a corresponding differentiation of spatial functions, and administrative responsibility for public urban space has become problematic. The borders between public and private are increasingly blurred and open to redefinition, while a segregative tendency towards privatisation can be detected in the design of public spaces. As Hanno Rauterberg (2002) notes, in a plea for the sovereignty of the public sphere, the difference between one's living room and the market place has become increasingly vague. In renegotiating the organisation of competences and responsibilities in new spatial orders, ideally all stakeholders should be represented. In this process of negotiation, many planners and architects have functioned as stooges of the new urban spatial order, aiding what Swiss architect Elisabeth Blum has called 'practices of dropping solidarity'. Poverty and homelessness are made invisible through the cleaning and standardising of public space (Blum 1996: 20ff). In such a context, urban space no longer serves as a setting for encounter and exchange, but as an aestheticised space of transition. When architectural frames no longer facilitate meetings between those who belong and those who do not, experiences with and from the urban Other become impossible. Assessments of the Other are based less and less on immediate experience and knowledge, and drift into 'imagined knowledge' (Gans 1995), fostering prejudice and stigmatisation.

Conclusion

What are the parameters for urban health[13] with respect to socio-spatial qualities? How can cultural studies contribute to a more sensitive architecture and urban planning? Historically, the characteristics of modern cities have been their openness and the possibility of unexpected encounters. A 'non-directional communication in open social structures' (Selle 2002: 16) was seen as a defining urban feature. Architect and sculptor Christoph Haerle (1997: 187) argues that the architectural form of public space must be modelled on a degree of indeterminateness and anonymity. Such models must allow the actual uses of public space to deviate from

12. *Die Wochenzeitung* 48, 15 November 2004, p. 27.
13. The Athens Declaration for Healthy Cities proposed the improvement of the city dwellers' health on the basis of the four key principles of equity, sustainability, intersectoral cooperation, and solidarity.
See http://www.euro.who.int/AboutWHO/Policy/20010917_1.

what is intended and enable the experience of cultural diversity and Otherness. It is in these forms of public space that physical encounters along with communication and even socialisation can occur (Wilson 1992).

The central mission in creating a healthy city, then, is to provide a public sphere. Developing and maintaining it should be one of the core applications of local policy. Public spaces are the basis for the appeal of a healthy city as urban culture is defined, according to urban planner Klaus Selle (2002: 19), by 'liveability, aesthetic quality and use of the public spaces'. Local policy must, therefore, enable citizens to sustain experiences with the Other; following Lévinas (1999). Another central task in ensuring a healthy city is to inform, and this task should not be left to road safety laws and police orders. How to develop and maintain the quality of public spaces cannot be devised at by committees (Breckner 2001: 145) but requires an understanding of planning that is able to take an 'eye level' approach (Lang 2000: 59) to historically shaped perceptions of everyday life.

References

Ayass, W. 2004. ' "Asozial" und "gemeinschaftsfremd": Wohnungslose in der Zeit der nationalsozialistischen Diktatur', *wohnungslos* 46 (3): 87–90.

Berking, H. 2002. 'Global Village oder urbane Globalität? in Städte im Globalisierungsdiskurs, H. Berking and R. Faber (eds), pp. 11–25. Würzburg: Königshausen und Neumann.

Blair, T. 2000. 'Values and the Power of Community'. Lecture at Tübingen University, 30 June 2000.

Blum, E. 1996. 'Wem gehört die Stadt? Stadt und Städtebau im Umbruch' in *Wem gehört die Stadt? Armut und Obdachlosigkeit in den Metropolen*, E. Blum (ed.), pp. 19–50. Basel: Lenos.

Breckner, I. 2001. 'Verlust des öffentlichen Raumes? Zukunft der Städte in Zeiten der Globalisierung' in *Zukunft Stadt: Die Stunde der Bürger in Zeiten der Globalisierung*, W. Schuster and W. Dettling (eds), pp. 133–45. Stuttgart: Hohenheim.

Buciek, K. 2004. 'The Un-Healthy and Misplaced Other' in *A Space Odyssey*, J.O. Baerenholdt and K. Simonsen (eds), pp. 183–96. Aldershot: Ashgate.

CNN. 2006. 'Boy George Snarls at Media during Trash Duty: 80s Icon Serving 5 Days of Community Service'. 14 August 2006. Accessed on 24 August 2006 at http://www.cnn.com/2006/SHOWBIZ/Music /08/14/boy.george.ap/index.html.

Corbin, A. 1984 [1982]. *Pesthauch und Blütenduft: Eine Geschichte des Geruchs*. Berlin: Wagenbach.

Dauskardt, M. and H. Gerndt (eds). 1993. *Der industrialisierte Mensch: Vorträge des 28. Deutschen Volkskundekongresses in Hagen, 7.–11. October 1991*. Münster: Ardey.

Gans, Herbert J. 1995. *The War against the Poor: The Underclass and Antipoverty Policy*. New York: Basic Books.

Girouard, M. 1987. *Die Stadt, Menschen, Häuser, Plätze*. Frankfurt and New York: Campus.

Grünes Bündnis Bern. 2006. *Anpassung der Wegweisungspraxis an neu festgelegte rechtliche Vorgaben und Einleitung des Verzichts auf ihre Anwendung*, 1 June 2006. http://www.gb-aves.ch/gbstadt-bern/vorstoesse/2006/anpassung-der-wegweisungspraxis-an-neu-festgelegte-rechtliche-vorgaben-und-einleitung-des-verzichts-auf-ihre-anwendung/index.html. Accessed on 16 August 2006.

Haerle, C. 1997. 'Stadt aussen Raum' in *Stadt im Umbruch: Chaos Stadt?*, B. Zibell and T. Gürtler-Berger (eds), pp. 185–212. Zürich: vdf Hochschulverlag AG.

Hofer, A. 2005. 'Barcelona – du Schöne!', *Die Wochenzeitung* 23, 9 June 2005, p. 20.

Hooper, J. and M. White. 2000. 'Blair Wants On-The-Spot Fines for Louts', *Guardian Unlimited*, 1 July 2000. Accessed on 16 August 2006 at http://www.guardian.co.uk/uk_news/story/0,3604,338584,00.html.

Hutter, J. 1998. 'Wem gehört die Strasse? Kritische Anmerkungen zur neuen Ordnungs- und Sicherheitspolitik', *Rundbrief der Deutschen Vereinigung für Jugendgerichte und Jugendgerichtshilfen e.V.*, *Bremer Regionalgruppe* 4: 1–5.

Keberlova, D. 2002. 'Drei hohe kommunistische Funktionäre zur bedingten Freiheitsstrafe verurteilt', Radio Praha, 12 February 2002, 19:12 UTC. Access on 17 August 2006 at http://www.radio.cz/de/nachrichten-/24041.

Korff, G. 1985. 'Mentalität und Kommunikation in der Grossstadt: Berliner Notizen zur "inneren" Urbanisierung' in *Grossstadt: Aspekte empirischer Kulturforschung*, T. Kohlmann and H. Bausinger (eds), pp. 343–61. Berlin: Staatliche Museen Preußischer Kulturbesitz.

Krebs, T. 1991. *Platzverweis: Städte im Kampf gegen Aussenseiter*. Tübingen: Tübinger Vereinigung für Volkskunde.

Lang, B. 2000. 'Zur Ethnographie der Stadtplanung' in *Kulturwissenschaftliche Stadtforschung*, W. Kokot, T. Hengartner and K. Wildner (eds), pp. 55–68. Berlin: Reimer.

Lévinas, E. 1999. *Alterity and Transcendence*, trans. M. B. Smit. New York: Columbia University Press.

Lindner, R. 2004. *Walks on the Wild Side: Eine Geschichte der Stadtforschung*. Frankfurt: Campus.

McCahill M. and C. Norris. 2003. 'Estimating the Extent, Sophistication and Legality of CCTV in London' in *CCTV*, M. McGill (ed.), pp. 51–66. London: Perpetuity Press.

Rauterberg, H. 2002. 'Wohnzimmer ist überall', *Die Zeit*, 10 January 2002, p. 33.

Reiners, D., G. Malli and G. Reckinger. 2006. *Bürgerschreck Punk: Lebenswelten einer unerwünschten Randgruppe*. Vienna: Löcker.

Rolshoven, J. 1991. *Provencebild mit Lavendel*. Bremen: Edition CON.

————— 2008. 'Die Wegweisung: Züchtigung des Anstössigen oder Die Europäische Stadt als Ort der Sauberkeit, Ordnung und Sicherheit' in *Intimität*, W. Egli and I. Tomkowiak (eds), pp. 35–58. Zürich: Chronos.

Sambale, J. and D. Veith. 1998. 'Der Raum als Beute: Sozialräumliche Konflikte in Berlin', *Berliner Blätter* 17: 35–50.

Sedlaczek, D., T. Lutz, U. Puvogel and I. Tomkowiak (eds). 2005. *'Minderwertig' und 'asozial': Stationen der Verfolgung gesellschaftlicher Aussenseiter.* Zürich: Chronos.

Selle, K. (ed.). 2002. *Was ist los mit den Öffentlichen Räumen? Analysen, Positionen, Konzepte.* AGB Berichte 49. Dortmund: Dortmunder Vertrieb für Bau- und Planungsliteratur.

Simon, T. 2001. *Wem gehört der öffentliche Raum? Zum Umgang mit Armen und Randgruppen in Deutschlands Städten.* Opladen: Leske und Budrich.

Vidal-Naquet, P.A. and S. Tiévant. 2005. 'Incivilités et travail de civilité', *Les Cahiers de la sécurité* 57 (2): 13–31.

Wilson, E. 1992. *The Sphinx in the City: Urban Life, The Control of Disorder, and Women.* Berkeley: University of California Press.

Wood, David Murakami (ed.). 2006. *A Report on the Surveillance Society. (Full Report).* For the Information Commissioner by the Surveillance Studies Network, http://www.ico.gov.uk/upload/documents/-library/data_protection/practical_application/surveillance_society_full_report_2006.pdf. Accessed on 20 September 2007.

CHAPTER 9

Social Equity and Social Housing Densification in Glen Innes, New Zealand: A Political Ecology Approach

KATHRYN SCOTT, ANGELA SHAW AND CHRISTINA BAVA

Introduction

New urbanism is characterised as concerned with sustainability in our cities and towns, with a focus on more compact forms of development. Compact, mixed-use, pedestrian-friendly developments are intended to reduce urban sprawl and reliance on cars, increase uptake of public transport, provide 'vibrant' public spaces, and make more 'liveable' communities. Increased levels of social interaction and cultural activities are also perceived to result from densification (Williams 1999). Spatial changes to urban form are therefore intended to improve social, economic and environmental sustainability in urban areas.

In the Brundlant Report (WCED 1987), social aspects of sustainability were expressed through references to equity within and across nations and also between generations. Yet investigations into social sustainability in urban areas have been guided by a planner's view of the world – city scale and spatially determined. The focus has been on whether the 'compact city' lives up to the promise of improved 'liveability', with attention given to social cohesion and social capital. Where social equity is investigated it is often limited to questions of access to services and facilities. Issues of access to jobs and poverty transcend city boundaries and are therefore outside the scope of liveability planning.

Glen Innes, a highly marginalised suburb of Auckland, New Zealand, was one of the first suburbs to be targeted for more compact development. Following international trends, liveability planning processes were undertaken to accommodate growth and improve liveability for residents. Ethnographic research in Glen Innes revealed competing definitions of what would make the place more 'liveable'. Fears about housing intensification (as it is known in New Zealand) ranged from future 'slumification' to gentrification. Despite positive feedback from state tenants living in the first social housing development in Glen Innes to be intensified, other residents continued to prophesy about such developments becoming 'future slums'.

Planning discourses of liveability draw heavily on social capital discourse and often ignore a long history of social science critique, relying instead on notions of 'community' as unitary, bounded societies, and ignoring issues of power, change, pluralism and conflict (e.g. Cohen 1985; Young 1986; Strathern 1982). Competing definitions of liveability and reinforcement of existing power relations revealed during liveability planning processes in Glen Innes are a clear example of this, and can be explored with reference to Douglas' (1970) concept of cultural pollution. Changes to the built environment create a threat to existing cultural values, requiring a reassessment of dangers and risks. Fears that intensification will endanger human health and safety are constructed through discourses of pollution and defilement; state tenants, for example, are constructed as the 'Other', 'people out of place'.

Examining the production of meanings and identities through discursive practices leaves some questions unanswered, however. As it was focused at a suburban scale and did not address entrenched poverty and social segregation, residents saw liveability planning as mere 'window dressing'. All stakeholders expressed collective anxiety that increased spatial concentration of poverty and vulnerability to future policy changes could result in the sale of state houses to passive investors.

A political ecology approach to social sustainability in our cities and towns investigates the relationship between the environment, social equity and the power to understand changes to urban form. This chapter uses this approach to examine the discourses and material conditions shaping the built environment, and effectively reinforcing existing power relations in Glen Innes.

Political Ecology

Environmental anthropologists develop knowledge of how culture mediates the relationship between environment and human societies, demonstrating that problems and solutions to environmental problems are 'as much cultural as they are physical or biological' (Milton 1996: 224). While recognising complexity and ambiguity, political ecology provides a framework for analysing the relationship between environmental change, historical political processes and socio-economic outcomes (Keil 2003).

Political ecology merges concerns with ecosystems and social equity (Harper 2004) and investigates the ways in which the environment 'serves as a locus for the enactment and perpetuations of patterns of inequality' (Brosius 1999: 280). Methodologically, political ecology investigates discursive, material, social and cultural dimensions of the human-environment relation from multiple scales of analysis: from the micro-scale of everyday life through to the macro-level national and global structural dimensions (Escobar 1999; Harper 2004).

The emerging field of urban political ecology is concerned with the 'interwoven knots of social process, material metabolism and spatial form that go into the formation of contemporary urban socio-natural landscapes' (Swyngedouw and Heynen 2003: 906, in Keil 2003: 727). Urban political ecologists have used critical social theory to challenge more positivist planning and policy-oriented perspectives that underpin much of the urban sustainability literature (Keil 2003), and to focus on social inequality and power as fundamental to understanding changes to the built environment. This provides a framework for the analysis of Glen Innes ethnographic data. Discourses of liveability are contextualised within historical political processes that have shaped material conditions within the built environment, and pathways are tracked between micro- and macro-scales. First, the ways in which social equity is examined in relation to urban form are reviewed, followed by the context of changing urban form in Glen Innes.

Social equity and urban form

Bramley et al. (2006) distinguish two core ways in which the relationship between social sustainability and urban form is examined: social equity (access to jobs, services and affordable housing) and 'sustainability of community' (social networks, community participation, sense of place, community stability and security). Investigations into social equity, like policy discourses of liveability, have been at a city scale and spatially determined. Compact and mixed-use settlements are seen as more socially equitable. Higher population densities are said to make local facilities and services more viable, and therefore provide more equitable access to goods and services (Williams 1999). Cultural values, practices and aspirations related to urban form and open space have, however, received little examination, and social justice issues have been narrowly focused on issues perceived as related to urban form.

Burton (2003), for example, investigated social equity outcomes in twenty five 'compact' UK cities and concluded such cities have the potential to promote social equity, particularly in redeveloped urban areas that are close to public transport nodes, services and facilities. The study focused on 'the goods that are most influenced by the built environment' (form, amenity, accessibility, affordability) but acknowledged that distributive justice could also be analysed from broader factors 'more closely linked to the management and ownership of the built environment than to characteristics of urban form itself' (2003: 541). Job accessibility and wealth were excluded from the analysis.

Intensification and community renewal in social housing estates have sparked debate about whether failed experiments in higher density social housing are due to concentration of housing (spatially determined) or poverty (socio-economically determined). Tenure and structural changes to employment are considered to have a greater influence on tenant wellbeing and social equity than housing density (Burton 2000). Increased poor health, crime and low amenity values are also more likely to be the result of concentration of poverty than housing type or density (Syme et al. 2005; Bramley et al. 2006).

Investment patterns are important in the shaping of urban form, with large investments of surplus capital being invested in speculative place construction (Harvey 1996). Urban renewal through new urbanism in the UK and USA is aimed at revitalising decaying city centres. In New Zealand, many inner city suburbs have been gentrified over the last thirty years, leaving a mix of affluent and more deprived fringe suburbs (Syme et al. 2005).

In Australia, Randolph (2005) determined that the current higher density market in major cities is distinctive as it is predominantly a rental market. Housing form is being determined by perceptions and behaviour of investors rather than people looking for homes to buy to live in. Smaller, two-bedroom dwellings are predominating, and high tenancy turnover, closely associated with the rental market, is a feature of higher density housing. Randolph raises concerns about the impact of these factors on social stability, community building, provision of open space, exclusion of children, and design and building quality.

Observations have been made in other parts of the world that discourses of accommodating growth are strongly linked to competitiveness between cities (Lehrer 2006), and that liveability strategies are more about investment protection, privacy and security than improving social and environmental outcomes (Helms 2005; Winstanley 2003).

Social equity does not appear to be a major driver for changes in urban form, although claims are made in policy discourse about potential for improving social justice. In this chapter concern with social equity underpins the analysis and ethnographic research informs the ways in which social equity is defined.

Context of changing urban form in New Zealand

New Zealand has been identified as a biodiversity 'hot spot', rich in endemic species but threatened by human activity; the number of households is rising at nearly twice the rate of the population (Liu et al. 2003). Rapid land and housing development is seriously affecting natural resources and the quality of human life in cities. New Zealand city dwellers have traditionally seen suburban life, with single dwellings on large sites, as the norm. A very strong cultural attachment to home ownership predominates. Single dwellings accounted for 82 percent of New Zealand homes in 2003 (Beacon Pathway 2006).

Auckland, where a third of the nation's population resides, is ranked among the top ten more 'liveable' cities internationally, but is also where social disparities are most evident in the country (Craig and Porter 2006). Population density in the Auckland region is low at 18.9 people per hectare (Arbury 2004), though this is changing rapidly. Former leafy suburbs have been carved up into 300–500–m^2 sections, and terraced housing, town houses, duplexes and multi-storey apartment blocks are becoming more common. Approximately 25 percent of building consents in Auckland are currently for multi-unit dwellings, and these are expected to outstrip single dwellings by 2016 (Beacon Pathway 2006).

Rapid growth in the Auckland region's population,[1] increasingly polluted skies, heavy reliance on cars, changing household dynamics and a growing demand for a greater range of housing forms have shaped planning strategies. So, while media representations tell us that citizens are extremely cautious and see intensification as a challenge to the 'quarter acre pavlova paradise',[2] societal changes are resulting in a proliferation of smaller households, creating a demand for a greater diversity in housing types (Liu et al. 2003).

In pre-European times, Glen Innes was the site of a strongly fortified pā (settlement), 'Taurere', situated on a multi-peaked scoria cone and with a capacity to hold 2000 people. Glen Innes takes its name from William Innes Tayor who settled in Auckland in 1843 and farmed in Glen Innes for 50 years. Glen Innes was developed in the 1950s as a state housing area, a dormitory suburb to service the freezing works and manufacturing industries in the nearby suburbs of Penrose and Mt Wellington. Glen Innes is approximately eight kilometres from the CBD and has Auckland's first

---

1. Increased from 700 000 to 1.2 million since 1970 and is projected to reach 2 million by 2030 (ARC 2006).
2. Colloquial expression referring to the standard suburban section of land in New Zealand; pavlova is a popular New Zealand dessert.

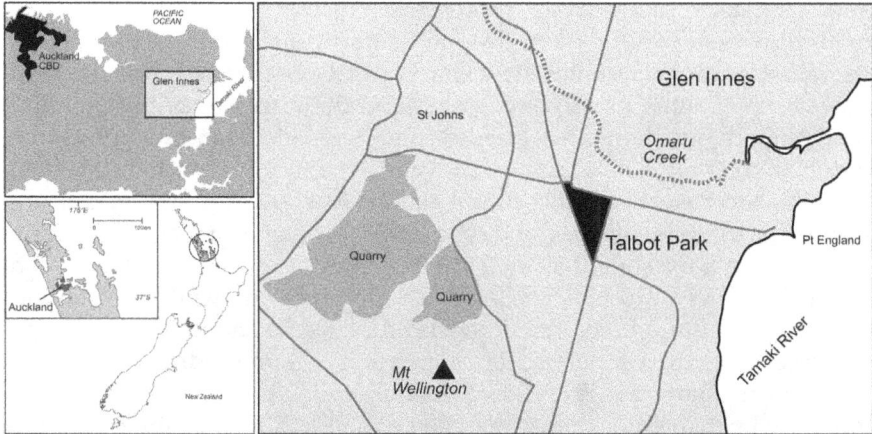

Figure 9.1. Area of ethnographic study: Glenn Innes, Auckland

comprehensively planned town centre (Auckland City 2004). The post-war baby boom, the migration of rural Māori to Auckland, and planning policies all contributed to a significant increase in the population in the broader Tamaki area within which Glen Innes is situated (Shirley 1979). Many of the new migrants to Glen Innes came from Freeman's Bay, an inner-city suburb that had undergone an urban renewal programme in the 1950s, leading to its gentrification. Current concerns about gentrification of Glen Innes therefore have strong links to historical experiences of urban renewal.

Social housing predominates in Glen Innes, accounting for over 60 percent of housing (and over 90 percent in some streets). This consists mainly of single dwellings, as well as some duplex and multi-unit blocks. In-fill housing, where 'standard ¼ acre sections' have been subdivided to fit two to three homes, has become increasingly evident in recent years. Parks and reserves are plentiful but are underutilised due to fears for personal safety.

Today, Glen Innes has a population of 17,500 (2006) and rates in the highest decile of deprivation in New Zealand. Very low relative household incomes and poor health are particularly implicated. Glen Innes' standard of living is especially low compared with adjacent suburbs that include some of the wealthiest in the country. Glen Innes has a youthful population and is ethnically diverse: Māori (14 percent) and Pacific (29 percent) populations being significantly higher than elsewhere in the city (7 percent and 11 percent, respectively). In New Zealand, poverty is entrenched among indigenous Māori and, more recently, among Pacific peoples, which is reflected in Glen Innes' statistics. Glen Innes was particularly affected by neoliberal economic reforms commencing in the 1980s: huge job losses occurred in industry and unemployment soared, particularly among Māori and Pacific people, heavily represented in manufacturing. Although unemployment figures have dropped significantly in recent years, the casualisation of the employment market and unrestricted global capital flows have resulted in very low wages and the displacement of low- and semi-skilled jobs. Benefit-dependant families face even greater relative deprivation as welfare is targeted at wage earners (Craig and Porter 2006).

Māori and Pākehā[3] families have lived in Glen Innes for many years, and waves first of Pacific peoples and more recently of an extremely diverse mix of ethnicities have shifted to the suburb. Ethnic and church affiliations are strong (reinforced by ethnicity-based service provision), while bridging ties between such community-based networks are weak, undermining attempts to build a sense of belonging, community connectedness and civic engagement (Bava and Scott 2006; Mathur et al. 2004). A large number of formalised networks have recently been established in Glen Innes to create cross-sectoral and inter-government links, some facilitated by Auckland City Council (henceforth referred to as Council) and Housing New Zealand Corporation (HNZC). This networking is aimed at strengthening links with community-based groups and building community capacity to 'rise to the challenge' of participatory democracy. Long time-frames, adequate resourcing and multi-sectoral commitment will be needed to create community readiness for collaborative action (Scott and Liew 2007). While some Council officers were involved in Glen Innes community development activities (most funded by Ministry of Health) during the period of the research, the Liveable Community Plan process was rarely mentioned and was not perceived as having any relevance to improving socio-economic conditions in Glen Innes.

Research approaches

This research builds on an earlier study of Council documentation and public submissions to the Glen Innes Liveable Community Plan and to Proposed Plan Modification 61 (PPM61) to allow higher density housing in Glen Innes (Scott and Shaw 2005). While home owners' and other stakeholders' views on community renewal and intensification were strongly articulated in submissions, many residents, particularly state tenants, had not made their views known. Many had signed pro forma submissions rejecting intensification in its entirety, and although all submissions were given credence, Council gave closest attention to submissions that gave reasons for rejection or support of the changes.

3. New Zealanders of European descent.

Subsequent ethnographic research therefore sought to draw in the unidentified voices through '[f]ine grained observations, narratives from everyday life, and testimonies in the voice of otherwise anonymous subjects...the basic material of ethnography' (Marcus 2005: 679).

Ethnographic research[4] (February to September 2006) including particiant observation, media reviews, and two focus groups, one with a group of six state tenants and another with ten Glen Innes residents and community development workers, together with other research and evaluation undertaken by the first author,[5] informs this study. Further participant observation and fifteen interviews with residents of Talbot Park were undertaken between February and May 2008. Participant observation involved attending community events, meetings and submission hearings and participation in several formalised social networks that support social environmental sustainability initiatives in Glen Innes. For the purposes of related research focused on the mapping of social networks and community governance processes in Glen Innes, a further twenty interviews were undertaken with other stakeholders – some of whom were also Glen Innes residents – including social service providers, *iwi*,[6] local government, government agencies and non-governmental organisations (Bava and Scott 2006). These interviews were also analysed in terms of discourses related to social justice, intensification and community renewal.

Research findings were presented to research participants and feedback integrated. This inclusion not only of residents but also of Council and HNZC officers throughout the analysis and writing stages of the research helped prevent the 'ethnographic distancing' (Levinson and Holland 1996: 19) of members of the dominant group (in this case, public servants) and retain the complexity and contradictory political realities (Ortner 1995).

---

4. This research is part of the Learning Sustainability research programme, a six-year programme (2003–2009), funded by the Foundation for Science, Research and Technology, aimed at examining different forms of settlements in relation to environmental, economic, and social performance. The programme is led by Opus International Consultants, with Landcare Research and the University of Auckland as project partners.
5. The Low Impact Urban Design and Development (LIUDD) programme http://www.landcareresearch.co.nz/research/built/liudd and evaluation of a Glen Innes community development project (Mathur et al. 2004).
6. Māori tribal and urban groups.

Policy constructions of community renewal and intensification

The Auckland Regional Growth Strategy (1999) was developed by the region's local councils to promote quality, compact, urban environments within existing metropolitan areas and focussed around town centres and major transport routes. Implementation commitment was then signalled by individual city and district councils through sector agreements. Liveable Community Plans were the key implementation strategy of the Central Sector Agreement.

The Local Government Act 2002 denoted a shift in government policy – the so-called Third Way, 'Inclusive' liberal turn – requiring highly consultative planning processes to determine Long Term Council Community Plans, based on 'four well-beings' (social, cultural, economic and environmental). This social governance model attempts to reverse the policy-operations spilt created through neoliberal policies of the 1980s and 1990s, shifting the focus on accountability of 'outputs' towards greater accountability of 'outcomes'. Collaboration within and between government and community sectors underpins both Long Term Council Community Plans and Liveable Community Plan processes, yet no implementation funding was allocated to either plan. Achieving 'outcomes' (four well-beings, liveability, social equity) therefore continues to be plagued by problems of departmental silos in budgeting, planning and strategising (Craig and Porter 2006). The social determinants of 'liveability', commonly acknowledged as related to political economic dimensions, were not addressed.

Glen Innes was selected in 2000 as a priority area to accommodate growth. Following four years of consultation and strategic planning, Council prepared a Liveable Community Plan (ACC 2004) and rezoned land to allow intensification. Rezoning was a two-step process. The initial 2004 plan change applied only to a state housing estate known as Talbot Park. The change supported the Talbot Park Community Renewal Project, a \$45 million project to provide 206 new and refitted homes. Following liveability planning frameworks, medium density housing, Crime Prevention through Environmental Design (CPTED) principles (Auckland City Council 2005) and environmentally-sustainable design features (Scott 2007) were used. On-site tenancy management and community development strategies were also implemented by HNZC.

Council subsequently notified a comprehensive plan change in 2005 to introduce suburb-wide, medium-density Residential 8 zoning. This rezoning applies to approximately 481 privately owned and 684 publicly owned residential properties in Glen Innes. A total of 586 submissions were made to Council, the majority opposing the plan, but the final decision was to allow the rezoning.

Reviews of planning documentation (Scott and Shaw 2005) showed that Council started from the point of accommodating growth by increasing housing densities (form), while placing controls on quality (design). Other themes of amenity, accessibility, vitality and viability of the town centre, and infrastructure were prioritised as necessary to create a 'liveable' community. As these themes are related to place, they fit within the traditional planning realm and are the core business of Council. Slightly less related were local economy and safety, which were assumed to be addressed by changes to form and design. While the theme of sustainability appears to be the driver for accommodating growth through changes to settlement form, it was not a strong focus in the discourse.

Council's expectation was that residents accept changes in form and, in return, would benefit from improvements to place. Nevertheless, Council planners reported feeling constrained by the context within which they worked. They felt constrained by regional growth management strategies that required accommodation of a certain level of population growth within city boundaries. Planners were concerned with the concentration of poverty within Glen Innes but were aware that Council was unable to influence the ownership and occupancy mix, nor attend directly to socio-economic issues in Glen Innes. Council responsibilities were therefore limited to zoning of land, resource consent processes, and facilitation of some community-development activities.

HNZC was also largely driven by a need to accommodate growth; in particular, to address the long waiting list for social housing in Auckland, particularly smaller two bedroom homes. HNZC was limited to increasing the number of dwellings on existing state-owned land; high land costs, limited resources for land purchase, and national policies that prohibit sale of HNZC properties meant HNZC was unable to sell some of its very valuable properties and purchase properties in a range of locations. There was also a lack of political will within local government to drive 'pepper potting' of state-owned properties in new developments in other parts of the city. HNZC was required to house those rated as 'high need' first resulting in a concentration of poverty in Glen Innes.

Residents' perceptions of community renewal and housing intensification

A common view throughout New Zealand, and strongly articulated in submissions, was that apartment blocks were not suitable for families with young children – lack of space including private outdoor spaces not large enough for children to play, and noise from children playing were common concerns. Numerous submissions and interviewees commented that 'children need green spaces to play', which was equated to private rather than public open space.

Another common view was that 'people are not designed to live in close proximity to each other'. Home owners and some state tenants living in single dwellings expressed concerned about a lack of privacy, noise pollution, tall apartment buildings shading neighbours, the potential for conflict between neighbours, security concerns for children in shared public spaces, and a general lack of control over the surrounding environment. These concerns were deeply imbedded culturally and cut across class.

Closer examination of ethnographic data suggested there were differences in perceptions of what would result from changes to urban form in Glen Innes and that these differences could be largely attributed to social class. In the following section, perceptions of two social groups – home owners and state tenants – are examined. However, it must be acknowledged that distinctions in perspectives often blur, conflict and change over time.

Home owners: 'Liveability' plans will lead to 'slumification'

Many of those who submitted opinions to the Glen Innes Liveable Community Plan, particularly home owners and social service providers, saw the plans as mere window dressing aimed at painting over the problems of poverty and inequality and the essential 'polluting' nature of a concentration of state tenants. A common concern among social service workers, private home owners and residents of neighbouring suburbs was that a higher concentration of low-income people would exacerbate existing socio-economic problems:

> At the moment the flats at Talbot Park are being re-vamped. They all look really nice then the tenants move in and they now look like a ghetto. There [sic] verandas look ugly, people drinking outside them and sitting under trees, throwing rubbish outside. It is a waste of money if people are not going to look after them and bring the area down. And now you want to put more of the flats in the area, bring in more people who don't care. On my street there is one area there [where] a lot of housing are put close together. It is the messiest, noisiest area on the whole street and you want us to say yes to more of this. NO THANK YOU' (submission to PPM61).

State tenants were framed as the 'Other' in these discourses; collective use of public outdoor space by state tenants was frowned on. Many home owners expressed the view that the number of state homes should be reduced not increased. 'The answer to Glen Innes' problems lies not with intensification of housing, but with addressing the income mix of its residents'. There was a strong perception that state tenants – and HNZC – did not take good care of their homes.

However, while there were repeated calls for HNZC to sell off some of their properties, there was also concern that medium-density zoning would allow poor quality development and that new, privately owned properties would be rented out with no maintenance or tenancy management. New Zealand rental properties are predominantly owned by 'Mum and Dad investors' and are commonly passively managed, under-maintained and sold every one to three years (Saville-Smith 2005). People feel vulnerable to future political changes that could result in sale of social housing:

> My concern is with these [higher density houses] if Housing New Zealand bought them, then forget it, it would just be terrible. But also if people started buying high density housing I could see what would happen, they would sell them like they do in the inner city and they would be rented out and you would get more of the same, and I think that's where the danger is. I think if they built them so they were nice apartments, expensive to buy so that people who had to live in them had a bit of money, that would help change the face of Glen Innes, but I can't see that happening (home owner).

Homeowners (and social service workers) were concerned that small apartments would become home to large, low-income families, with dire consequences for families and the community. One long-term home owner who had observed that garages in Glen Innes always became homes to families commented:

> I remember when they first talked about [Talbot Park] I said to [HNZC] now don't put garages in, just put carports and maybe a little shed for the bikes. If you do put a garage in, make sure it's fully lined and preferably has toilet facilities and is carpeted and sound proof so that people can live in them comfortably.

Families, meaning two adults and children, were commonly considered best for community building by homeowners. Single people were thought to make bad neighbours and could threaten others' feelings of security. People reminisced fondly about when Glen Innes was first established as a state housing area for low-income families.

The discourse of slumification was also evident in views of renewal of the town centre. One submitter commented, 'The only shops that will benefit through the extra people in the neighbourhood are the TAB [betting agent], takeaways, Lotto and pub'. Home owners expressed a desire for a more diverse range of shops and community facilities, including repeated calls for an arts centre. Residents in affluent neighbouring suburbs, many of whom make use of the Glen Innes train station and supermarket, expressed strong concerns in submissions about the potential for 'slumification' in Glen Innes through intensification. Although not articulated in submissions, it is likely that these home owners felt threatened by the potential of having even more 'high need' state tenants at their doorstep.

Middle-class attachment to low-density living and private outdoor space was strongly evident in discourses of liveability. Claims by home owners that intensification would lead to slumification implicated concepts of cultural pollution in the discourse, and also pointed to strongly entrenched poverty and historical political processes that impinge on experiences of urban form.

State Tenants: 'Liveability' plans will lead to gentrification

A common theme in submissions from state tenants was fears of gentrification due to 'liveability' plans – 'As happened in Ponsonby [an inner city suburb] in the 1960s', 'fear of being pushed out to Otara', or as one person said in an oral submission, 'I am afraid this is shorthand for moving some of the community out'. This fear was heightened by close proximity to comparatively wealthy suburbs. State tenants often commented that Glen Innes was well situated, easy to walk around and well-serviced by public transport. Car parking had become a problem since renewal of the train station as many residents from neighbouring suburbs parked in central Glen Innes to make use of the train service. The local shops were considered very affordable, and state tenants feared 'liveability' processes would change this:

> Glen Innes has got everything you need, all the shops here, it's convenient. You can walk to the supermarket, you can buy clothing here, you can buy everything you need…I know people which moved out of the area…and they all complain that everything is just so much more expensive…they just can't afford a lot of things and especially having big families. Here even second-hand clothing and so on for the little ones [make it affordable]… (state tenant).

State tenants were cynical about the dominating presence of a new police station in Glen Innes since it was known as a regional centre for traffic police rather than a community policing centre. Authorities claimed a reduction in reported crime in Glen Innes, while residents complained that it was 'a waste of time' to report crime as 'nothing ever happens' as a result. State tenants (and community development workers) made repeated calls for more community police presence. A residents' group was engaged in removing graffiti, actively eliminating this symbolic threat to social order. If liveability strategies were about attaining improved social order, as claimed in other localities (Wacquant 2003), then residents would generally be extremely supportive.

Affordability was a key issue for state tenants. Intensification was perceived as helping meet the need for more affordable homes in Glen Innes:

> [Medium density housing] for a great number of people to be housed in the smallest space and low maintenance, and that brings the cost of housing down, and at the same time providing for some accommodation for some people who can't afford it, including families. Because at the moment we have about 4000 people waiting for housing in Glen Innes alone, and we haven't got any houses. Something like [medium density housing's], I guess, practical in a sense but it's a matter of getting used to a new kind of lifestyle to fit in with what's available, I guess that's what it is (state tenant).

Ethnographic research suggested that residents enjoyed living in the revamped 'Starblock' and new apartment blocks in Talbot Park. They were perceived to be healthier and more comfortable to live in, with improved ventilation, security, and outdoor public space. Concerns about personal safety in Talbot Park had largely been addressed by reconfiguration of public space and tighter controls on tenant behaviour. Some liked the fact that apartment living meant they did not have the expense or work of maintaining private outdoor space, and for this reason were prepared to live in a smaller living space. Social service and community development workers in Glen Innes also reported that Talbot Park residents were generally happy in their homes, and that some of these tenants have a 'new lease on life', feeling good about where they live, which has a positive impact on other parts of their lives.

Residents identified some issues associated with living in close proximity to neighbours, including noise, feeling 'jammed in' and the resulting 'strong tenancy management' approach by HNZC. One Starblock resident liked her flat but, commenting on the construction of apartment blocks in close proximity to hers in Talbot Park, said, 'our road is real narrow, imagine when they've finished all the buildings, you'll be stuffed in like a [sardine], won't be able to get out of there'. Lack of privacy did not emerge as an issue for these residents, and some expressed feelings of security and comfort with having people nearby. While one single parent said she liked the opportunity for social interaction, most appeared to operate under a system of 'polite avoidance' of their neighbours in order to preserve people's privacy.

Tenancy control measures produced contradictory responses from tenants: they wanted restrictions on other people's behaviour but at the same time resisted controls over their own freedom. Much of the talk about living in Talbot Park centred on the tenancy control measures, seen by some as too heavy handed and making some feel fearful. Some residents saw them as the only thing they did not like about living in the area.

Affordable, safe, healthy homes were strong themes in state tenants' discourses of liveability, and results to date in Talbot Park were positive in this regard. Middle-class concerns about privacy and adequacy of indoor and outdoor space were less evident. Vulnerability to national policy changes in relation to state housing underpinned concerns of potential gentrification of Glen Innes.

Comparing discourses of 'liveability'

Examination of discourses of liveability showed a clear mismatch between Council and HNZC objectives of accommodating growth and residents' goals of addressing socio-economic issues. This mismatch reflected the competing political, institutional, social and economic processes at various scales that shape urban form at a city scale.

Home owners and social service workers wanted to see significant improvements to the socio-economic well-being of residents before more people (especially 'high need' HNZC tenants) were housed there. Liveability planning processes raised expectations that their concerns about socio-economic issues would be addressed as priority concerns. This contrasts with the Council's expectations that the community would accept changes in form and, in return, would benefit from improvements to be made to place. Fears that intensification of housing would endanger human health and safety were constructed through discourses of pollution and defilement; state tenants were constructed as the 'Other', 'people out of place'.

In contrast, state tenants, a marginalised group that is in most need of a more 'liveable' environment, valued the efforts of HNZC to provide attractive, healthy homes in a suburb that is well serviced by public transport and a local town centre. Despite concerns about the perceived 'big brother' approach of HNZC to tenancy management, Talbot Park had become sought after by state tenants. Talbot Park residents' desire for a range of housing styles and construction materials so that they 'don't look like state houses', for example, was accommodated. People liked apartment living, in part because of, rather than in spite of, the lack of private outdoor space. Tenancy turnover in Talbot Park has been greatly reduced by the redevelopment (from 50 to 4 percent p.a.) and there is now a waiting list of people wanting to live there. A shift in views became evident over time among state tenants, social service and community development workers, from anxiety about 'town cramming' in Talbot Park before construction, to 'watching with interest' during construction, and finally being impressed with the post-construction results and hopeful that more such renewal programmes would be undertaken in Glen Innes.

The need for locally specific indicators of liveability was recognised by Council and HNZC through a process of consultation and collaboration. Government strategies have aligned to create more affordable homes, improving community stability, safety and amenity values. However, the participatory governance model on which the Liveable Community Plan was based was undermined by the lack of resourcing of its implementation (Scott and Park 2008). The plan relied on collaboration between residents, HNZC, police, Council, and community organisations, many of whom were already stretched to meet existing socio-economic challenges, 'core business' or contractual requirements. In effect, this points to the ways in which government agencies failed to link place-based strategies and the lack of power that each agency had to control just how intensification of housing will be applied and by whom. This supports Craig and Porter's (2006) observations that 'the outcomes orientation [in government policy] is not in fact primarily about producing social change outcomes, but about attempting (and largely failing) to widen narrow public service accountabilities' (2006: 245).

Conclusion

Auckland City has little available land to accommodate even natural population increase, and while the public generally does not want urban sprawl, it also does not support intensification. Critical dialogue on intensification is badly needed. Changes to the built environment are forcing people to reassess cultural assumptions about urban form and associated dangers and risks. Environmental problems such as air pollution and threats to natural resources are also impacting on quality of life in cities and raising questions related to the urban form. More compact forms of development could provide affordable homes and therefore contribute to social equity. However, as this research shows, provision of affordable homes is only part of the equation. Concentration of poverty and other issues associated with material conditions have a bigger impact on social equity than urban form. The fact that Glen Innes, the most impoverished suburb in the city, was the first to be targeted for liveability planning raises questions about whether those already in highly marginalised positions stand to bear the brunt of bureaucratic agreements to accommodate growth within city boundaries. Current material conditions of Glen Innes residents' everyday lives – and high levels of cynicism about urban renewal – are strongly shaped by historical political processes as well as discursive practices. Social equity emerges as a priority in any examination of urban sustainability.

Low-density housing is a symbol of middle-class New Zealand, signifying stability, independence and control over private indoor and outdoor space; and these representations, though under threat from new urbanism, are far from eliminated from discursive constructions of the built environment. This study suggests that more compact forms of development may provide well for marginalised people in Glen Innes, and their perceptions and experiences of intensification deserve further investigation. However, their marginal position is unlikely to change as long as broader socioeconomic issues are not addressed and cultural concepts of urban form that value single dwellings remain dominant in the public arena (and equate intensification with 'slumification').

Based on Douglas' notion of cultural pollution, policy and home owner discourses of liveability in Glen Innes could be explained as an attempt to impose social order and protect property values. In Glen Innes, liveability planning is not rhetoric to sell homes but rather rhetoric to sell intensification, and if social order is improved in the process, Council, HNZC and residents alike will be happy. This matches findings from ethnographic research in low-decile high schools in USA where rather than seeing surveillance and controls on students as being inappropriate 'power over', people wanted stronger social order imposed in order to create a safer learning environment (Devine 1999).

Nevertheless, the core issue in both ethnographic examples is concentration of poverty and socio-economic problems. These are arguably more strongly linked to a deregulated economy and employment than to the built environment. Liveability planning processes shaping the built environment in Glen Innes are largely detached from economic processes that shape the socioeconomic context that are of primary concern to residents. The focus of liveability planning processes on issues of security and social order can be understood as dealing with the symptoms rather the cause. As Wacquant (2003) observed, it is ironic that in the neoliberal state, 'more state' is required to maintain public order 'to remedy the generalised rise of objective and subjective insecurity that is itself caused by 'less state' on the economic and social front' (2003: 198).

Once a vibrant hub of commercial activity during pre-European times, Glen Innes was established as a state housing area in the 1950s, became homogenised in terms of class, and stigmatised as a result. Nevertheless, 'GI' became home for several generations of people who lived in single dwellings, duplexes and apartment blocks. The suburb is now being reshaped to house more people in apartments and townhouses, meeting the needs of some residents, while creating a threat to others. Whether this leads to gentrification, slumification or something in between remains to be seen.

Acknowledgements

Our sincere thanks to Michael Krausse, Alison Greenaway and two anonymous reviewers for reading and commenting on earlier drafts of this chapter. This research was supported with funding from the Foundation of Research, Science and Technology.

References

Arbury, J. 2004. 'What Contribution has the "Compact City" had to the Search for Urban Sustainability?' Working Paper, prepared for Objective 1. Learning to be Sustainable: Tool for Adapting the Shape of Existing Cities and Settlements. Auckland; School of Geography and Environmental Science, The University of Auckland.

Auckland City. 2004. *Glen Innes into the Future*. Auckland: Auckland City Council.

————2005. Safer Auckland City: Introduction to Crime Prevention through Environmental Design. www.aucklandcity.govt.nz/auckland /introduction/safer/cpted

Auckland Regional Council. 1999. *Auckland Regional Growth Strategy: 2050*. Auckland: Auckland Regional Council.

————2004. Central Sector Agreement, 2004. Auckland: Auckland Regional Council.

Bava, C. and K. Scott. 2006. 'Visualising Community: An Ethnographic Approach to Social Network Analysis in Glen Innes', Presentation to Anthropology Department, The University of Auckland, 12 October 2006.

Beacon Pathway. 2006. Market Segmentation – Notes for Strategic Planning Day. Auckland. www.beaconpathway.co.nz

Bramley, G., N. Dempsey, S. Power and C. Brown. 2006. 'What is "Social Sustainability", and How Do Our Existing Urban Forms Perform in Nurturing It?' Planning Research Conference, Bartlett School of Planning, UCL, London. 5–7 April 2006.

Brosius, J. P. 1999. 'Analyses and Interventions: Anthropological Engagements with Environmentalism', *Current Anthropology* 40(3): 277–309.

Burton, E. 2000. 'The Compact City: Just or Just Compact? A Preliminary Analysis', *Urban Studies* 37: 1969–2001.

————2003. 'Housing for an Urban Renaissance: Implications for Social Equity', *Housing Studies* 18 (4): 537–62.

Cohen, A.P. 1985 *The Symbolic Construction of Community*. London: Routledge.

Craig, D. and D. Porter. 2006 *Development Beyond Neoliberalism? Governance, Poverty Reduction and Political Economy*. New York: Routledge.

Devine, J. 1999. 'Postmodernity, Ethnography and Foucault', in A. Chambon, A. Irving, L. Epstein (eds), *Reading Foucault for Social Work*. New York: Columbia University Press: 248–67.

Douglas, M. 1970. *Purity and Danger*. Middlesex, England: Pelican Books.

Escobar, A. 1999. 'After Nature: Steps to an Antiessentialist Political Ecology', *Current Anthropology* 40 (1): 1–30.

Harper, J. 2004. 'Breathless in Houston: A Political Ecology of Health Approach to Understanding Environmental Health Concerns', *Medical Anthropology* 23: 295–326.

Harvey, D. 1996 'The Environment of Justice', in A. Merrifield and E. Swyngedouw (eds), *The Urbanization of Injustice*, pp. 248–67. London: Lawrence & Wishart.

Helms, G. 2005. 'Cleaning up the City: The Liveability Agenda as a Means for a Socially Just City?' Conference presentation, Royal Geographical Society – IBG Annual International Conference, London, 31 August–2 September 2005.

Keil, R. 2003. 'Urban Political Ecology', *Urban Geography* 24(8): 723–38.

Lehrer, U. and A. Winkler. 2006. 'Public or Private? The Pope Squat and Housing Struggles in Toronto'. *Social Justice* 33 (3): 142–57.

Levinson, B. and D. Holland. 1996. 'The Cultural Production of the Educated Person: An Introduction. In Levinson, B., Foley, D, Holland. D. (eds), *The Cultural Production of the Educated Person: Critical Ethnographies of Schooling*, pp. 1–55. New York: State University of New York Press.

Liu, J., G.C. Daily, P.R. Ehrlich and G.W. Luck. 2003. 'Effects of Household Dynamics on Resource Consumption and Biodiversity', *Nature* 421: 530–3.

Marcus, G. 2005. 'The Passion of Anthropology in the U.S., Circa 2004', *Anthropological Quarterly* 78 (3): 673–95.

Mathur, N., K. Scott, S. Strang. 2004. 'Ka Mau Te Wero-Health: Spinning the Web of Change through Organisational Networking'. The Social Policy, Research and Evaluation Conference 25–26 November, 2004, Wellington, NZ.

Milton, K. 1996. *Environmentalism and Cultural Theory: Exploring the Role of Anthropology in Environmental Discourse*. London and New York: Routledge.

Ortner, S.B. 1995. 'Resistance and the Problem of Ethnographic Refusal'. *Comparative Studies in Society and History* 37: 173–93.

Randolph, B. 2005. 'Higher Density Community: Current Trends and Future Implications'. Strata and Community Title in Australia for the 21st Century Conference, 31 August–3 September 2005. Gold Coast: Griffith University, Service Industry Research Centre.

Saville-Smith, K. 2005. Keynote Presentation, National Community Housing Conference, 3–5 November 2005, Auckland: Waipuna Lodge.

Scott, K. 2007. 'Talbot Park'. Retrieved 12 Novermber 2007 from http://www.landcareresearch.co.nz/research/built/liudd/casestudi es/case_tamaki.asp#talbot

Scott, K. and T. Liew. 2007. ' "I Just Come for the Chocolate Biscuits": A Fresh Look at Community Networking in Aotearoa'. National Local Authority Community Development Conference, 19–21 September 2007, Novotel Hotel, Hamilton.

Scott, K. and J. Park. 2008 'Creating a Liveable Community? Linking Participatory Planning with Participatory Outcomes'. 46th International Making Cities Livable Conference, 2–4 June 2008, Santa Fe, New Mexico.

Scott, K. and A. Shaw. 2005. *Report on Local Community Perceptions of Liveability.* Auckland: Opus International Consultants.

Shirley, I.F. 1979. *Planning for Community: A Mythology of Community Development and Social Planning.* Palmerston North: Dunmore Press.

Strathern, M. 1982. 'The Village as an Idea: Constructs of Villageness in Elmdon, Essex', in Cohen, A.P. (ed.), *Belonging*, pp. 247–77. Manchester: Manchester University Press.

Syme, C., V. McGregor and D. Mead. 2005. 'Social Implications of Housing Intensification in the Auckland Region: Analysis and Review of Media Reports, Surveys and Literature'. Report prepared for Auckland City Council, Waitakere City Council, HNZC and Auckland Regional Council.

Sywngedouw, E. and N. Heynen. 2003. 'Urban Political Ecology, Justice and the Politics of Scale', *Antipode* 35: 898–918.

Wacquant, L. 2003. 'Toward a Dictatorship over the Poor? Notes on the Penalization of Poverty in Brazil', *Punishment & Society: The International Journal of Penology* 5 (2): 197–205.

Williams, K. 1999. 'Urban Intensification Policies in England: Problems and Contradictions'. *Land Use Policy* 16 (3): 167–78.

Winstanley, A., D. Thorns and H. Perkins. 2003. 'Nostalgia, Community and New Housing Developments: A Critique of New Urbanism Incorporating a New Zealand Perspective', *Urban Policy and Research* 21 (2): 175–89.

World Commission on Environment and Development (WCED). 1987. *Our Common Future.* Oxford: Oxford University Press.

Young, I.M. 1986. 'The Ideal of Community and the Politics of Difference', *Social Theory and Practice* 12 (1): 1–26.

CHAPTER 10

Afterword: Impure Thoughts on Messy Cities

AIDAN DAVISON

Understood as a physical threat to human and non-human health, pollution attracts considerable attention in the form of management regimes, public controversy and technical discourses of risk. Within the academy, there is an associated focus on pollution in fields such as economics, engineering, medicine and biology. Pollution nonetheless fits poorly with the academic division of labour into natural sciences, social sciences and humanities. As the illegitimate offspring of technological systems, pollution appears to be the antithesis of ecological order and social order. The category of pollution threatens to pollute modern disciplines of knowledge by seeming to originate from neither the realm of nature nor the realm of culture. This category has, not surprisingly, been subject to stringent intellectual management.

   In the introduction to this book, the editors observe that urban pollution, in particular, has been constituted as an object of technocratic analysis. In this frame of reference, pollution is objectively – that is, purely – impure materiality. This is not to say that technocratic colonisation of urban pollution is total. This book, after all, takes its cue from Mary Douglas' (1970: 36) study of what she called pollution behaviour, or 'the reaction which condemns any object or idea likely to confuse or contradict cherished classifications'. However, many following Douglas' lead in the fields of anthropology and cultural studies have left untouched objectivist accounts of 'pollution material', choosing instead to balance the ledger with constructionist accounts of pollution behaviour. Ironically, then, cultural accounts of the dialectics of impurity often hold fast to cherished classifications that deny the messy but productive coupling of representational practices and material realities.

The effort contributors to this volume have made in bringing cultural analysis to bear on facts as well as on ideas of urban pollution is thus welcome. Generating ethnographic and historical insight into the production of impurity in a rich variety of contexts, this collection challenges the impulse to clean up the messy reality of cities. This is not to deny threats that may be posed by urban pollution, and posed most severely to impoverished and oppressed human groups and to similarly silenced non-humans. It is, however, to resist efforts to strip pollution of its qualitative constituents. It is to draw attention to the enculturation of pollution. It is to expose ambiguous freight in the stuff of pollution. It is to widen the definition of urban pollution to include, as does this book, questions about migration and ethnicity, morality and social control, bodily distinction and public space, artifice and naturalness. Although the authors of this book widen the circle of concern in the study of urban pollution, their motivation should be familiar to urban managers. The focus of attention may have shifted from water quality and cancer incidence to social identities and cultural narratives, but the practical intent remains that of improving the lot of urban residents. What is perhaps less familiar is the implication that such improvement does not have to be harnessed to visions of the pristine city. The great value of ethnographies of urban pollution is that they not only leave intact the untidy tangle of relations that makes the city possible, they shed light on the ways in which attempts to cleanse the city only proliferate problems of impurity.

The editors point out in the introduction that this collection presents a parallel analysis of material and symbolic substance in urban pollution. This analysis is explicitly ambivalent as authors strive to remain aware of the way in which the 'materially and sociality of urban pollution are relational entities that produce each other', while relying on a 'symbolic-material dualism' to produce recognisably cultural studies of ' "symbolic" social pollution' (Jaffe and Dürr, this volume). While urban pollution is acknowledged to be a hybrid entity, to be an impurely impure, the research methods and scholarly conventions that underpin many chapters handle semiotic subtlety with greater dexterity than they do material subtlety. Urban pollution is shown to be shot through with powerful cultural agencies, such as morality, solidarity and rivalry. Yet so too is urban pollution shot through with powerful physical agencies, such as the reproductive vigour of *E. coli*, the toxic persistence of mercury or the warmth of a blanket of carbon dioxide. With cultural practices often in the foreground of analysis, these physical agencies are at some risk of appearing to be an epiphenomenon of representation. In practice, the risk is that the way is left clear for technocratic institutions to lay claim to the threat of urban pollution.

I am not suggesting that the analytical ambivalence in this book is a flaw. The avowedly tentative grasp on the stuff of pollution attempted in this volume invites and should stimulate dialogue across disciplines. Although occupied with description more than with theory, the text draws close to lively debate about non-dualistic ontology and methodology, especially, but not exclusively, in sociology and geography (e.g. Haraway 2008; Law 2005; Latour 2004; Thrift 2007). The multiple trajectories of this debate attract terms such as posthumanism, culturenatures, actor-network theory and non-representational theory, and are cross-cut by themes of embodied performativity and material hybridity. Importantly for the present volume, these trajectories are leading to experimentation in the study of cities and, to a lesser extent, in the study of pollution. These experiments intersect much analysis in this book, offering the promise of mutual exchange between ethnographic detail and socio-political critique. Consider two examples. First, Maria Kaika's (2005) *City of Flows* offers an account of the role of water in the physical and symbolic cleansing of Athens during its nineteenth century transformation in modern European imaginaries from Eastern Other to ancient seat of a newly minted Western identity. Kaika's study of the interplay of modernist meta-narratives and urban infrastructure invites complementary ethnographic accounts of the lived experience of urban water. Second, in *The Ethics of Waste*, Gay Hawkins (2006, 75) locates waste, 'the afterlife of things', in the context of a systemic paradox in commodity capitalism. She points out that the logic of efficient production pushes towards the elimination of waste while the logic of maximal consumption pushes towards the production of waste. As with all social paradoxes, ethnographic questions arise about how such dissonance in the materiality and symbolism of waste is maintained in human experience.

Experimentation with non-dualistic ontologies and methodologies in the social sciences and humanities is bringing them into new forms of contact with the natural sciences. So too the exploration of urban pollution in this book opens up avenues for future inquiry about the material semiotics of nature. Despite the influence of ecological metaphors in urban studies, social scientists commonly represent cities as social artefacts and cultural arenas in which nature is fully subordinated, if it is not erased altogether. To the extent that the idea of urban nature has not been rejected as an oxymoron, it usually refers to gardens, parks and other 'green' spaces. Similarly, urban environmentalism has often been split off from forms of environmentalism inspired by visions of nature. Issues such as urban pollution have typically been framed within 'brown' environmental discourses of risk and efficiency rather than within 'green' discourses of natural purity and balance. Although discourses of pure nature, centred on ideas such as wilderness and nativeness, have primarily taken hold within urban constituencies, they have nonetheless presented the city as inherently impure, so much so that the idea of urban pollution has been regarded as a tautology. Over the last two decades, however, assumptions about the unnaturalness of cities have come under increasing challenge within the natural sciences, prompted by study of non-equilibrium ecologies and attempts at integrated management of social-ecological systems (e.g. Alberti 2008). Reciprocal inquiry within the social sciences into cities as more-than-human realities has also recently gathered pace, as have urban environmental movements that blur old distinctions between nature and technology (e.g. Heynen et al. 2006; White and Wilbert 2009). Ethnographic studies of urban pollution, such as those presented here, promise to contribute to understanding of the hybrid materiality and more-than-human agency of cities. Rich cultural description of the dialectics of impurity presents cities as ambivalent realities, as material-semiotic relations which could ever be otherwise. Such description asks how humans construct cities as material culture. Such description also pursues symmetry in asking how cities construct humanity: How is the human condition made in more-than-human urban worlds? The study of urban pollution, then, promises not just lessons in hubris and loss, but also lessons in modesty and recovery. Such study promises to show how the rejected content of cities and of humanity is never beyond reclamation.

References

Alberti, M. 2008. *Advances in Urban Ecology: Integrating Humans and Ecological Processes in Urban Ecosystems*. New York and Dordrecht: Springer.

Douglas, M. 1970. *Purity and Danger: An Analysis of Concepts of Pollution and Taboo*. London, Boston and Henley: Routledge and Kegan Paul.

Haraway, D. 2008. *When Species Meet*. Minneapolis: University of Minnesota Press.

Hawkins, G. 2006. *The Ethics of Waste: How We Relate to Rubbish*. Sydney: University of New South Wales Press.

Kaika, M. 2005. *City of Flows: Modernity, Nature and the City*. London and New York: Routledge.

Latour, B. 2004. *Politics of Nature: How to Bring the Sciences into Democracy*, trans. C. Porter. Cambridge, MA and London: Harvard University Press.

Law, J. 2005. *After Method: Mess in Social Science Research*. London and New York: Routledge.

Heynen, N., M. Kaika and E. Swyngedouw (eds). 2006. *In the Nature of Cities: Urban Political Ecology and the Politics of Urban Metabolism*. London and New York: Routledge.

Thrift, N. 2007. *Non-Representational Theory: Space, Politics, Affect*. London and New York: Routledge.

White, D.F. and C. Wilbert (eds). 2009. *Technonatures: Environments, Technologies, Spaces, and Places in the Twenty-first Century*. Wilfred Laurier University Press: Waterloo.

Notes on Contributors

Christina Bava is currently involved in research on consumer behaviour at the Horticulture and Food Research Institute of New Zealand Limited. She received her MA in Anthropology in 2006 from the University of Auckland. Here she worked on a variety of projects as a research assistant which ranged from consumer behaviour to community networking. Her current interests involve the application of qualitative research for understanding consumer behaviour particularly with regard to food-related practices.

Aidan Davison is a Senior Lecturer in human geography in the School of Geography and Environmental Studies at the University of Tasmania, and is formerly Program Chair of Sustainable Development at Murdoch University. The author of *Technology and the Contested Meanings of Sustainability* (SUNY 2001), Aidan has published on topics ranging from public perceptions of biotechnology to Australian urban history to environmentalism. His research interests follow socio-cultural questions generated at the intersection of themes of technology, nature and sustainability.

Anouk de Koning lectures in History at the Free University and in Anthropology at the University of Amsterdam. Her contribution is based on ethnographic research that focused on Cairo's experience of economic liberalization in an era of globalization. It culminated in a study, *Global Dreams: Class, Gender and Public Space in Cosmopolitan Cairo* (American University in Cairo Press, 2009), that explores what happened to a post-colonial middle class that was once the carrier of national aspirations and dreams. The book elaborates how young middle-class professionals navigate Cairo's increasingly divided landscape and discusses the rise of a young upper–middle–class presence in the work, leisure and public spaces of the city.

Eveline Dürr is a Professor at the Institute of Social and Cultural Anthropology at the Ludwig-Maximilians-University in Munich, and previously held a position as Associate Professor in the School of Social Sciences, Auckland University of Technology, New Zealand. She received her PhD and *venia legendi* (Habilitation) from the University of Freiburg, Germany. She has conducted fieldwork in Mexico, the USA, Germany and New Zealand on patterns of culture change and identity formations. Her current research interests focus mainly on urban anthropology, cultural identities and transnational linkages between Latin America and the Pacific.

Rivke Jaffe is a Lecturer in the Institute of Cultural Anthropology and Development Sociology at Leiden University. She previously held teaching and research positions at the University of the West Indies, Mona and the Royal Netherlands Institute of Southeast Asian and Caribbean Studies (KITLV). She has conducted fieldwork in Jamaica, Curaçao and Suriname on topics ranging from the urban environment to the political economy of multiculturalism to alternative governance structures. Her various research projects and publications evidence a concern with urban life; the spatialisation of power, difference and inequality within cities and states; and the historical trajectories that have shaped the present.

Szabina Kerényi is currently a PhD candidate at the Masaryk University, Brno, Czech Republic, with research on collective action strategies of the urban environmental movement. She has an MA in Cultural Anthropology from ELTE, University of Budapest (2004), an MA in Political Science from the Central European University, Budapest (2003), and an MA in Bulgarian Philology, ELTE, University of Budapest (2002). She has received scholarships from the University of Copenhagen, the Open Society Institute and the Hungarian Ministry of Education and she has been a visiting student at the European University Institute, Florence.

Damaris Lüthi did her postgraduate studies at the London School of Economics and at the University of Berne, Switzerland, from where she has a PhD in Social Anthropology, focusing on South Asia. From 2001–03 she conducted research on social change among Sri Lankan Tamil refugees in Switzerland, funded by the Swiss National Science Foundation. She is an associated researcher of the Department for Social Anthropology of the University of Berne. She is also an independent documentary filmmaker (*1000° Celsius*, 1993; *Silk, Muthappar and VHS*, 1998; *Hippie Masala*, 2006), and she is responsible for the women empowerment programme in India of the Swiss League of Catholic Women.

Johanna Rolshoven has a PhD and Habilitation in Culture Studies and a diploma in Ethnology. She is currently Professor for Cultural Studies at the Institute for Cultural Anthropology, University of Graz, Austria. She has held positions as professor, lecturer and researcher at universities in

Switzerland, Germany, France and Finland and as scientific director of the CCSA (Centre for Cultural Studies in Architecture) at the Swiss Federal Institute of Technology in Zurich. Her main research areas are epistemology and methodology of the social sciences of culture, urban studies, material culture and consumption, biography, cultural theory of space and liminality, mobility and multilocality. She has conducted fieldwork in Hungary, France, Corsica, Switzerland and Germany.

Kathryn Scott is a researcher on the Sustainable Settlements team at Landcare Research in Auckland, New Zealand. She received an MA in anthropology at The University of Auckland in 1995, and since then has undertaken research in the areas of health, urban sustainability, low impact design and community development. Kathryn is engaged in long-term ethnographic research in Glen Innes, Auckland and is currently undertaking doctoral studies in the area of community engagement in urban renewal processes.

Angela Shaw has worked for Opus International Consultants in New Zealand for nearly ten years. She specialises in social impact assessment for major infrastructure projects, environmental policy and consultation. Angela trained in sociology at the University of Canterbury and environmental policy at Lincoln University, both in New Zealand.

Magnus Treiber is currently a lecturer at the Chair of Anthropology, University of Bayreuth, Germany, following a teaching position at the Institute of Social and Cultural Anthropology, University of Munich, from 2005 to 2008. His fields of special interest are migration studies, the state in Africa and the Horn of Africa region. He has conducted fieldwork in Asmara (Eritrea), Tigray and Addis Ababa (Ethiopia), Cairo (Egypt) and Minneapolis and Washington, D.C. (USA). While his Ph.D. thesis *Der Traum vom guten Leben* (2005) deals with the life-world of Asmara's urban youth, recent publications focus on migration from Eritrea.

Susanna Trnka is a Senior Lecturer in anthropology at The University of Auckland. Her work focuses on political violence, pain, and Indo-Fijian sociality in Fiji and on nationalism and historical memory in the Czech Republic. Her most recent book is State of Suffering: Political Violence and Community Survival in Fiji (2008).

Index

www.ingramcontent.com/pod-product-compliance
Lightning Source LLC
Chambersburg PA
CBHW060038030426
42334CB00019B/2379